# Life in the BUS LANE

Have you ever wondered what happens on the road to rock and roll stardom, when the coin you toss lands heads up, when you shouted "Tails?"

Well, you're just in time, to hitch a ride on a journey through the gutter of the music business, with the guarantee that you will laugh along the way.

Tony Bell is indecent, obscene, shocking, honest, humorous and truthful. He wrote this so you don't have to.

Losers don't come any more successful!

# LIFE IN THE BUS LANE

# Tony Bell

## Life In The Bus Lane

Vanguard Press

VANGUARD PAPERBACK

© Copyright 2007
**Tony Bell**

A CIP catalogue record for this title is
available from the British Library

This book contains some strong language and may not be
appropriate for young readers.

The cover design is credited to Steve Kenny

ISBN-13:  978 184386 266 6

*Vanguard Press is an imprint of
Pegasus Elliot MacKenzie Publishers Ltd.*
www.pegasuspublishers.com

First Published in 2007

**Vanguard Press
Sheraton House  Castle Park
Cambridge  England**

Printed & Bound in Great Britain

# Dedication

"For the little girl I met very briefly, once upon a time, and the star she sent to save me."

# Introduction

All night parties with Van Halen, celebrity fuckfests, global coverage, sold out arenas, private jets, fan clubs, paternity suits... we had none of them. When measured on the Richter scale, the impact we had on the music business wouldn't have knocked the ash off your fag. If we had been a band of Wild West outlaws, there would no doubt, be seven more wooden crosses in Boot Hill cemetery.

From the start I had a dream. I wanted to be in a rock band and I did it. For one brief moment, I caught a glimpse of the bottom rung of the ladder. I couldn't reach it, but I saw it, I swear. If you want a classic rock and roll book, stop now, I won't waste your time. Go and buy Dave Lee Roth's "Crazy from the Heat", I don't come close, not by a long shot. Sure, we sweated the same sweat and dreamed the same dreams, but that's where the similarities end. "Everybody wants some, I want some too!" Yeah, that was me.

I was born on 24 April 1963, which means that I was infected with the trashy, zit-popping rock of the early seventies, and the cool rock of the late seventies. I grew up in a technicolour star-spangled world, wishing I had an uncle called Sam. The closest I got was "Bob" on a few occasions. I couldn't have been born at a better time, as I lived and breathed the greatest music ever. To travel the path alone would have been enough for me, but I was fortunate enough to meet some great people along the way, before being thrust together with the six lads who shared my ideals, my humour, and my dreams. As a Bobsleigh team, we would have been sat on the ice with wet arses, watching the empty Bobsleigh career helplessly off the track; but give us a few beers, our guitars, and an evening together, we were unbeatable.

We tinkered under the bonnet, and to nobody's great surprise, we couldn't get the fucking thing moving, because none of us were mechanics. However, we found that if we got behind the metaphoric automobile that was our band, and all pushed like fuck, then the engine roared and we were off. Of course there were faster, flashier

13

models around, but we were cruisin' with the hood down, all gleaming teeth, long hair and sunglasses, acting like we owned the road, so move over buddy. Every mirror on the car was angled inwards so we could check how cool we looked. Consequently, we didn't see the headlights of the cars behind us, carrying every other 80's rock band, whizzing right past, until it was too fucking late. What's the rush? We'll all get there in the end. Chill out, enjoy the scenery, there's plenty for everybody when you finally get there. Major record deals were ten-a-penny in the '80's, especially if you played "dancey" rock, and had long hair and tight buttocks.

Dancey rock? Well, we were all brought up on the best pop music ever, which glided without a hitch, into the best foot-tapping rock music ever, and set us up with a wealth of melodic inspiration. It wasn't a conscious thing at all, it couldn't have been, but by the time I started going to rock clubs, I found that beautiful girls were dancing in a suggestive, provocative, sexy manner, to the songs I loved. As well as being "ginger", I couldn't dance, so I stood on the periphery, an outcast, watching babes dance to my favourite songs, while I mouthed the words like a cunt, drunk on cider, hoping one of them would take pity on me, and fuck me for a bet. Don't get me wrong, I tried to dance, but I was fucking rubbish. Anyway, I went out to get drunk and get laid, so dancing was way, way down on my list, but unfortunately, unbeknownst to me, it was above getting laid.

No matter how much I loved a song, there was no way you could get me up dancing, but as I began to relax, my body stopped spasming and I tried to teach myself how to dance in the privacy of my bedroom. Two left feet didn't help, but I danced like I had three of the fucking things anyway. Not only that, but it looked like I had a flip flop, a clog, and a platform shoe on each of them, so there was no stability or uniformity to my pathetic attempt at winning over the opposite sex, while swinging my ginger hair all over the place. It soon became obvious that I couldn't rely on my dancing skills, so I channelled my energies into comedy, which was also met with utter disdain, and doubled up as some kind of fucking chastity device.

By the time I teamed up with the lads, we could all bump and grind with our instruments, with a degree of nounce, from the years of practice. However, if you attempted to fly your kite one inch higher than anybody else's, then the rest of the lads would fight for your strings and aim you straight into the nearest tree. Fugsy didn't spend hours ironing his "Mozart" style frilly shirt, just to be fucked off by me, pulling out a polka-dot beauty, which was held together by two buttons. Just in the same way that Rob wouldn't soak and starch his jeans, only for Steve Kenny to waltz in, wearing a tighter more faded pair. Noel didn't spend two weeks in the gym, just for Andy to do more press ups than him in the rehearsal room, as we loaded the van for another gig. It was a healthy challenge to everybody concerned that benefited all of us in some way.

We were decent enough musicians, but we weren't academic or driven enough, to even try to enter the realms of serious, disciplined, trained musicians. We could have all locked ourselves away, learning theory and notation, but that reduced drinking, laughing, and fucking time, something our rock n' roll heroes placed higher than anything remotely rudimentary musical. Steven Tyler or Wolfgang Amadeus Mozart? Hey, don't worry; I'm with you on this one. I know where I should go, but "Tyler" taught me "groove", so you can go and dig Mozart up while I tap out "Same old song and Dance" on his teeth, and then you can sling the fucker back, with an Aerosmith T-shirt on him. It may all sound a bit "cut-priced", and undeserved, but every great rock n' roll band on the planet has opened a beer, with fingers that had recently been inside some young ladies underwear, before churning out a life-changing riff for their fans. And that was all we ever dreamed of doing. Glyn, the manager of our band, was a modern day "crucifixion" bolt that went straight through the lot of us, and kept us from falling apart.

Anyway, back to that car we were in. Now I can't remember who was holding the map, but we took a wrong turn somewhere. I got the blame, I always did, but I distinctly remember, I had a beer in one hand and my hairspray in the other, so it wasn't me. As this story unfolds, the names and traits of strangers will become familiar, but as yet you've barely been introduced. Fugsy couldn't have had the map, because that would mean him having to put one of his beers down, something he would never do. Glyn was driving, so that rules him out. Rob was too busy trying to cause a rumpus between the other lads just for his own amusement, to be bothered with a map. Besides, he was too fucking lazy to apply himself to a task that held no personal gain, so I know it wasn't him. Anyway, he was hogging the wank mags, so he wouldn't be interested in a map at this particular point in time.

Steve Kenny was clunking the back of our heads with his

acoustic guitar in the claustrophobic space, churning out some "Bad Company" so he's off the hook as well. That leaves Andy and Noel, who, to be quite honest, couldn't read a map, with their bat like eyesight. Cometh the evening, and cometh the gig, they had 20/20 vision, courtesy of some big heavy duty "Jodrell Bank" powered contact lenses, but during daylight hours it was, well, the blind leading the blind to be honest. It may well be that we didn't have a map after all, and therein lay the problem. Anyway, by the time we found the road again and caught up with the pack, the very last record deal had just been handed out, and we saw the wet signatures drying in front of our eyes. I can't remember who it was, but they looked just like us, only with shorter hair, blacker teeth, and uglier birds. I wouldn't mind, but this wasn't "Last Chance" records, it was CBS, EMI, Phonogram, or BMG. The last big deal handed out to a melodic rock band, and we missed it. Glyn looked at his watch, and a smile broke out across his face. The pubs were still open.

The music business has always been a ruthless, cut-throat, greedy, mercenary, fickle, cruel, back-stabbing industry. It is run by shallow, insincere, false people, who don't possess one fucking ounce of loyalty once your album sales take a nosedive. So, they turn their attention to some other "sap" to pay their cocaine bills and keep their pool heated all year round. So, there's a certain amount of pride about the fact that we didn't quite fit in with it all. This story is about friendship first, and then music, but one could not have existed in the way that it did without the other. If you have ever been in a band, ever had close friends, ever loved laughing at the spectacularly trivial, or have been lucky enough to experience all three, then you will understand.

# CHAPTER ONE

*"Raindrops Keep Falling On My Head"*

It was raining. Fuck me was it raining! November 1991, and I had just left the Apollo Theatre in Manchester, after watching Extreme play to a full house. As usual, I was with Glyn and Rob. It was a far cry from the night before, when we played our first, and only headline gig at the Marquee Club in London. It's awesome to watch a really good band on top form, but these fuckers were just rubbing our noses in it, after we had breezed in and out of the capital unnoticed, twenty-four hours earlier. We couldn't get a fucking parking ticket.

London can be a lonely place, even when you are not homeless. Just ask the woman in the ticket office at the "Marquee" that night. At least she managed to finish her knitting. We strode into the "Marquee" with chests like Norfolk Turkeys, puffed up and proud. Yep, that was my Marshall stack on the stage there. Funny, but if you "dusted" the handles on the fucking thing for fingerprints, you would only find my set of "dabs" on it, the lazy twats. Fugsy's bank of keyboards was next to Steve's guitars, and I could read the green "Trace Elliot" on Rob's bass stack from where I stood. In the middle of it all was Andy's gleaming kit, which was attached to some hi-tech frame. Although it was normally seen in a pub, club, or shitty rehearsal room, tonight our set-up could be seen at the "Marquee" club. London, England, if you don't fucking mind.

When the doors finally opened for the evening's trade we tried to get on with whatever we were doing, but we all had one eye on the door, not knowing what to expect. I didn't expect a rush, I'm not a fool, but I expected some kind of trickle from the busy Soho streets. I went into the foyer just to make sure they had opened the doors, then I wandered outside and mooched around. Well, every Italian restaurant that had a couple of candles on the tables had a queue outside. Every take-away had a queue outside, and the "Angus" steak house was doing a roaring trade. People wandered

17

around looking at fuck-all, rather than come inside the "Marquee" that cold winter's evening. It pissed me off because I believed in my band 100%, and I wondered if it would eventually turn into one of those U2 situations, a legend. Remember? The late 70's, they played their first gig at the "Marquee", a place that held a few hundred punters. Well, since that gig, I've met loads of people who swear that they were there. If you believe every fucker you talk to, it should have been like "Live Aid."

Our chests and cocky swagger diminished by the second, as I looked at my reflection in the glass of the ticket office. My hair was fantastic, and ready to be enjoyed by girls from all over the Southwest. The woman in the booth was now doing the crossword as well as her knitting, and as she lifted her head, she didn't even acknowledge me. I must have cut a lonely figure standing on my own, desperate for somebody, anybody, to come through the door. It was the world famous "Marquee" for fucks sake. What I had failed to take on board, as I teased my hair, was that the words "world" and "famous" were yet to be used in a sentence containing our name.

A few people drifted in, and I wanted to go up and hug each one of them, but rock protocol clearly stated that I kept my distance, and remained aloof and mysterious at all times. By approaching "Joe Public", it would have raised the question of whether we were out of our depths by headlining the "Marquee", but I'm sure it wasn't what the punters expected anyway. By the time we went on stage, around forty people had turned up. I asked the woman at the ticket desk if she would lock the doors to keep the crowd in, trying to make a joke of it all. She peered over the top of her glasses, and I'm sure I heard her mutter "Fuck Off" under her breath.

It has only just dawned on me, but were these people curious, drunk, fulfilling bets, cold, or actual fans? Although there was plenty of room to lean against the stage, nobody rushed forward to get what would have been the easiest chance ever, to touch their heroes. At first, I thought there was another band playing behind the bar, because that's where everybody was standing, with their backs to us. I nearly stopped playing and grabbed Noel's microphone, and shouted, "Oi, do you fucking mind? That's just bad manners you ignorant twats!"

The floor space between the stage, and the bar at the other end of the room was exaggerated by the lack of punters on it. By the end of our set, I recognised every person in the crowd, because I had been staring at them one by one, for the last hour and a quarter. It all started well enough. We had a great intro tape that Fugsy spent ages making. Big booming cellos, and orchestra shots panning left and right, swirling like crazy with some eerie stabs on some quirky off beats, gradually getting louder and louder, with a hypnotic fucker of a heartbeat mixed in the middle of it all. Andy gave us our cue, and we all dived in, chugging on this big fuck off "A", that twisted and writhed into the smash U.S. Number One hit, "Why can't love Survive?" It was big, it was loud, it was majestic, and we were dishing it out like any top rock band, littered with sex gods would have done. Fucking hell, we were worth three quid of anybody's money. We built to the climax at the end of the song, rocking like fuck, as it ended with a big "A Cappella" chorus. The song finished, and all I heard was the sound of a bag of change being emptied into the till. Earlier in the day, I'd been eagerly practicing my autograph on a McDonald's napkin for fuck all.

Four hours back up the M1and M6 in a van is bad enough, but to share the journey with a collection of gaping, operatic sphincters, at least two of whom you would swear blind had actually shit themselves, is not my idea of fun. Don't get me wrong, I love a kebab, but something is lost in the translation when it is presented through your bass player's arsehole, mixed with everything he supped the night before. We spent more time in that fucking van than Scooby Doo and the gang. A social club with a sliding door, a bedroom without the bed, a bathroom without a shower, a shithouse without a flushing toilet, a sperm bank without the cubicles, that was our van.

Before long, it became clear that only the strong survive in the world of the van. Go on; drink as much as you can. Enjoy the night, because the more pissed you get, then the more you become the prime candidate for getting slung in the back of the fucking thing for the long journey home. This cuts down the amount of people vying for a seat in the front next to the heater, and your odds increased as the drunks fell by the wayside, in the battle for the seats. I've been the dribbling idiot thrown in with the "Marshall's", and I've been the guy next to the heater, so I knew where I should be, but most of the time I supped like a cunt, and ended up with a sleeping bag thrown over me, to fend off my old mate hypothermia, while breathing in Rob's sulphur specials.

Like I said, Glyn was the manager of our band, A.O.K. He drove the van, booked the gigs and bought the porn. "A.O.K.?" I hear you ask. "What the fuck's all that about?" Well, it's from I.G.Y. a song on "The Nightfly" by Donald Fagen... "Well by 76, we'll be A.O.K." So now you know. What's in a name anyway? Did it hold us back? I don't think so, but in hindsight I think we could have picked something a bit more fitting. I always loved "Laughing Boy" as a name for a band, and "Big Mouth" came a close second. Towards the end I wanted to call us the "Love Vandals" after we had gained a few pounds each, from the years of decadence. Geddit? Love handles? Oh, fuck off then. Don't start pissing me off, or else this thing will go straight in the bin, and you'll never find out what happens next, will you smart arse?

Anyway, anybody who has been to Manchester will know that Manchester rain is the wettest rain you will ever encounter. Big ugly drops that explode continuously. Pennine piss that defies gravity to find the safest, warmest, driest parts of your body, until it soaks your soul, and almost makes you question your love of the red and blue football crazed metropolis. What could possibly be worse than this incessant barrage? Glyn's methane filled time bomb, that's what. Desperate to continue our limited life of rock and roll, but not half as desperate as we were for a lung full of relatively clean air, me and Rob jumped out of the van in the town centre and headed for the pub. After the long journey in the back of the van, I looked like Columbo's scruffy brother. Still, we had a few quid between us, so there was a good piss up in our pockets, and enough for chips on the way home. Glyn took the van back to the mill in Ancoats where we rehearsed, and arranged to meet us later. Smelling like a couple of wheelie bins, we trudged on through the pissing rain, watching each others precision engineered hairdo turn to shite. We ended up in a bar underneath the Piccadilly Hotel, slightly the worse for wear.

There is something totally romantic about being able to return to the place of your birth after being away for even the shortest period in your quest for success, no matter what field it encompasses. To return to a rain sodden town, and still feel that "tug" deep inside your gut, no matter what may or may not be promised elsewhere, is almost ethereal. We weren't away for eighteen months on world tours, in fact the longest I was away from the place was three weeks; but I was out of town almost every other weekend, be it gigging or clubbing, for years. Manchester isn't the easiest place to love, but that's why I love it. Murders became almost a daily topic on local news bulletins. Some people in the city got a shit deal regarding education, jobs and homes. The youth of the city weren't prepared to put up with the spectre of a dismal future full of failure before their lives had begun, and unfortunately, the Police were the only tangible face they could vent their anger against. Drugs, guns and violence became a feasible way of paying the rent and keeping the bailiffs from the door, but people always believed there was another way.

Manchester is now a massive success story, and the city has been transformed over the last decade, into a hi-tech, vibrant, multi-lingual, multi-cultural, multi-sexual, big fucking bouncy castle, just like it always should have been. This didn't happen by chance or by accident, this was down to the people of the city, from the councillors, the investors, the traders, and most importantly, the ordinary, hard working, honest people of Manchester. Oh, and a big fucking bomb! Of course there are still problems, there isn't one fix to cure everything; but the people still struggling with their own personal demons have somewhere to turn. New York, Milan, Cannes, Sydney, I've known people who could afford to live in any of these places, but they chose to save on the cost of sun tan lotion, and splash around with the rest of us, like Gene Kelly, "just a singin' and a dancin' in the rain."

Now, to continue without mentioning hair would be to negate the story. For us at least, everything began and ended with long hair. Soft I know. Basically, the longer the better, but you had to have style. It was the benchmark for judging "cool", it was an invite to parties, it was an extra "star" out of ten for your band, but most of all, it was popular with the girls. Some lads missed the point completely, but it was perfectly clear to all of my mates, that if you looked good, then girls will fuck you. Throw in a guitar, and the long hair they had grown to love, and you were laughing. Within minutes of meeting Rob, we were heavily into a discussion about the benefits of various hair products, and the ones to avoid. The conversation progressed into our top ten of rock hairdos. This was a man after my own fucking heart alright. Next we threw in a good hour about women and our favourite porn stars, just to re-affirm that neither of us were gay, despite the obsession with grooming, and cleanliness.

Gay, straight, it never bothered me, I was too busy enjoying myself, but facts are facts, and the fact is, I'm straight. I'm not "dissing" any kind of sexual proclivity, and I'm certainly not trying to appease the "politically correct", as you'll see as the story unfolds. If you both enjoy it, whether it's boy/girl, boy/boy, or girl/girl, steady there lads, then its positive energy being expelled from both people, so what's the fucking bother? Oh, I almost forgot, girl/boy/girl. Well I can dream can't I? Anyway, I can't see the problem myself. People have the flimsiest excuses when voicing their opinions on sexuality. "Well, it never happened in my day." Maybe it didn't, or people were too scared of the repercussions, but hey, guess what, slavery and Nazism were around in the past. Does that make it alright, you wankers?

Hair was a big deal in the rock community, and the bigger you could make the fucking thing on a Saturday night, the better you felt, the more people would talk to you, and the more girls would want to shake your bones. Not once, but as many times as was physically possible between 3am and the sun rising. Luckily, it was a time when the length of your hair, and not the length of your knob, got you into the most sought after panties around. I spent ages learning how to back comb it, how to tease it, how to twist it, trying to perfect the "just got up" look. I bought a new hairdryer that had something called a diffuser. I had a shower, opened a beer, and put on some Van Halen. Fuck me! Twenty minutes later I was Adrian Vandenberg. "Somebody's gonna get some leg tonight for sure!!!" I ferreted my way into some crazy, dirty situations, all because some tasty girls fell for the long hair and slim torso. I didn't even have to try, I just sat back, let my hair grow, and ate every thing I could lay my hands on. It doesn't matter in your twenties; every fucker has got the metabolism of a cocaine addict, so you remain stripped of any body fat for the whole decade. I was practically see-through for ten years.

For years I had been a barren wasteland, desperate for some female attention. Do you know what I craved most? All I ever wanted was for a girl to put on some perfume, just to smell nice for me. Of course, if a girl did that it might lead to sex, but a girl taking time out, to make herself nice, just for me, well that was beyond me, but I lived in hope. The key to it all is that lads are idiots, and girls are cool. There you go, I've told you the secret, and it has cost you fuck all. Well, not if you've borrowed the book anyway. Lads are too busy checking over their shoulders, to see if their buddies are watching, as they fuck it up and miss out on a beautiful girl. Girls sit at home and plan exactly what they want to happen. Once they have decided what they want to happen, they orchestrate it down to the last minute detail, before making you think that it was all your own doing. Yes, it's just fucking struck you hasn't it? You've been "had" by the most beautiful girl you've ever met. Well go buy her another diamond just for being the girl she is. I did.

I wouldn't describe myself as superficial, because that takes away the history that led me to where I am. You might not like me, or the musical path I chose, but don't you fucking dare question what drives me. I was a complex mix, somewhere between Les Miserables, and Les Dawson, but with mighty long hair. Once my hair started attracting attention from the girls, I took my foot off the gas, and let them chase me a bit, but that's what any lad on the planet would do, given half the chance. They had planned it that way anyway, so what was I to do? Try and scupper their plans of doing a striptease for me, in their co-ordinated black stockings and suspenders? I don't fucking think so my friend.

As my hair took on a life of its own, so my own life changed, with girls appearing out of nowhere, wanting to take me home and cuddle me. Absolutely fuck all had changed except my hair. I always thought I was mildly amusing, but not to the point where girls laughed at the slightest thing. In fact, I became less funny, because I didn't have to try as hard anymore. Like Rapunzel, my hair was my way out, so I made every effort to make sure that it always looked its best, night out or not. Throw in a gig, and it was bedlam. Manchester Rockworld, Cardiff Bogeys, Norwich Waterfront, Bristol Bier Keller, Edwards Birmingham, Wolverhampton Wulfren Hall, The Tivoli in Buckley, The Night Owl Gloucester, The Astoria London. The list goes on and on, but I never forgot my VO5 gel spray… not once.

My heroes all had cool hair. David Lee Roth, Paul Stanley, Steven Tyler, they all had it going on…big time. These were all "big hitters" from the '70's, who had almost two decades of looking outrageous under their belts. There must have been some rigorous fitness regimes involved, because these guys had the bodies of athletes. Tyler was like Iggy, with his "stripped" body wrapped around his mike stand. Roth had the whole martial arts thing going on, with an amazing set of oblique muscles to boot.

Stanley? Well he was like a fucking Greek god, with the

23

shoulders and biceps to match. He looked like he'd been rowing the Argonauts' boat under the Mediterranean sun for a couple of summers, while the rest of the crew slept off the wine. I must admit, that if I ever saw any of them walking down the road towards me, then I'd cross the street. Not for any other reason, than that if you hold these people in such high esteem, then any chance meeting can only be a let down. Can you imagine meeting any of the above, after they had just spent the day being grabbed and pulled this way and that by their fans? You may be the final straw that enthusiastically snaps that camels back. Tempers must fray in these situations, after years and years of being recognised and mithered. Can you imagine? "Hey Dave…" "Fuck off." I enjoyed the man far too much to ever chance it ending that way.

By far the biggest band in the world when I was getting into rock music was Led Zeppelin. They had a cool logo, with that Icarus type chap on the Swan Song label, and I was aware of all the destruction they left behind at the "Hyatt" on "Sunset" and the infamous "Red Snapper" fish at the "Edgewater Inn", but I was too young to "get" Led Zep, having only been five or six when their first album was released. No, I tell a lie, by the time I was listening to them, I did get it, but I just never liked them that much. Probably ten songs that blew my fucking socks clean off my feet, but you can keep the rest. "Sacrilege!" I hear you scream, but who gives a fuck? I certainly don't. They were spoken of in hallowed, revered tones, and respect is obviously due, but you have to be true to yourself with something as important as music.

My favourite Zeppelin member? Well, seeing as you're asking, it's got to be Richard Cole, the tour manager. For those four guys to get on stage each night, it took a lot of planning. Not only did it take planning, but it also took love. Zeppelin was a tight unit, that worked because of the devotion of Grant and Cole, who did whatever was required, to get the band the best deal in town. Now I'm getting sick and tired of recommending other authors, but you've got to go and read Richard Cole's book, it's fantastic. Anyway, I could have bought all of their albums and pretended to like them, just to fit in with the majority; but there was something about Joe Perry's Les Paul slung around his back while he played his "Strat." Something about Dave Lee Roth's and Eddie Van Halen's youthful exuberance in the face of dinosaurs; and something about Stanley's voice and songs that removed any possible need for Led Zeppelin in my life. It matters not one iota that all three of my favourite bands cite Zeppelin as one of their major influences. It works the other way too, because Motley Crue will enthusiastically acknowledge that Kiss, Van Halen and Aerosmith were massive influences on them, but I managed to plug that leak before they seeped into my world. Like I said, it's probably an age thing, but those red marks on my sleeve come from where I chose to wear my heart.

The '70's was the decade when I started to recognise different tastes and smells. A time when I came alive, and forged my own opinion based on what my mates told me, and what I actually thought for myself. Out of all of the bands that were already established during the '70's, I think the music of Deep Purple has grown the most gracefully over the years, making me return again and again, to listen to the magic I just didn't understand at the time. Like me, there were thousands of lads the World over, impressed just as much by a great haircut as by a great melody. As the '80's clambered on top of the '70's, these lads relocated to Hollywood California, to instigate the '80's "hair metal" phenomenon. Taking their cues from Roth, Stanley, and Tyler, they wrote heavy metal pop songs and added two handed hammer on guitar solos. They had all reached a plateau of musical excellence, and then decided to compete for the biggest rock and roll hairstyle, west of the Capitol Records building.

Then came Adrian Vandenberg, the guitarist with Whitesnake during the late Eighties and early Nineties. He looked like a male Kim Basinger, churned out "Give me all your Love" down on one knee, and wore a Phil Lynott style military jacket. Put the best picture ever taken of me, next to the worst picture ever taken of him, and then drink ten pints. See, I look just like him don't I? I totally got it with this guy. I got all my stage moves off of him, and I deliberately left magazines with pictures of him in, open on coffee tables, praying that somebody would notice the similarities. Despite coughing like a cunt, and rustling the magazines, people either ignored me because I didn't even register in their brains, because I was absolutely nothing like him, or it fucked them off totally, because I was that man. Yeah, well I don't need you to tell me do I? Like me he was tall. Like me he had some fucking long hair about his personage, and like me, he was at his best in "soft focus." At this point, the blue of the sea may seem to merge with the blue of the sky, but like I said, I am not gay. Not that there's anything wrong with being g... Aaaah, Fuck Off, this isn't the book!!

# CHAPTER TWO

*"I Don't Want A Rock DJ..."*

Back in Manchester it was still raining. Fuck me was it raining! In the bar we bumped into Chris Tetley, who presented the rock show on Piccadilly Radio. He was holding court with a crowd of young kids, recounting tales of excess he had been told first hand, by their heroes.

Although he was the local DJ, he had met everybody. He has interviewed every top rock star you can think of, and his interviews were released as picture disc vinyl, with a picture of the relevant bands on the disc. Needless to say, he interviewed Gene Simmons and Paul Stanley, so I was always into him about them. I could tell that they weren't his favourite band, but it was a "power" thing. If he knew you liked them, then he had you. He changed in a split second, into this gregarious character, dangling snippets of your heroes' right under your nose, as you fought your way to the bar to buy him a drink.

He played our songs on his show, and also featured us in his music column in the Daily Sport newspaper. Now you can already see that there is room here for conflict and tension from the off. On one hand you've got an experienced DJ, with a foot in the door of David Sullivan's media empire, who says "Yay" or "Nay" as to whether we end up on the radio, or in the press, and who is very, very drunk. Then you have two council house gobshites, who have never had anything from anybody, suddenly finding that they are part of a band, who, although we had no record and no deal, were starting to get the odd bit of recognition from here and there. Oh yeah, we were very, very drunk.

I was born in Ardwick, right around the back of the Manchester Apollo. Inner city living, where the love you received, painted a "sunshiny" picture over the "unbombed" houses left over from the war. Rob was a child of Wythenshawe. Newall Green, to be precise.

Wythenshawe was Ardwick with fields. Only you couldn't play in the fields, because they were part of the fucking airport. Living on a council estate opens your eyes to sex at a very early age. Not because everybody was at it, or because there was some bizarre initiation ceremony when you reached the age of twelve. Well not for me anyway. No, what it was is that every time you turned a corner, there were a couple of dogs shagging in the street. Open your curtains first thing in the morning, and there were two dogs humping away on your lawn, next to a steaming pile of shite. While you were waiting for the bus, there were two dogs hammering away in the bus stop. It didn't matter that one of his back paws was resting in a big dollop of dog shit, he carried on regardless. Sometimes there were packs of dogs roaming the streets, just jumping on each other at will, and banging away until they swapped over to another dog, barking and growling like fucking crazy. And then you go and ask me why I was like I was!

Anyway, answer me this one if you can. Why is it, when you get an itch in between your shoulder blades that you can't reach, by the time you've contorted your body into the most ridiculous shapes, and managed to reach the fucking thing with the very tip of your little finger, the itch is "off", on a full tour of your back, darting as you chase the bastard thing everywhere, but it's always one step ahead of you? This carries on for ten or fifteen minutes, and before you know it, your clothes are in a heap on the floor, and you are wanking like a fucking madman. Well? Right then, give me a couple of minutes to get dressed, and we'll carry on with this fucking thing. Yep, that's better.

For some reason, Tetley called me Rob, and Rob, Tony. I used to think that he was taking the piss because we looked similar. Well, if you flattened Rob's hump with a spade we did. Anyway, after correcting him several times we gave up, and I became Rob and vice versa.

Tetley was pushing fifty, maybe older, and was always turned out in black jeans, black T-Shirt, and a black leather biker's jacket. His look was finished off with the whitest pair of trainers you have ever seen.

Tetley. "Alright Rob?"
Me. "I'm Tony."
Tetley. "I played two of your songs on Wednesday."
Me. "Yeah, Glyn told me."

Rob pays for the beer and hands out the drinks.

Tetley. "Thanks Tony."

Rob. "I'm Rob."

Tetley. "What?"

Rob. "I'm Rob. Anyway, what happened on Wednesday? You played our songs at the wrong fucking speed. The tape was running slow. It sounded like a demonic message played backwards."

Tetley. "Well, all of your songs start slow anyway. How was I to know?"

We were far too drunk to argue, so we jumped in a taxi, and headed for the Apsley Cottage, which is a cosy little boozer next to the Apollo, and was always bursting with rockers whenever there was a gig on. Tetley said that he had some passes for the Extreme concert, so we bought him a few drinks and he handed over the passes. The passes had the Extreme logo on them, along with the bouncer from the cover of the "Pornograffiti" album. Now these had to be applied with precision. To plaster it over your chest would give the game away, you're trying too hard. I think it was Freud who said, "The less you show, the more you know." So, bearing this in mind, I stuck the pass on the inside of my black leather, and folded the edge of the pass over on to the lapel. You could still see that it was a pass, but only the "E" and "X" of the band's name was visible. Fucking cool or what…!! "Good evening ladies!!!"

I had been in the "Apollo" bar dozens of times before, watching total fucking nobodies from the local rock scene wear out a good pair of shoes, while parading up and down, with a backstage pass they had embarrassed themselves whilst getting. This was the biggest night of their lives, so they made sure that the rest of us having a pint noticed the "Sammy Hagar" or "Scorpions" logo slapped on their leather. As they pranced up and down in the cramped "Apollo" bar, they missed out on the all girl sex show going on backstage (which they had a free ticket to, slapped on their chests) just because they wanted to let us know that they had a pass.

It was this kind of fucking nonsense that made me cringe as I stuck the pass on my leather, but the beer had dulled my senses, and I was out to get laid. That's why I hid the majority of the pass on the inside of my jacket. I didn't want to hear people shout "wanker" as I passed them in the bar. I was one of them, I was there all of the time, and I wasn't pretentious in the slightest. I knew who I was, and I knew where I belonged. There again, why didn't I hide the pass completely? So, there was an element of me that wanted to be noticed after all. Wanker! My place was with the rockers out front, not with the sycophants back stage, whose lips bore the faintest whiff of shite, from being around the arseholes of total strangers. I had no intention whatsoever of using the pass, neither did Rob, but I intended to put it to some use in a sexual experiment, at some point during the evening. This was the only benefit of having a pass. There was nothing else to be gained from having one. Can you imagine being sat backstage with AC/DC, and everybody is ignoring you, as people fall about, laughing and drinking? All of a sudden, somebody notices you sat on your own, and asks all innocently.

"Excuse me, but who are you?"

"Err, nobody really."

There is nobody but yourself to blame, because you thought you were somebody, when you slapped that fucking pass on your chest. You thought you could compete. Let me tell you now, if you stick a pass on your jacket, and you haven't got a pussy, then you are a fucking idiot to think that you will be included in anything slightly rock and roll by your heroes. Think about it, where did your pass come from? If the band didn't give it to you personally, then you are not relevant, no matter what you think. They don't know you, and they certainly don't care about you in slightest. You might be the best looking fucker on the local rock scene, but that doesn't matter where millions and millions of album sales are concerned. You are fuck all, and you will have to wait until long after the local "slappers" have finished, before you hand over your shitty demo tape to a pissed roadie. Then, you will stick your rose tinted spectacles on, and bore people for months, that it was the best night of your fucking life, you sad twat. Grow up.

Anyway, if we were quick, we had time for another drink in the "Apollo" bar. "Right." said Tetley, "I won't be a second. I'm just going to get ready." He staggered off, and disappeared into the toilet. Rob's expression mirrored mine. It was a look of puzzlement, with a hint of "Hurry up you cunt" thrown in. Tetley had silver wiry hair, which was just past his ears, in a kind of "Sir Bobby Charlton" sweep over. Thick bushy sideburns continued where his hair finished, and went right down to his jowls. Rosy red cheeks completed the "Amos Brearley" makeover. Tetley returned from the toilet with a red bandana tied around his head. Now I've not sniggered for fucking years, not properly. Remember the sniggering you did at school?

Well I turned to look at Rob, and his shoulders were shaking up and down in complete silence. His head was bowed down so I couldn't see his face, and he was biting his beer glass, trying to stifle his chuckles. Oblivious to our new source of amusement, Tetley finished his beer and left the pub ricocheting off every wall, like a well played Pinball. To be fair, we got a higher score on the way out after him.

Now to be honest, I don't remember too much about the gig, apart from the light years' difference between them and us the night before. Oh yeah, Nuno had this cool knee brace on, as he had apparently injured his leg earlier on the tour. I searched for weeks afterwards, but I couldn't find one anywhere. After the gig we shuffled out on to Stockport Road, and ended up talking to a group of girls. We had met up with Glyn in the Apollo bar, so Larry, Curly and Mo set about their comedy routine, for the benefit of the ladies. I forgot to duck a few times, as the "Plank" of irony twatted me full on in the face. Then the blonde bailed me out.

"Is that a pass?"

"Why, do you want it?" I enquired.

"It can't be a real pass or else you wouldn't be offering it."

I could understand her reasoning. After all, passes weren't that easy to come by, and they carried a certain amount of status in some peoples' eyes, so why give it away?

"Look" I said. "Rule number one. Get as many passes as you can. Rule number two. Never ever use them."

She didn't understand. Like I said, the thought of joining a queue to kiss somebody's arse never appealed to me. If you were male and had a backstage pass, and used it, you were a cunt. Surely that makes sense? Passes were invented for girls, and should only ever be used by them.

"O.K. I'll have it", came the doey eyed reply.

"Right then, that'll be one blow job please."

The girl laughed nervously. "I can't do that."

Mentioning the words "Blow job" in the vicinity of my knob is like shouting "walkies" to a dog. Before I knew it, the fucking thing was straining this way and that, but to no avail. She was calling my bluff, wasn't she? Needless to say, the relationship went quickly downhill. She never did take up the offer of short-term employment, and the pass is now in a scrapbook somewhere.

We made our way back to Glyn's car, which was parked on a street nearby. As we approached the car, we noticed a group of maybe a dozen people talking. All of the cars on the row had been broken into, and these were the victims. There was glass everywhere, but Glyn's windows were intact. It looked like he had escaped the vandalism. He went to open his door, but there was no fucking lock there. Someone had punched the lock right out, and the door opened without the key. Upon further inspection, the boot had been opened using the release lever on the floor.

Glyn had not emptied his car from the previous night's gig, and had left two boxes of the band's T-Shirts in the boot. They were gone, along with our bags. Unruffled, we began discussing where we could still get a drink, when somebody shouted.

"Hold on."

A guy picked up something from the bonnet of his car. "I've got a black Waiter's jacket here."

"Actually, it's a fucking Bolero jacket and it's mine." I replied. I snatched it from him, half gutted, half elated.

Somebody else shouted. "I've found some ripped jeans, with paint splattered all over them."

I scurried over and claimed what was mine. Sitting underneath a street light, I checked my jeans, to see if there was one more night out to be had from them. I wasn't a proper Doctor, but it was clear even to me, that they were 50/50 at best. I felt a tap on my shoulder and turned around. Without saying a word, a girl handed me a silver bracelet with purple stones all around it.

"Thanks", was all I could muster.

I found one of my cowboy boots in the middle of the road, and not long after, the other was found. I couldn't decide whether they had been run over, or if they were just encrusted with the shite engrained in them, from the floors of a thousand rock clubs. It was a result, even though my complete existence had been "dissed" by a total stranger. Some people have no taste.

These were "Happy Mondays" scallies or "Stone Roses" fans who did this, we were sure. After all, the "Stone Roses" or their fans desecrated Central Library, and a few other high profile places for fucks sake, so a few cars was no problem. We blamed anybody local that was doing better than us. 808 State, James, The Smiths, Simply Red, M People, Lisa Stansfield, and anything "Hookey" touched. Yeah, this was a fucking conspiracy all right. As the city threw unassuming stars into the nation's eyes, the rock and heavy metal bands of the city sat patiently, sure that the explosion would reach us all eventually. We were right. The explosion came, and I felt a wave of ecstasy, that had been missing for a while. Unfortunately, the explosion took place over a pair of pert breasts in an alley somewhere not far from "Rockworld", and had nothing to do with my band. Something to do with my hair, apparently.

It was weird really. I have no shame in admitting, that girls were just as much the driving force in my quest for stardom, as the music I loved and the lifestyle I craved, but I could draw the line, and separate the two in order to get things done. I auditioned and jammed with bands that would have a crowd of girls sat giggling away, or one miserable tart draped across a "Marshall", pulling a face because nobody was giving her any attention. Usually she was the singer's, or guitar player's girlfriend. This kind of carry-on snowballed for two reasons. Firstly, some pussy-whipped musician, with spandex pants and a shit hairdo, didn't have the balls, because of his own insecurity, to tell his girlfriend to fuck off and leave them alone, while they got on with what might make her redundant. Secondly, they were in a band that didn't really consist of mates. Not real friends, you could scream at and square up to, and then go for a pint. So, undercurrents raged, and these bands didn't really last too long.

Of course, a few weeks later, they were back together as a new band, with a couple of new members, and they were all scowling at the same fucking girl as they played away. A truly dreadful state of affairs I know, but it could turn much worse. After a couple of rehearsals, the girl on the "Marshall" starts humming as you play. When you stop for a break, she tells her boyfriend that she has been singing along in her head, to the tune being played. Before you know it, she's got the microphone in her hand, singing her ideas, and she is the new lyricist. Don't laugh; I've seen it all before. Or, what about the embarrassing moment when the singer stops for a snog, when he should have his mind on the pussy he'll be chasing when she's not at the gigs, the soft twat.

Then, there was the chemistry. Chemistry; it's a big word that conjures up some fucking bizarre experiments that can result in history changing cures and discoveries, right down to Frankenstein's monster. I was a fool to myself, because of my desperation. I travelled far and wide in my search for a few guys that wanted to do the same as me. Nothing earth shattering, nothing too radical, just an honest, justified attempt at getting on the payroll. Some of these bastards shouted the "odds" so loudly, that they didn't need a phone. I could hear them across the junkyards of the city.

One such guy tricked me into a journey up Ashton Old Road to audition for his band. I knocked on a rotting front door, and was greeted by Uncle "Fester", no word of a lie. He was fucked. Usually, I would have pirouetted like "Roth" and fucked off, but he grabbed me while I gasped, and before I knew it, I was inside the "Addams" residence. I couldn't hear the harpsichord, but true to form, "Lurch" made his appearance, ducking under the doorframe without saying a word. They led me into "Fester's" bedroom, where the ugly band members were kept. Fucking hell, the walls were painted matt black, with glossy black crosses on them. There were books lying around with "magick" in the title. Not "magic", but "magick", so you could tell that these fuckers couldn't get laid for love nor money. We made our way to some lock up that they used as a rehearsal room, and played "Am I Evil?" for about an hour; by which time I thought I was on the set of "Beetlejuice", so I called an end to it all and fucked off. I bet they searched around for one of my hairs once I had left, so they could make a Voodoo doll. Well I hope they backcombed the fucker first.

So, there are loads of band politics to deal with that have got nothing to do with the music, before you even start playing gigs. Clothes being another gem. I've never had any smart clothes, I didn't want them, but I did want to see a common link throughout a band that at least made them look like they gave a shit about what they were doing. Go on; wash the fuck out of your jeans. Fade the bastard things. Lie in the bath with them on; wear a black leather jacket with nothing underneath. Show the girls you fucking well mean it, and woe betide their tight little asses if they doubt you for a second. Do they know who they are dealing with, standing there all innocent in their shimmering lip-gloss, with not a fucking scrap of underwear under that tight short dress? Attitude, that's all they wanted from you. They wanted to be told what was going to happen to them, if they stared at you for one second longer. They needed to know that you would be every bit the dirty bastard they expected you would be. They needed you to be the fucking animal they were desperate to shout about at the tea point on Monday morning. Hell, you fucking well dressed like that, so you might as well act like that. Don't let them down, that's what I say.

Anyway, I could never be doing with girls hanging around rehearsal rooms. Girls are what happened after you had spent days moulding ideas in a shitty, damp, smelly, hole of a room. If you went into a room with all of your creature comforts, and that includes girls, then where did your desire and your hunger come from? There have to be sacrifices, there has to be risk, there has to be heartache, there has to be rejection, and there has to be complete fucking lunacy, to think that you can sneak up along the rails, and cross the finish line as the 250-1 outsider. If you could succeed at this without any heart, without any conviction, without any sacrifice, then every fucker would be out there living the life of a rock star.

A.O.K. was perfect for me. Not a single woman around in the daytime, and hundreds of them at night. Yeah, right. When we first got together, we immediately agreed that there would never, ever, be any girls in the rehearsal room. You don't know how refreshing it was, to hear that from a gang of lads, who, when we weren't rehearsing, were trying to figure out where our next fuck was coming from. From previous experience, I thought I was the only fucker around that cringed when the rehearsal room was littered with girls, no matter how great they looked. Like I said, it was nothing personal, but we needed space to let our minds run wild, while trying to pluck up the confidence to goad each other on, to pose like the stars we aspired to be. I didn't need the distraction of trying to come up with an idea, while trying to look up a short skirt, hoping for a glimpse of a gusset, or if I was very lucky, a split second sight of a real life, living, breathing, pussy, which, by the way, would have belonged to one of my mate's birds.

We raced along, without any real master plan, confident in the music we played and the way we looked, believing that this was enough to elevate us to superstar status. We weren't big-headed, we just believed in what we did. We believed that we did it well, and we believed that we looked shit hot while we were doing it. After that, your conscience is clear to do whatever the fuck you think necessary to get there, because you have met the criteria for success. The rest is down to chance, fate, timing, commitment, and the ability to kiss some fat arses along the way. We all fell at the same hurdle, determined to give not one ounce of respect, credence, or acknowledgment to anybody who thought they might be able to make a dollar off the back of us, especially if they had a fat arse. And believe me; we saw some big arses between us over the years. Mostly, it was while getting changed, ready for a gig, but I digress. The stage was set early on, by a gang of "gobby" individuals, determined to get drunk and have a fucking good laugh. There was no room for middlemen, leeches or wide boys, so, by making it clear that there was no free ride for anybody, to anywhere, we avoided insufferable fools from the start.

# CHAPTER THREE

*"Have You Seen Junior's Grades!!!"*

Music wasn't a frequent visitor to the Bell household. Not in its' Sunday best anyway. Sure, my Dad could croon some wicked songs while he was shaving, getting ready to go to the pub, and you knew that they were classics of their time, but crotchets, minims and quavers couldn't reach the fucking door knocker. My younger brother Steve was the first to take the musical plunge. One day he came home from school with a violin, signalling his retirement from football at the ripe old age of eight. He rolled up the sleeves of his Bay City Rollers tartan jacket, let out a nervous fart, and then proceeded to amaze us for a good fourteen seconds, before being told to button it. Fourteen seconds, and not one correct note. Something that came back to haunt Bell the Elder on a few occasions, years later.

A few weeks later, Steve came home without the violin, the beast he could not master. Everything was back to normal, and I could get back to watching Shaggy and Scooby unmask the villains in peace again. The following week Steve came home with what looked like a tiny suitcase.

"What's that?" I asked.

He lay the case down on the chair and opened it. It was a fucking trumpet. I found out later that it was actually called a cornet. At least this was a laugh, watching him go cross eyed, while his bulging red cheeks looked set to burst. It looked like he was sucking air in through his arse, to help him reach the final notes of "Three Blind Mice." Luckily it didn't last too long, and Mum was soon back to washing two filthy football kits.

In a way I felt sorry for Steve, because once rock came to Burnage, he was right in the thick of it with me. He had no choice. One morning he went to school, sick and tired of staring at my Abba posters. When he came home, Paul and Gene were pouting and snarling at him from every corner of the bedroom we shared. Turn

37

away from them and you were met by Ace's smoking Les Paul, or Criss's levitating drum kit. He didn't stand a chance, as I took over every scrap of spare space on the walls. If you are a Kiss fan from the '70's, you will be aware of those fucking huge posters you could buy. I'm not even going to describe them, because you know exactly what I'm talking about don't you? The cherry in his mouth? Yeah, that's the one. Steve not only put up with my adolescent nonsense, but he kinda grabbed the tail of it all, and he opened his mind and loved a lot of the rock music I brought home.

I will always remember my very first day at work, after I'd left school. Not because it was such a great job, or it was great money. No, what I remember is walking in the house, fucking starving. My Nan had the chip pan going, and I was given a cup of tea and told to go and sit down, after a hard day. Steve was in the kitchen with my Nan, and he brought my tea in to me. He handed me the plate, and I immediately noticed that he had cut the chips in a perfect Kiss logo. Each letter was one massive chip. He must have had the potatoes in the bedroom, as he followed the shape of the Kiss logo as true as possible. Star.

As I daydreamed about rock music and playing in a band, Steve started turning up with armfuls of shields, medals, and plaques from the football team he played for. Suddenly, every shelf had a medal or award on it. It was like the fucking "Oscars" in our house some nights. I was really proud of him, because he loved his football at the time, and he was good at it. In fact, I'm sure I let him use the shelf above my bed to store part of his growing collection. Well, there were no medals with my name on, putting a strain on my shelf, or gold discs come to think of it. So, from a distance, I started to look successful, as long as you couldn't read the name.

If you have a younger brother, there is only one time you are going to hate the fucker with a passion, and it was a horrible experience. I am a couple of years older than Steve, and consequently left school before him. No big deal really, until it comes to the six weeks holidays in summer. All of a sudden, I'm the only fucker up in the house, and Steve was lay there, wondering what to do with himself for a month and a half. I felt violated that I had to get up and go to work, while he woke up to a cup of tea and a plate full of toast all bastard summer. Oh yeah, and all of the next summer as well! What could I do? I'll tell you what I did. I walked in and woke him up every day. It didn't faze him at all. In fact one morning he said, "You've just missed your bus, idiot." Consequently, Steve stored this information, and as soon as he started work I was fucked. Any day I wasn't working, when he was, I suffered. He sat on the edge of my bed, tapping my foot, saying "Tony, Tony, Tony, Tony, Tony, Tony", for fucking ages. It was like Chinese water torture.

The Seventies are so well documented that I don't feel the need to dwell on them, and that's a real big pity. A week rarely goes by without a retrospective television programme or CD for sale that evokes everything from that era. I've been raped of the most treasured memories of my childhood, as they are blazed across all sections of the media. That was supposed to be private. They can't tell my childhood in two thirty minute episodes, not even with the best intentions. The only point I will make, is that communication on a physical level, the thing that made this planet thrive, is in decline. The kids, who are our future, live in a world of e-mails and text messages. People will tell you that it's evolution, and all part of the journey, but I think it is sad that a child can now be recognised by the ring tone on their mobile, rather than the sound of their voice. But what of the future? America believes they can colonize the Moon before my toes turn skywards. So, I expect to read about the first rape or murder on the Moon before I die. It will probably be next to a picture of a Moon buggy on bricks. We don't deserve this fucking planet, so we should be trying our hardest to keep human scum off any other.

The only "plus" I can make out of all this technology, is the DNA machine I am going to invent sometime in the future. The plan is that if you are a sad, unloved, ugly, bad breathed, virgin, then I can help. Firstly, you pay around £500,000 for the machine. Then, all you have to do is obtain a loose hair from the coat of an absolute babe. Stick the hair in the DNA machine, and leave it switched on overnight. Next morning you have a perfect clone of the babe you saw, and you can fuck them senseless for the rest of your life. Obviously, it will be aimed purely at the male market, because girls just don't need this kind of thing, because girls are in charge. Yep, sad lads everywhere will be sleeping out around the clock, just to get their hands on one of those babies. I'm gonna get awards for that fucking thing, you just wait and see.

My best mates were Mike and Chris Harris, who are twins. They lived two streets away, and I've known them since I was four or five years old. We grew up together, went to the same schools, played for the same football teams, hung out together, laughed together, cried together, and said goodbye to loved ones together. Our shoulders were all at different heights but they all seemed to be at the same level when we needed somewhere to turn to. I might have been the slowest runner out of the three of us, but they always slowed down while I caught up.

After thirty six years, I know I can still knock on their doors and get a hug that might break my fucking back. Sometimes I don't see them for months at a time, but whenever I hear their voices, I remember a corker of a goal scored in Fog Lane Park. Yeah, so what if I was in nets? Or a great song we listened to in their garden, or a ridiculous pair of flared pants I wore to one of their parties. We all had the same number of stars on our jumpers, and nobody's centre partings were as symmetrical as mine, but guess what? Apparently I was the only one who looked a cunt. My excuse is that I was a rocker caught up in a world of punk, which was always going to be hard. What people forget, is that while punk was at its pinnacle, so was disco too, and I loved Nile Rogers as much as Steve Jones. There were some talented people knocking about, turning out some great music. Ian Durie, Glen Tilbrook, Debbie Harry, Edwin Starr, Earth Wind & Fire, The Jacksons, Elvis Costello, Jake Burns. However, in my world they were all bit part players in the world of Paul Stanley, who ruled the planet.

Mike and Chris have an older sister Debbie, and an older brother called Dave, who I think, is around ten years older than me. It might as well have been a hundred years difference. Dave had cars, motorbikes, records and girlfriends, and from what I can remember he had loads of each. I lost my musical virginity in the Harris household. If Dave was in, he used to play his records and tell us about the bands. If he wasn't in, it didn't matter, we'd rummage through his records anyway, to find something we liked. Abraxas by Santana, the first four Zeppelin albums, Deep Purple, Cream, Simon and Garfunkel, the Beatles, Black Sabbath, the Beach Boys. It was all great stuff, and mixed with a healthy dose of Abba a few years later, definitely set me off in the right direction.

School came and went practically unnoticed. I'm quite laid back, so I'm sure this is why. Captains of industry will disagree, and tell you that school is where they were moulded. Criminals will probably tell you, that school was an angst-ridden battle from start to finish.

Football ruled my life from 1969 until 1977, which is a long, long time. In fact, the majority of my youth was spent chasing a plastic bag of wind around a cold playground. I wouldn't mind, but I reached my sporting peak around 1970; so I kind of faked the next decade by smiling, and occasionally shouting the odd tactic over the playground; oblivious to the severity of the situation I had just created, as I read my "Sounds" while running aimlessly up and down the pitch.

School, really was about what you made of the options available to you. My option was to rock. In 1978, there were about seven lads in my class who liked rock music. We sat and compared who had the longest hair, when the best any of us could offer was a bad David Cassidy. One of the lads turned up one day, clutching "Rainbow Rising." I nearly shit myself, and that was just looking at the cover. I was almost scared to listen to the fucking thing. That Ken Kelly painting lent itself perfectly to the brilliance etched in the grooves. He had a good 1976 that Kelly bloke, as he also did the artwork for "Destroyer" by Kiss. There was a network of borrowing and taping albums, so that nobody need miss out on what the others were talking about, and it worked well. AC/DC, UFO, Scorpions, Rush, Thin Lizzy, Alice Cooper, Rainbow. My collection was growing quickly, until some fucker knocked on the door and I had to hand half of it back. I soon separated the wheat from the musical chaff. I was up and running, and there was no fucking stopping me.

By making time and taking time, I was finding some truly amazing music that just wasn't played on the radio back then. I think that people who settle for chart music, no matter how much they like the individual artists, are just lazy bastards, waiting to be fed what programme controllers decide we should hear. Dare to look deeper and you would be amazed at the passion and feeling waiting for you, if you could only be arsed. It was just like finding gold. After your first nugget there is a wave of euphoria, and the excitement at possibly finding another. When the second one comes, you realise that you have located something special. However, just like finding gold, you keep your mouth buttoned, because you want it all for yourself. The only time you are interested is when you meet somebody who knows where there is even more gold. Well, I turned into "Klondike" Pete, as I shared my wisdom and my gold, for fuck all. What did I want in return, after being so frivolous with my life changing discoveries? Well, one of my mates could have at least turned up with a babe of a sister, or cousin who was colour-blind, and hence could not recognise the colour ginger.

Born ginger. It sounds fucking awful doesn't it? People with cleft palates used to take the piss. I'd be walking down the street next to a big fat cross eyed hunchback with a gammy foot and people would point at me, the twats. Strip me down to get the full "orange" effect.

A few people actually liked "ginger" hair, but a certificate from the Home Office, got those insane fuckers off the streets, sharpish. Some people were happy with their own "gingerness", but again, it was a temporary arrangement, and could be easily rectified by hypnosis, mind bending drugs, or a good fucking kicking. Once puberty hit, hair started sprouting from everywhere. Not just a bit around each nipple, it was like a bastard rug, from just under my chin, right down to my ankles. Every fucking one of them ginger. I looked like I was on fire. If I'd have had any sense whatsoever, I would have avoided rock music like the plague. It was plain obvious, that if you were a "ginge", then you became a skinhead, and shaved the lot off, and adjusted your braces accordingly. To make any kind of impact in the world of rock, you had to be prepared to let your hair sprout forth and multiply.

So, as you can see, the predicament I found myself in was an absolute bastard. I looked like an extremely pissed off cross, between the lion from "The Wizard of Oz", and "Pan." Aye, that mythical fucker covered in ginger hair with hooves for feet, that's the chap. Alright, he had better feet than me, but I never wanted to be an open toed sandal model anyway.

Short ginger hair was bad enough, but long ginger hair? That was gonna take some fucking doing alright. It was going to be a bumpy ride if I committed myself fully, but I wasn't ska or reggae enough to give myself a choice, so "rock" it was. Cilla Black, Neil Kinnock, Rula Lenska, Bonnie Langford, Lulu. There wasn't even much of a celebrity "ginger" list to attach myself to, if I ever got there.

So, let's recap. As I took my Abba posters down, my face broke out in spots, which at least averted the gaze from the ginger hair creeping slowly down my neck. I was getting pretty handy with my hairdryer, and was quite adept at the old "centre parting" carry on. Once I was happy with the style of my hair, it suddenly dawned on me that it was still ginger. Bastard.

Things couldn't possibly get any worse, could they? At least I had reached rock bottom, and the only way from here was up. A smile broke out, as I was convinced that Mother Nature had done her worst, and I was still alive. I ordered up a pint of lager and lime, and sat in silence, knowing that things could have been a lot worse. All of a sudden, the doors flew open, and in steamed Mother Nature, twatting me around the head with a barstool, catching me completely off guard. Yep, my arse hairs were ginger too. Ouch.

Well, you can't exactly be sexy being a "ginge." There is no horny way of taking your pants off in front of a girl, when there is a big mound of "ginge" heading their way. It looked like I'd been rubbing down a rusty old bike with wire wool, for fucks sake. Best thing, is to get the fucking lot off as fast as you can, and make the most of the time available. That's if you can stop them laughing for long enough.

Now, if that wasn't bad enough, there was the total indignity of meeting a fellow "ginge." If you knew a "ginge", or were known by a "ginge", it was easy, you just avoided each other at all costs. It didn't matter that they might have turned out to be the greatest fucking mate in the entire universe; we were out of bounds to each other, forever. It wasn't planned it was just the rule, passed down through two millennia of "ginge." Thinking back, I never liked the ginger kids at school anyway, just as they probably didn't like me. Like them, I was a constant reminder of what Mother Nature could get up to after a night on the piss. My only saving grace was that my hair was straight. One of the ginger lads at school was a white, anaemic looking fucker, with freckles the size of cornflakes, but get this; his hair was wiry, like a big afro. I felt like Cary Grant next to this poor twat. Locally, I knew all the gingers, and the places to avoid, but out there in the big wide world they were around every corner, the ginger twats.

Bumping into a "ginge" by surprise was fucking horrible. If you saw each other coming, you could both adopt the Pink Panther "shuffle", and avoid each other by the skin of your teeth. Other times there was no warning, and from nowhere, "Boom", you were stood awkwardly face to face, like some bizarre experiment. In these situations, I just convinced myself that I wasn't as "ginger" as the ginger twat I had just encountered. It's only just dawned on me, that my poor brother had a ginger brother. I'm sorry Steve.

By the mid to late 80's I had a big full mane of blonde hair, which to be honest, should have been in place since birth. Some bird bought me a leather jacket that had a kind of carpet sewn into it, all the way around the middle. It was a bit Red Indian in its appearance, and I wasn't too happy with it. She took her clothes off, leaving only her black stockings, suspenders, and high heeled shoes, and convinced me that it was actually a great jacket. Anyway, I kept the fucking thing, and gradually became less embarrassed about it. One day I was fighting my way through a crowded Piccadilly station, when I came face to face with an old dosser, wearing the same jacket as me. I might as well have been bright ginger again. No amount of stockings and suspenders would get me to put that fucking thing back on again, but she didn't know that.

# CHAPTER FOUR

*"Kiss Me, Honey Honey, Kiss Me"*

Early 1978, and it was around this time that I first started listening to Chris Tetley's rock show on Piccadilly Radio. I can still remember, it was a cold evening, and I was lying on my bed. He played "Shout it out Loud" from Kiss Alive II, and I was hooked. I'd never heard of them before, let alone seen a picture. He described their make up and stage show, and how they would never play in the UK, partly due to their popularity in the States, but also because no UK venue could accommodate their huge stage show. Now this was fucking interesting. I immediately had a weird conception of them looking like "Nosferatu", from that old black and white film from the '20's or '30's that was made on that boat. Yeah, kind of like him, but with long hair. The chorus of "Shout it out Loud" buried itself inside my brain, until I could take no fucking more. I made it my quest to track down the band, and it didn't take long. Piccadilly Records came up with the goods. The first Kiss album, "Destroyer", and "Hotter than Hell", were nestled behind Carole King. Over the years, I came to associate "Tapestry" with Kiss, even though it was Carole King's album. She was always perched right next to Kiss, and I used her as a mental bookmark. In the end, I bought "Tapestry" and fucking loved it, so there you go. Some kind of moral in there somewhere, but you can pick the fucker out yourself, because I can't find it.

Anyway, back to Kiss. I was mesmerised. I inspected the covers and I wanted "in." Dry at the mouth, I put the albums back while I decided which two I would buy. From nowhere, and without warning, four guys in make up, high heels, and Lycra outfits, dared me to not like them. Dared me to put their albums back, dared me to laugh at them, dared me to buy "Led Zeppelin", who were hovering within arms reach. Dared me to lick my lips, to alleviate the unexpected dryness, dared me not to pick a favourite band member, dared me to keep quiet about them, dared me not to join them on their journey, dared me to dismiss their androgynous, sinewy, foot stomping assault as fake. I daren't. I can't explain what happened; this was beyond Noddy's hat and Dave Hill's silver boots. But there was more. From the corner of my eye, I spied a record out of place in the rack. I picked it up, it was Kiss Alive II. After being greeted with that massive Kiss logo on the front of the album, I turned to the back cover. Whoa! Those evil soulless eyes, the face dripping with sweat, the menacing look, and the blood. Aah the blood, it was splattered everywhere. Now that was fucking cool.

Albums were not vacuum packed at the time, so I opened the sleeve, expecting more group photographs. Fucking hell, this was getting serious. There was fire and lights everywhere, as the band descended on to the stage in the now legendary, Barry Levine photograph. You don't even need to listen to Alive II, just look at this picture. Sodom and Gomorrah at 33 1/3 RPM. I was soon on my way home with Alive II and their first album. The first album contains the classics they are still playing today, and a couple of "not so" classic tracks, but this was my calling. My road ahead was made of brick, a strange yellow colour, and was a one way street. What can I say about Alive II? I felt like Wylie Coyote, when the Acme bomb goes off in his hand. You're either with me 100% on this one, or not at all. If you're not, then fuck you.

I am the first to acknowledge the fact that most rockers ridicule the band, and the media tear savagely at them. From the uninspiring music; to the image they hide behind; to divert the spectator from their musical ineptitude; to the juvenile merchandising machine. Yeah, yeah, yeah. I fucking loved it, and collected every article I could find. They didn't understand, it only made us stronger. Every other band, before or since, has not had this effect on people. Other bands can wrestle indifference from a neutral. Not Kiss. People loved them or hated them, and it's still the same today. Kiss force an opinion, either totally positive or totally negative, and they wouldn't have it any other way.

Have you ever read Rolling Stone magazine? Rolling Stone inspired latter day publications like Q, and Mojo, and applied the lipstick for the arse kissing of Bob Dylan and Jerry Garcia to continue. At the end of the day, music is about entertainment, pure and simple. It's not hard to understand. From Beethoven to Marilyn Manson, it's all the same. From Chopin to the Spice Girls, they are equally as valid. My eleven year old niece will get as much enjoyment from the latest Pop Idol winner, as a Professor of music will get from Mozart's Concerto N° 40 in D Minor. And nobody will ever tell me any different.

Charles M. Young wrote an article for Rolling Stone during the Seventies, which compared the music of Kiss to a Buffalo fart. Apparently, according to "Chuck", Dung Beetles recognise the smell of a Buffalo fart, because they promise shit. Pretty much in the same way that the music of Kiss promises shit. "Is that the best you've got?" I thought. This guy obviously sat down and thought long and hard about this. So intellectual, so fucking clever, so smart, what a guy. Then he researched this whole fucking angle. He sat there with thick encyclopaedias, ruminating over different texts, cross checking it with nature periodicals and "Dung Beetle" monthly; the sad, sad man. Once he was convinced he had a whole new twist on the Kiss phenomenon, he actually thought somebody would be interested, and his point would be valid. For me, Paul and Gene reigned supreme as the architects of my destiny, while he ended up looking a twat. It was obvious, that while Gene and Paul were tearing the world apart, fucking every age, shape and colour, this clown was sat at home, clutching Kiss Alive close to his chest, wishing that he had somebody to "Rock and Roll all Nite, and party every Day" with. "Italian for one tonight Charles?" …Cannelonely.

I couldn't understand why, if these people didn't like a band, not just "my" band, but any band, they didn't find a new group to champion, and add something positive to the debate.

Then again, if you are writing about the biggest band in the world, people will read what you have written, rather than stumble across your inane offerings, when they have run out of text to read, whilst taking a dump. At its most basic, its $75 per 5000 words, compared to $300 per 5000 words for the big boys. You might have already guessed, but Kiss was the biggest.

The detractors did nothing, but multiply my belief, tenfold. Similarly, the great reviews I basked in were only for the chosen few. I don't think anyone was converted, no matter how good the review. It wasn't long, before me and Mike Harris would enter record shops, purely to look for Kiss Alive II. Once located, we would open the cover, and leave the fucking thing propped up on the end of the rack for the world to see. Kiss Alive II was our "Watchtower." Spread the word. Nowadays, bands everywhere will tell you what an influence Kiss have been on their careers. It's funny, but back then I can only ever remember me and Mike shouting it out loud. Over the years, I've lost girls because of Kiss, and met girls because of Kiss. I caught Stanley's plectrum during "Love Gun" at Bingley Hall, on September 5th 1980. I caught Eric's drumstick at the same gig. The last time I saw them, was the fifteenth Kiss gig I had been to. I'm by no means the biggest Kiss fan in the world, and I'm not trying to pass myself off as that dude, because Kiss has some fucking loyal fans. Besides, I know that some fans go to fifteen gigs on each tour, and will laugh out loud at my paltry attempt to take their crown. Something I wouldn't dare.

Conviction, is a big word, unless you are actually wholly convicted, then its fuck all. Go on, love a band, any band, it's great. Put your fist up and punch that fucking air for no other reason than you can, and that it feels fantastic. Fight your corner because you love them; tell a lie because you love them; miss a train because you love them; lose a bet because you love them; fuck an absolute "howler" because you love them; lose face because you love them. It doesn't fucking matter, because if you can do any of this with conviction, then you are the winner. Music separates you from every other teenage shmuck in the neighbourhood. If you didn't have music and the "raggle taggle" bunch of friends you met through the bands you loved, then you would be just another silent face in an ever increasing crowd.

I noticed a trend developing, which can be applied to practically anything in life. A psychiatrist will know exactly what I am talking about, and no doubt there is a popular term for it. I think there is an element of wanting to feel secure in unfamiliar surroundings, when you have no real information about the situation, but there is a touchstone to identify with in the middle of it all (or some bollocks like that). If I was in a crowd, and I recognised somebody with say, a "Kiss" or "Van Halen" T-Shirt on, then I would stay close by, and probably make an effort to break the ice with them. Now if this person turns out to be a right twat, I would persevere and tolerate them longer than normal, just because I knew we liked the same music. It doesn't matter, that the guy ten feet away, in the "Jethro Tull" T-Shirt might be the funniest fucker in the world, I just wouldn't entertain him because I didn't like the band. Take the T-Shirt off, and change it for race, colour or religion, and you finally "get" the world.

# CHAPTER FIVE

*"I'm A Yankee Doodle Dandy"*

Intrigued by what America had to offer, I dug deeper. I didn't have far to go until I found Aerosmith. They were amazing. I started with "Rocks", and then "Toys in the Attic." Tyler and Perry ran the show, and are two of the coolest fuckers I have ever had the pleasure of losing the feelings in my legs to, whilst watching. Behind them were Kramer, Whitford and Hamilton, playing out of their skins for third place.

The Seventies were mythical times for rock bands, and Aerosmith defined the Seventies more than any other pill popping, line snorting, self-destructing, bourbon guzzling, stadium fillers. If you've read the Stephen Davis book, "Walk this Way", you will be as amazed as me that "Live Bootleg" was ever made in the first place. If you have not read "Walk this Way", may I suggest that you take this book back, explain that it is shite, and get a credit note, with which to purchase the aforementioned Stephen Davis book. How many times will you hear that from an author? See, I'm honest. Too fucking honest for my own good sometimes!

"Live Bootleg" was made to look like an authentic bootleg album. The cover looked like it was made from poorly printed cardboard, and it had two coffee cup stains on the back. I adapted mine by actually adding a third cup stain on the back. Not only was mine now an original, but I could also check if some shifty bastard was trying to "lift" it from a party. I truly believed that every girl's "Kitty" was in the middle of a swing like they didn't care. "Back in the Saddle", "Sweet Emotion", "Toys in the Attic", "Dream On", "Chip away the Stone", "Walk this Way", "Lord of the Thighs", "Mama Kin", "Come Together", "Train kept a Rollin." Could I take any more?

"Ladies and Gentlemen, I give you Van Halen."

"Fucking Hell, go easy on me guys, I'm only fifteen"

"Fuck Moi", as they say in France.

I didn't think that anything would come along and challenge

Kiss, not so soon anyway. After all, we'd only been seeing each other for a while, and I was still besotted, but Van Halen had shorter skirts, higher heels, and made me laugh. Like any great first love, I was over-protective of Kiss. I couldn't relax in company, I was nervous when introducing them to friends, and I could only hope that people found them as much fun as I did.

Van Halen hit me like some kind of fucking baseball bat wielding freight train, but they always made sure they kissed me better afterwards. Simmons and Stanley, Tyler and Perry, and now David Lee Roth and Edward Van Halen, I was definitely on to something big. My brains were at bursting point, as wave after wave of sheer Van Halen brilliance washed over me, and left me tingling. They had the songs, the musicianship, the "Beatles" harmonies, and the looks. Dave and Eddie took their respective roles to the max and all for little old me. Hands up, if you wanted to be in a band after this. Man, I'm scraping the paint off the fucking ceiling. Like Mike Tyson years later, they swept everybody aside, and went straight to the top. Undisputed heavyweight champions of the World.

The delight in the music they created was the fresh uninhibited approach they had. Blessed with a painful amount of talent, they never let me, or millions of others down. David Lee Roth is articulate, witty, clever, and is a raconteur of the first order. There are countless stories and tales that have been told and retold over the years, so please forgive me while I open a beer, raise it to Van Halen, and in particular to Mr. Roth, while I recall my favourite.

Dave was working with an Orchestra, which I was led to believe was during the "Crazy from the Heat" EP. You may need to check that with him. Anyway, these people are professionally trained musicians, and Dave could sense that an air of animosity was developing. In America, there are strict Union breaks that Musicians need to take while working. During one of these breaks, Dave had a wander round the empty studio. He picked up a violin, and gave one of the tuning pegs a gentle tweak. A short while later, the Orchestra returned, and continued playing.

"Whoa, stop." said Dave

The Conductor looked puzzled, and asked Dave what was wrong.

"Somebody is out of tune."

The conductor waved his baton and continued. Dave stopped them again, pointing as he shouted. "Hey, you at the back."

"Who me?" came the reply.

"No, the guy sat on your right." said Dave.

The guy checked his violin, and of course, the fucking thing was out of tune. He sheepishly corrected the problem, and the recording continued. Dave had them eating out of his "arseless" leather chaps. This guy does more on his lunch break than most of us do in our whole lifetime.

While reeling from the "Force 9" of Van Halen, I stumbled across the first Montrose album. I couldn't believe that this fucking thing was released in 1973, and I had never heard of it. No bastard had even mentioned it to me. Was it some kind of conspiracy? If it was, I was "Agent Bell", at your service. Big dirty guitar riffs, heavy pounding drums, and Sammy Hagar giving it everything. Then there were the songs themselves, every one an absolute gem. "Rock Candy", "Make it Last", "Bad Motor Scooter", "Space Station N° 5", "Rock the Nation." My neck aches just thinking about the fucker. Tremendous! My spiritual co-pilot, Lieutenant Mike Harris, joined me on many an inaugural journey, as we turned up at each other's house with a bag full of albums, which we sat and listened to for the first time, together. Two cups of tea, a handful of digestives, and a big tub of Vaseline. Oi, fuck off. I know exactly what you are thinking you weirdo. Well think again, I don't fucking like digestives!

My love affair with music was blossoming, and in addition to the music, I bought albums because a band looked good, or because I recognised a producer's name. North America provided an endless stream of bands that I could immerse myself in. Starz, Angel, Journey, Loverboy, Foghat, Cheap Trick, ZZ Top, Boston, Styx, Ted Nugent. They all hit the spot.

Then there was the music press. "Sounds", "Melody Maker", and "NME", they all gave me my weekly fix. There was a shop in Manchester called Paperchain, where I bought magazines imported from the States. "Hit Parader", "Creem", "Circus", and for fucking reasons I cannot to this day explain, on a couple of occasions, "Rolling Stone." Yeah, let it be known for the record, that any reference to "Rolling Stone" magazine be struck from the story from this point forward. This magazine made me question artists I maybe should have had a bit more respect for; but to see their names in "Rolling Stone" had me gritting my teeth and snarling, as my heckles brushed against the top of my cage. Bearing in mind what I have just said about "Rolling Stone", all of these publications were instrumental in the metamorphosis of this boy; but first I had to work on removing the words "Ginger", "Specky" and "Twat" from any description of me. This was not going to be easy.

# CHAPTER SIX

*"There's A Star Man"*

In the late Seventies and early Eighties, Geoff Barton was the Editor of "Sounds", and he was a huge Kiss fan. In late '78 early '79, one particular copy of "Sounds" boasted, "Next week, Geoff Barton's exclusive interview with Paul Stanley." The clock limped around like it needed a fucking walking stick, but the day eventually arrived. The interview was accompanied by a couple of pictures. One was a silhouette of him looking out of his balcony. The other picture was full-page size, showing him without his make up. His right hand covered his face to protect his anonymity. His hair was a work of art, a magnificent thick black mop, teased and lightly backcombed to perfection. And he could sing; boy could this fucker sing. Gripped by Rock fever, I did what any lad would do.

"Hello, is that Hairline?"

"Yes."

"How much is a perm?"

"They start at ten pounds."

"Can I make an appointment please?"

The girl took my details, and I was booked in for Saturday morning. Fucking hell, ten quid? That was a bit steep, the robbing twats. Then again, I'd have probably handed over fifty quid if she'd have asked for it, knowing how desperate I was to be curly. Until then, I had sported the "Richie Cunningham, "Happy Days", Ginger Cunt special." Nothing to be proud of I know, but now it was time to stand up and make a statement, my statement. Saturday came and I headed off to the hairdressers with my "Sounds" under my arm. After being seated and given a drink, I was handed several magazines, showing different hairstyles for me to ponder. I told the guy that I had brought my own picture of how I wanted it, how I needed it. He looked at the picture, and said it would be no problem. Relaxing into the chair, I felt at ease.

"Go ahead Raphael, fucking paint me!"

It was an uncomfortable experience, but I had to focus, and look to the future. This was my re-birth, and I was coming out fighting. People were going to stop and stare when this "baby" was finished. Two hours gave me plenty of time to drift off, deep in thought. Would I be a mean and moody type, or would I be the life and soul of the party, "Mr. Popular"? Maybe I could be a mixture of the two, some kind of unpredictable loose cannon, but always interesting, yes, always interesting. I knew a lot of lads that had long hair, but there was no style involved in the late '70's. They all looked like Geddy Lee or Uli Jon Roth, so I reckoned it was time to bring a bit of American glitz to the streets and clubs of Manchester. Alright, alright the street corner, the park, and a pub now and again; if I was lucky, but I was dreamin'. I could feel the excitement welling up inside me as I prematurely crowned myself the saviour, the phoenix, the forefather, the catalyst, the leader, the pulse; of the re-birth of long hair as we knew it. Someone had to break away from the old generation, on the horizon of the '80's, and I stepped forward without any qualms. New decade, new attitude, new blood. It wasn't advertised anywhere, but this was the job for me all right.

Suddenly, I shouted out "Fucking hell!"

The teeth on the roller dug into my head as the hairdresser wound the fucking thing too tight.

"Sorry."

"It's OK."

Somewhere in Manhattan, Paul Stanley was going through exactly the same. Not this particular day, but somewhere in Manhattan, somewhere in time. This kept me focused, as the foul smelling potion was slapped all over my bonce. It smelt like cat piss burning my poor nostrils. Then the itching started. I was pulling the most contorted faces, hoping that they would move the skin on my head, in a desperate attempt to bring some relief to my frazzled scalp. I looked like a stroke victim going through physiotherapy. There was no respite; there was no "give." It was a fucking intense sweaty experience that managed to make two hours seem like twelve.

Finally, the hairdresser started to remove the curlers and my heart began to race. As he dried my hair, the curls tightened and shrank towards my skull. It looked like a fucking old ladies perm.

"Oh no, what the fuck's gone wrong?"

Close to tears, I searched desperately for some reasoning

behind this heinous crime. I flicked frantically through "Sounds" just to see if there was a Leo Sayer interview, and the hairdresser had used the wrong picture. The hairdresser noticed my distress immediately, and obviously sensing my displeasure, gave me the biggest beaming smile I had ever seen.

"Hey don't worry; they all look like this to start with. It'll drop, trust me. They all do."

Was there any truth in what he had just said, or did that mean he just fucked up every single perm he ever attempted? I paid the man when I should have belted him, and ran home. I went straight to my room and stayed there, for about two months, fucking gutted.

Now then, my next-door neighbour was a great girl called Jackie. She was a couple of years younger than me and she loved rock music. I made the mistake of telling her I was going to get my hair permed. I was sat upstairs staring into the mirror, pulling and stretching my hair for all it was worth. There was a knock at the door, and I knew it was her, just coming to check out the "new" me. She loved Led Zep, and especially Robert Plant. I made the most ridiculous mistake, of telling her that my hair was gonna turn out like a cross between "Stanley's" and "Plant's." Well, maybe Ada Stanley's and Gladys Plant's, from the Bingo Hall, but that was as close as I was gonna get. I answered the door, with my shoulders somewhere around my knees. She set off laughing, and finally ended up on the floor. I felt like crying, and the longer it went on I got more angry. She couldn't fucking well speak, and I managed to break out into the smallest smile imaginable. She didn't even look up to see my smile, and the anger raced through my veins again. She stopped to catch her breath, and I jumped in.

"The hairdresser said it will drop."

That was it, she was off again. I shut the door and left her there.

# CHAPTER SEVEN

*"Another Piece of Meat"*

Despite the number of new bands I was finding weekly, I had not yet been to a gig. This was all set to change, as I had a ticket to see Whitesnake at the "Apollo." It was worth the price of the ticket just to be part of the brethren. This is how it felt to be truly alive. I can honestly say that up to this date, the Whitesnake concert was my first religious experience. By religion, I mean a faithful devotion; not the pious, racist, biased, murderous, intolerant, sexist, homophobic, torturous God, you have created, to try and justify centuries of sadistic abuse against each other. If there really is a Day of Judgement looming, then you're fucked, I'm fucked, we're all fucked. I've never really believed, I've never needed to; but if there is a God, he could use a good "Spin Doctor" at the minute. Any sad crackpot, weirdo, misfit or lunatic can cause carnage in a school with a machete or a gun, and then try and hang their straight jacket on God's coat peg. Me? I'm happy to sit on the fence, trying to figure it all out. It's not ideal, but at least I hope I'll be ready to shout "Yes Sir", if my sins are read out. I only hope that I'm behind the old bastard in the robe, trying to explain why he tied his rosary beads and his cross together, to stop them jangling, while he fucked a choirboy from behind. Now give me a "bottom E" while I tune this fucking harp.

Anyway, most of the people wore denim jackets, embroidered with the names of their favourite bands. These jackets were works of art, painstakingly completed to meet the concert deadline. I spent ages wandering around, standing so close to people, just to see if any of their "Rockness" would rub off on me. I remember Rob way before I ever met him. He had a faded Wrangler jacket, with "Sheer Heart Attack" on the back. However, it would be a while yet, before me and my soul mate became "Morecambe & Wise" style bed partners. I had a fucking corker of a jacket, that one of the girls at school spent hours embroidering for me. I had to mither her to make sure I had it for the Sammy Hagar gig at the "Apollo", so she put the time in, while phoning me with regular updates, letting me know how cool I was gonna look.

I knew she liked me, and she spent hours on my jacket, hoping I would take her out. In the end, I bought her some chocolates for doing it; when in hindsight, I know I should have stripped her naked, and eaten the chocolates off her young, taut, unblemished, virginal flesh, and unloaded months, no, fucking years, of pent up aggression all over her breasts. Then again, she would have looked like a fucking snowman. Ah well, at least Hagar was brilliant.

Whitesnake came blazing onto the stage in a sea of lights. As they tore into the opener, Coverdale greeted us in his regal English accent.

"Good evening my serpents... Are you ready?"

I stood there motionless with my mouth wide open, while all around me people were going ape-shit, shaking their heads and punching the air. I wasn't prepared for any of this. Had I gotten in too deep? By the second song, I was holding my ears flat against my head, to stop my glasses falling off. This was my initiation. Almost two hours later, I walked out of the "Apollo" like Frankenstein. I couldn't move my head, and I had to twist the whole of my upper body, just to look around. My ears were ringing, and I was soaked in sweat. Clutching my tour programme, I staggered to the bus stop, physically and emotionally drained. Later, I lay on my bed staring into darkness, unable to sleep. Images raced through my mind, reliving the spectacle, over and over.

"Goodnight John Boy."

"Goodnight Pa."

The next day I went into Manchester, and bought "Lovehunter", the latest Whitesnake album. Another love affair had begun.

To fund my addiction, I worked in a Butcher's shop while I was still at school. Nothing too strenuous, a few hours after school, and all day Saturday. I had to be in the shop for 6.30 on Saturdays, which, during the winter was a bastard. I could tell that I was slowly being introduced to the real world. I suddenly started to recognise the smell of warm kiddies pyjamas. The ones I had just stepped out of, to be precise. Blue paisley "Sitcom" specials, that wore at the knee before anywhere else. It didn't matter, all I wanted, was the means to go and buy albums and posters, and fucking loads of them. "Butchery" may not be the obvious choice, but you go and get the "music" bug, and then decide what you are prepared to do, to get the cash to let you indulge in the thing that takes up all of your living moments. Not only was rock music the best music on the entire planet, we had the dirtiest, sexiest, horniest girls, ready to shake their asses, free of charge, to my favourite songs, time after time after time.

On my first day, the boss, John Higgins, set me my first task. I had to fill a bucket with hot soapy water and scrub the kitchen floor. It was a stone floor that sloped gently towards the door.

"Don't forget to pull the cooker out and clean behind it", he said.

Armed with my brush, I scrubbed like fuck. When I moved the cooker, I noticed a piece of paper on the floor. It was a crisp new ten pound note. John had obviously planted it there to test me. Ten pounds would have bought me three albums at the time, but I had a better plan. I dropped the banknote in my steaming bucket, and held it under the bubbles with my brush. I kicked the bucket over, and the banknote slid across the floor. It came to rest in the corner, where I proceeded to mash the fuck out of it, grinding it into the sawdust. It was in tatters, all faded and shredded. John reappeared to inspect my work. He wandered around, looking at the floor. Hands behind his back, he peered behind the cooker.

"Was there anything behind here?"

"No."

"What do you mean?"

His eyes fixed on my brush. He reached down and picked the shreds of paper from between the bristles. "Oh, for fucks sake."

"What is it?"

"This… this… it's my fucking money."

I bit my lip to try and stifle my laughter.

"It was a fucking tenner this, how did you miss it?"

He stormed back into the shop, my first paying customer.

John employed a lad called Kevin Reeves as a full-time butcher, and there were three of us that worked part-time. I hit it off with Kev straight away, as he was fucking mad. He took the piss out of my hair and the music I loved, the least I deserved. He was one funny guy, always dreaming up pranks. It was like living in a comic for three years. I was half expecting "Roger the Dodger", or "Minnie the Minx" to drive past the shop, in a home made Go-Kart.

John had a fruit and veg stall outside the shop, which was situated at the junction of Fog Lane and Kingsway. One busy Saturday I was serving on the stall, when I heard somebody shout my name. I looked up, and saw one of Kev's mates, called Myles. He was sat in his open top MG, stopped at the red light. It was sunny, and two of his mates were in the back.

"Hey Tony, throw us an apple."

I picked up a shiny red apple and threw it. He caught it, and handed it to his friend. I threw another, which he gave to his other mate. At this point Kev appeared, and I told him what I was doing.

"Hurry up, only one more." Myles shouted.

Kev started rummaging in the box of tomatoes, and pulled out the biggest, dirtiest "Fuck Off" tomato he could find. One side of it was white, due to the fact that it's sell by date had long gone. He picked it up, and lobbed it into the car. The tomato, exploded up the side of Myle's face, and over his shirt. The debris hit the dashboard and sprayed on to the windscreen. He was covered in tomato shite. He tried frantically to clear his windscreen, but the tomato smeared his view perfectly. The lights turned to green, and the drivers behind started honking away.

"Fuck off, I've been hit." Myles shouted.

He crawled off at a snail's pace, waving his fist in the air. "I'll get you pair of twats." His voice trailed off into the distance. I'm still waiting.

We were busy serving customers in the afternoon, when Kev walked out through the back of the shop, into the kitchen. I assumed that he was going to use the toilet, but he picked up a tray of eggs that were kept in the kitchen, and he walked out into the yard. I was still serving a customer, but I could see out of the corner of my eye, that he was throwing the eggs over the roof of the shop, onto the pavement at the front. All of a sudden, it was raining eggs. Shoppers were ducking, and running for cover. Most of the eggs exploded on the floor, but I remember one guy running into the shop for cover. He stood there with raw egg dripping off his nose, down on to his fag, which was still dangling from his lips.

"What do you know about this?"

My face was contorted, I dare not reply.

"It's nothing to do with him, he's serving me."

A hastily assembled defence was provided by the woman I was serving. However, under cross-examination, I would have been fucked.

There was a lad called Billy who used to do some work with us occasionally. Now I use the term "work" loosely, as he is the laziest cunt I have ever met. I never knew the full facts of the story, but John owed him one, and he was always given a job when he turned up. He had a scar on one of his hands, so I suspect that the injury happened while working for John. Then again, if it involved work, the accident wouldn't have happened at John's, the lazy twat. He turned up to work in a dirty blue suit, that was around six or seven years old. Bearing in mind this was 1978, it put the suit's heyday around 1972. The lapels were huge, but nowhere near as big as the pants. You could probably make three suits from the material that was hanging off him. The fashion police needed "back up" with this one, especially when they saw his Marc Bolan platform shoes. Once in the shop he would change into a pair of trainers. To give us credit, we never grassed him up, but as soon as John left the shop, "laughing boy" always made an excuse to get out of the shop, and go missing for a couple of hours. One day, he had been missing all afternoon.

"This isn't fucking on Kev. He's taking the piss."

"I know; I'll sort it today."

I didn't ask how, I was prepared to wait and see. All I was certain of was that something would happen today, and I would probably get a laugh out of it. Closing time came, and Billy was still missing. I filled the huge steel mixing bowl with boiling water, which was used to clean the knives. The water was so hot, that it popped and hissed like a madman's experiment.

"Pass me his shoes," said Kev.

I could see what was coming, and like Peter Lorre, I obeyed my master. Kev dropped the shoes into the bubbling water, and cackled like a witch at her cauldron. He weighted the shoes down under the water, and we carried on cleaning. Twenty minutes later Kev removed the shoes from the water, and dropped them into a sack of sawdust, shaking it like a cocktail.

He grabbed them out of the sack, and threw them on to the floor, where they lay still, steaming from their encounter, totally fucked. Billy returned later and took off his apron. He found his shoes where he had left them hours earlier.

"Oi, what the fuck's all this?"

"What?" said Kev.

"My shoes, they're fucked." he confirmed.

"I'm sorry Billy, they must have been near the steel bowl," I replied.

"Why didn't you move them?" Billy was desperately flicking sawdust off his shoes.

"Too busy. If you'd have hung around you could have moved them."

Billy sat on the step cursing us, while trying to shoe horn his feet into his shrunken pride and joys. As he stood up and walked towards the door, he fell over. What we didn't realise, was that the heat of the water had warped the shoes, and neither heel was flat on the floor. The soles were also arched, but by no means equally. He told us both to "Fuck Off", as he made his way out of the shop like Dick Emery in his "Ooh you are awful" sketch. That night, we celebrated our victory by going to watch Bob Marley. I never saw Billy again.

# CHAPTER EIGHT

## *"Cranked Up Really High"*

I knew that I wasn't really ready for alcohol, because I drank cider. Sweet, sticky, gassy, sugary, cheap rubbish, sold in two litre, lemonade style, plastic bottles. You know the script though, don't you? You reach an age, when alcohol is thrown at you, whether you like it or not. Spirits, beers, cocktails, cider, they all head your way. Naively, I thought that girls would follow a similar sort of pattern. Maybe they did, but not in my neck of the woods, I can vouch for that. So, alcohol stood behind me, and instead of fucking me up good and proper, it took pity on me, and unleashed a kind of cross between a panto horse, and a stand-up comedian. There was always something to hide behind, if my comedy went "tits up"; but I could also take the horse's head off if anybody loved what I did, and I could say, "Hey, look, that was me." This must look so obvious to you, but this thing has manifested itself for twenty years inside me, as I have ducked and dived through the "gingerness" of my teenage years, right up to the date that I strutted out, knowing I could compete with any fucker on the block. Not just my block, but your block as well!

Anyway, apples? What damage could an apple possibly do? I soon found out. Cider puke is one nostril burning, sweet then sour, smooth then lumpy, fizzy, smelly, son of a gun. Discretion is, of course, the Ace in your pack at any party.

"Guffaw guffaw, simply marvellous."

You're in control, cohesive, and sharp. As the night goes on, you find yourself forgetting what you are talking about, as soon as the sentence finishes. Then, you know you are in trouble, so, like "Rigsby", you interject with a witty comment, then excuse yourself impeccably. Absolutely charming. Once outside, your legs buckle like they are made of elastic, and you yak your lungs up, frothing like a horny Werewolf on a full moon. You can't see, because of the stinging tears running down your face, and you can't stop because the phlegm and chest sewage is stuck in your windpipe, turning the whole fucking process into a cycle.

Remember discretion? Well cider won your discretion in a Poker hand, early doors. There are no witty comments, there is no charm, there is no fucking exit. Oh no Sonny, cider is here and cider is now. Everything happens in exactly the same way as explained, except you don't leave the room. If you are still standing, you are very lucky. By this stage, I was on all fours, retching as the involuntary spasms offered up, what was basically shit, dragged back from my small intestine. People were dancing around me, to "Don't fear the Reaper." Will someone change the fucking record?

I woke one morning in a flat, after an altercation with a gang of apples. Big fuckers mind you, nothing to be ashamed of. I was clutching an electric guitar, an Epiphone SG copy. The party, or the abridged version I attended before I passed out, was great. Somebody was playing along to "Kick out the Jams" on the Epiphone, as the smallest apple started "gobbing" off. Before I knew it they all dived in, and I was mincemeat. The guy who owned the flat was selling the guitar, and I was the new owner. Well it was either me, or some other lad that wanted it. Whoever could produce thirty pounds first could have it. I tiptoed over a crowd of bodies who looked like their parachutes hadn't opened, and legged it home for the cash.

Fucked beyond imagination, I hammered on the door after the return journey. I walked home triumphantly with the "Golden Fleece", suddenly realising that I couldn't play a fucking note.

I bought a battered old combo amp, and hid myself away with Bert Weedon's "Play in a Day" book, the lying bastard. I phoned a guitar teacher and booked a few lessons. All I wanted to learn was how to do the Pete Townshend "Windmill" chords without hitting the light hanging from my bedroom ceiling. In the process, I learned "I shot the Sheriff", "By the time I get to Phoenix;" "All along the Watchtower" and "Detroit Rock City", which I begged him to work out. In total, I had about ten guitar lessons, which speaks volumes.

From the amount of time I spent practising, I should have become a far better player than I turned out to be. My time was now spent 50/50, between playing my guitar and wanking, so you can appreciate how much guitar I was playing. I would love to be able to say that twenty six years of playing the fucking thing has made me a genius, but all of the players that stand out have a natural talent, something I don't possess. Ambition? Desire? I had it in bucket loads, but the spark? No, not me. Most of the guitarists I met were the same. Everybody was writing their own songs, me included.

"Yeah, I write songs."

That was always the reply when I met a guitarist. Most of the time, it was like me saying,

"Yeah, I can paint."

I can paint a big pair of comedy tits, and that's about it. Come on, "Bridge over troubled Water" is a song. "Mr. Blue Sky" is a song, for fuck's sake.

I met Danny Hope when he was nineteen. He studied at the Guitar Institute in Los Angeles from the age of sixteen, and is a phenomenal talent. He can play anything; all styles, and unlike anybody else I know, he can sight read. He is tasteful, flashy, classical, bluesy, and it all seems effortless. Gobby fucker with the girls, and he liked a beer as well, so he had all bases covered. He got paid for transcribing "Pornograffiti", before the songbook was available, solos and all. Dan's favourite guitarist is Jeff Beck, so there is also a wonderful quirk to his playing. He lost his cherry to a Hollywood hooker, saw a murder, and was in the same guitar class as George Lynch. Billy Sheehan even gate crashed one of his parties, for fuck's sake. Ba-da-bing.

However, for the overall package, I would have to go for my mate Steve Kenny, who also played guitar in A.O.K. Half lounge lizard and half Mediterranean Rock God, this fucker loved a good time. Loads of dark brown hair, on a tanned, zero body fat, Budweiser soaked frame. Steve ripped his clothes to bits, and then rebuilt them with paint, studs, chains, beads, and taste. He studied Art at college, and found an outlet for his talents on the gear he swaggered about in. Like me, he was caught up in the moment, and dreamed bigger than Rip Van fucking Winkle. We had a bit of a battle going on, to find great songs, and then try and casually slip them on while we were having a quiet beer, confident in the knowledge that we were about to blow the other fucker's mind. Steve was someone you knew you could rely on 100%.

Although I knew he would never drop a note when playing live, I also knew that when we were out for the night, he would turn up with some big fucking hair, accompanied by a bony tanned chest jutting out from beneath a leather, with a quality set of white teeth, and a heart melting smile. He had the whole "Italian" thing going on, which I applaud to this day. Do you remember playing football on your dinner break at school? All the best fuckers get picked first, and then you look around, to find yourself left with the twats that can't even kick the fucking thing straight. Well, if it was a game of "Rock & Roll" I was choosing for, then Steve Kenny would be on my team every fucking time.

Steve was the smallest in the band, and took loads of shit because of it. Nothing vicious, just a celebration of the fact. We were having some photos taken in a studio, and Steve had to stand on a couple of bricks to give him a bit of a lift. At the very next gig, he turned up with a pair of black leather chaps he had customised from a pair of pants. Down one leg he had painted the words "Think Big" in white, the cool fucker. I've played with Steve for sixteen years on and off, and I've watched him turn into a great guitar player, with a big groove to his playing.

# CHAPTER NINE

*"I've Got You Under My Skin"*

The blue touch paper that had been lit by Whitesnake on that cold October evening exploded. "Sounds" was totally biased towards rock music, and each week I was educated, entertained, informed, teased, and cajoled. Rumours of tours were almost whispered across the news pages, and I was left hanging for a week or two, before "Wham." Whole tours were unleashed before my eyes, along with the latest picture of the band, and a track listing of the new album that the tour was promoting. I was a total sucker for all this carry on, as I let myself be immersed totally in the unrelenting force that was rock music. I couldn't understand how anybody would not want to be enlightened by the music I had fallen for. Finally, music became serious, and I understood where I fitted into the whole fucking scheme of things.

Whitesnake, Van Halen, AC/DC, Ted Nugent, Y&T, Scorpions, Motorhead, Rainbow, UFO, Blue Oyster Cult, Gary Moore, Ozzy, Cheap Trick, Sammy Hagar. The "Apollo" box office held me to ransom, as I turned over my hard earned cash, again and again. The bar in the "Apollo" sold "Tulip" lager. Never heard of it before, never heard of it since. Tepid, insipid, nondescript, tinted water. This beer was not fun. This was fucking Quaker beer, and could have been brewed by John Calvin himself. It was meant to taste shite, and woe betide if you extracted any kind of pleasure from it. For me, it was something I could actually handle, so I didn't make too much fuss that it tasted like toenails soaked in piss. Anyway, I couldn't lose; it was either one of the great English bands I was watching, or those damn Yankees.

Around this time, came the New Wave Of British Heavy Metal, or NWOBHM. This started in "Sounds" and it spread like wildfire. I didn't like it, because I couldn't see any reason for it. Up to this point, English bands had been majestic; but all of a sudden, I was listening to the same dodgy riffs that were being hummed to me as I helped yet another pissed guitarist out of the "Phoenix" on a Sunday night. There were loads of bands, Angelwitch, Tank, Raven, Vardis, Jaguar, Samson, Grim Reaper, Sledgehammer, Split Beaver, Bitches Sin, Geddes Axe. In fact, you can join in here if you want. Just think of the most fucking ridiculous, savage, misogynistic, macho names you can imagine, and you have the name of a heavy metal band from the late '70's, early '80's.

I sat there laughing into my "Sounds" each week, as the names of these bands got more and more bizarre. It seemed to be split, between a blatant disrespect for females, a tough macho name, or a naive "big toe" dipped in the boiling waters of occultism. If I was faced with a choice, I'd have had to go for some sad, Devil worshipping, idiot kind of name, because it would have been far easier to pass myself off as that kind of fucking numpty, than ever pass myself off as someone who hates women, or who is "tough" for that matter. Woman gave me life, woman sustained my life, woman drove my life, and knowing me, woman will probably end my fucking life. The two bands that made it big were Maiden and Leppard, but they were destined to be big whatever. The horse must have swallowed a couple of rings, because these two diamonds were pulled out of its shite. The NWOBHM took my beer off me, pushed me into a corner, and punched me full on in the face, as hard as it could. I knew I could never write "Dream On", "Sweet Emotion" or "Walk This Way, but surely I could match this shite.

Without considering the social repercussions, I locked myself away, and played and played and played. Music became an all-consuming affair, and anything that threatened it was pushed aside without consideration. This is a massive gamble, because all of a sudden your mates stop calling, and Saturday nights hold no attraction, as they are now identical to any other night, sat in your room. The ideal outcome is that you are very successful, and the hard work pays off. Girls fight for a piece of you, and all of your mates work for your band, while surfing with you in Hawaii between tours. The flip side of the coin, and the "odds on" bet, is that your biggest gig ever is in your bedroom, and your only fan is your Mum. I couldn't even contemplate failure, so I turned up my amp and ploughed on. Every inch of my room was covered in posters of slim, long haired men in tight pants. Although it was never mentioned, my parents must have wondered if this macho world of Heavy Metal excess was having an effect on my sexuality. No need to worry, there was a big pair of tits just around the next bend.

# CHAPTER TEN

*"In The Windmills Of Your Mind"*

"Dynasty" had been released the day before, and I was up early trying to work out "Sure Know Something." I went downstairs humming the bass line, and found my Dad putting the bin bags out, ready for collection. There was a pile of bags in the middle of the street, so he dumped the bags on top. Amongst our rubbish, there was a bag of lawn cuttings, and a bag full of dog shit, that had been collected over the week. Before the refuse truck arrived, a Transit van screeched to a halt next to the pile of bags. Two guys got out of the van, and started loading the bags into the back. We recognised one of them, as a neighbour who was moving house. Tears rolled down my Dad's face as he struggled for words. "Oh fuck."

One sunny Sunday, my Dad had been out on the piss all afternoon with his mates. He came home and went straight to bed, hammered. He reappeared at seven in the evening, showered and shaved, ready for another session. It was still warm and sunny, and he had his beige pants on, and a crisp white shirt. So far so good, but Mum was mopping the kitchen floor, pissed off.

"Where do you think you're going?"

"I'm just going to the Pub for a couple of hours. I won't be late."

"Oh no, you had a skinful at dinnertime, you can stay in tonight."

Mum blocked the doorway, as my Dad tried to dodge his way around her. She dipped the mop into the bucket of black water, and slapped it around his face. While he was spluttering, she rubbed the mop all over his shirt and pants. He was pissed wet through and filthy. He managed to slip out of the house in a change of clothes while we were still laughing.

This was the Seventies, and the summers lasted forever. So, the next weekend my Dad was decked out in exactly the same togs, heading for the Pub in the sunshine. Me and Steve were playing

69

football in the garden as he made his way out. My Dad always thought he was Tony Curtis, so he sauntered coolly down the path.

"Come on lads, let me have a shot."

Steve threw the ball in the air, and Dad controlled it on his chest. As he pulled his leg back, to let fly with Geoff Hurst's last goal against Germany, he caught his foot in a rose bush, and lost his balance. As he fell backwards, he twisted his body, to avoid a prickly fate. He missed the rose bush, but ended up rolling in the damp, recently watered soil. For the second week running, he was covered in shite, and for the second week running, me and my brother were reduced to tears. After yet another change of clothes, he was way behind schedule, as he ran down the path.

"Keep that bleeding thing away from me."

Or, try this for size. My Mum made a rice pudding one Sunday after dinner. I was playing in the doorway with Steve, blocking her entry into the room. She stepped over both of us, taking care not to tread on us. She lost her balance slightly, and as she put her foot down, it went straight into the pocket of a cardigan that was hanging on the door handle. She fell head first, throwing the fucking lot all over my Granddad, who was sat in the chair next to the door.

# CHAPTER ELEVEN

*"Send In The Clowns"*

I bought this badge, fucking massive it was. It was the picture from Kiss Alive, and wasn't much smaller than the album cover. I put it on the lapel of my school blazer, and my eyes just managed to peer over the top of it. It was like a Gladiator's shield, with Gene Simmons and the gang blazed across it. I felt a bit of a twat really, but it was better then those "Old Grey Whistle Test" badges, with the guy kicking the star, that all the hippies wore. Wankers!

I loved the "Whistle Test", you couldn't knock it. Bowie, UFO, Thin Lizzy, Roxy Music, Alice Cooper. "Whispering" Bob loved his music, but why oh why did you only see the "Whistle Test" badge on Hush Puppy wearing, rainbow jumpered, frayed jeaned, "Keep Music Live" stickered, eight O Level taking, twats?

I mean, "Keep Music Live." What the fuck was all that about? You either went to see a band play live, or you listened to their music on the radio, or on your stereo in your bedroom. Programming sequencers and drum machines, was two days ride away in the USS Enterprise at this point, so there was no threat to live music, despite the fucking rubbish they spouted, courtesy of the Musicians' Union. In fact, you were stuck for choice, because there were so many gigs to choose from in the '70's. Now, a "Keep music Pretty" badge I could have understood, and I would have supported them in their quest. There were some ugly bastards around that were picking up guitars and getting on to "Top of the Pops" and in the charts, and I'm tempted to start a list of the fuckers right here and now. However, some might point out that the only reason I'm not on the list myself, besides the "Top of the Pops", and "chart" issues, is because I'd be typing the bastard myself.

I liked hippies, because they only went and researched half of the subject they kicked up the fucking fuss about in the first place. "Hippies", basically 'A' level students, listened to any fucker they thought might be good for quoting; if it was related to politics,

Animal Welfare, Palestine, Che Guevara, Fascism, Communism, Idealism, Marxism, Cubism. In fact, anything they could buy a poster of. So, Hendrix, Marilyn Monroe, and cannabis leaves, also found themselves draped across the walls of bed-sits that "mummy" and "daddy" subsidised, while the "hippy" carried on living the same quality of life they had if they were back at home in Gatley; while they sympathised with the monetary restrictions of the roll-up smoking, out at 6am, not home 'til 6pm, hard-working, rent-paying, family-loving, pub-loving, Labour voter, they could never fucking be. And incidentally, never fucking wanted to be.

What did piss me off, were the "Anti-Nazi League" badges they all swaggered about wearing. They thought that just because you didn't have one of these badges, then you were a Nazi. Now, it was plainly fucking obvious to me, that anybody with the slightest bit of common sense, could see right through the outdated, badly thought out ideals of National Socialism, to give no credence whatsoever, to a handful of racist bigots still ranting on about issues they didn't understand, which they picked up from a handful of wankers, on a predominantly "white" football terrace on a Saturday afternoon.

These idiots didn't understand that at the end of World War II, the Nazis still had enough Zyklon B crystals, to kill 20 million people, even though there were only three million Jews left in Europe. So, who do you think would have "copped" for the rest? Yep, anybody that wasn't a Nordic "Aryan." Well, that's you and me, all of our forefathers, and every twat that has ever supported them on a football terrace, or anywhere else for that matter. Their plan was to exterminate ten million people a year, after they had dispensed with the Jews. I know that the Nazis also killed seven million Christians, and countless others, including gypsies, homosexuals, the infirm, and their own people; and I'm not ignoring anybody for a second, but I'm so fucking disgusted, at the actions of educated men, under the guidance of Eichmann, that the Jews as a people were to blame for Germany's "declassed" society.

Still, in a desperate attempt to appeal to anybody, and hopefully, to lose their virginity in the process, "Hippies" dwelt far too long, on issues that the rest of us "Thicko's" knew in the first place, would never ever, take root in an England that had been defended to the hilt, for freedom, twice in a row, before I was even fucking born. I don't take my "Liberty" lightly either, so I am indebted to everybody who has lived or died for my freedom, and I mean that from my heart.

"England" means so many things to so many people. To me, I can sit at home, tapping away on this fucking thing, whilst having a quiet beer. Nothing spectacular, but the fact that I can do it, is down to a bunch of guys who dived into Spitfires, trenches and tanks, when they were half my age, with bollocks made of steel, to carve out a safe and permanent haven for the unborn, of which I was one. I'm so fucking glad that I wasn't around at the time, because I don't know if I could have been relied upon, to go that extra mile for the Union Jack. I'd love to think that I'd have taken on every aggressor bare-handed, but these "Old Boys" kicked the shit out of anybody that challenged us, defending my right to wear as much hairspray as I wanted; and I love them for that, even though they didn't know what they were creating in the long run.

Consequently, nobody values their "freedom" anymore, which is just taken for granted, and expected, with scant regard for the sacrifices that made it possible. It has been so long since we have been threatened, that we have become a dysfunctional nation, because there is no need, or urgency, for national unity. You get a rare glimpse of it now and again, when the England football team gets through to the latter stages of a football competition. After that, it's a fucking struggle to find anything that makes so many people "pull" in one direction at the same time. We are an "island" nation, with an in-built need to defend ourselves; but when we don't need to, when there is relative peace, then everything goes "tits-up", as we run amok amongst ourselves, unleashing the fury within.

So, this country is over-run with scallies who hang around outside Post Offices, waiting for some old "hero" to limp out, before they give him a quick thump, and "leggit" with his only source of income, in this unjust land of ours. I bet the "Old Boys" wonder why they bothered in the first place. The sooner a "Time Machine" is invented, the better.

When they are eventually invented, they should be placed outside every Post Office in the land. As the illiterate, baseball cap wearing, sovereign ring flashing, inbred twat approaches the old guy, the old guy is given a chance to say to him, "If you just bear with me for a minute, I'm gonna nip in here." Our hero jumps in the time machine for 60 seconds, and steps out, the guy he was in 1940.

Obviously, he tears the skin right off the bones of the big-eared, goofy fucker that was expecting to run off with his pension. I would volunteer to scrape up the bodies of every piece of human shit that littered the pavements, laughing, as I sold them to McDonalds. Fucking "Nuggets" the lot of them.

I'm like Ronnie fucking Corbett with my stories aren't I? Where was I? Oh yeah, I'd just wandered through the school gates with that badge clanging away. My mate "Quinny" came running over as I made my way into school. I knew what he wanted. I put my head down and tried to lose him in the crowd. I'd had his "Tokyo Tapes" album for about a month, and this lad loved the Scorpions.

"Tony!"

"Hiya Quinny. Look, I'll bring your fucking album back tomorrow. Gimme a break."

"No, forget about that. Have you seen Sounds?"

"No, why?"

He reached in his bag, and handed me his "Sounds." The front inside cover said "Kiss announce UK tour."

"Fucking brilliant. Do you fancy going?"

"Nah, it won't be like a real concert. It's not proper rock music. It will be just like watching clowns."

"Hold on, you've dragged me to see Rush enough times, and I didn't complain. Even when I had to pay for the matchsticks, to keep my bastard eyes open. So don't fucking start, By-Tor."

As I became animated, my Kiss badge rattled loudly in agreement with me.

"Nice badge."

"Fuck off. And for that, you can wait another month before you hear Steamrock Fever again."

Another lad noticed us reading the "Sounds" magazine, so he joined us. He "sided" with "Quinny", as they pointed at the picture of Kiss, and laughed at the make up, trying to relegate me to some kind of second division rock fan.

Now there are a few things I considered, that "barred" you from rock music, and took you out of the set up completely. The main one being "fatness." It took a lot to be a rocker, but if you were a fat rocker, to me, you might as well be fucking bald, or ginger. I nipped this scenario in the bud, straight away, as the fat lad expressed his hatred of "Kiss."

Me. "Do you like "Rush" as well?"

74

Lad. "Yeah, they're great."

Me. "I thought so, you remind me of one of their albums."

He flexed his arms.

Lad. "What, "Caress of Steel?"

Me. "No... do you know "Twenty One Twelve?"

Lad. "Yeah, it's my favourite album."

Me. "Well you look like you weigh twenty one stone twelve pounds, you fat cunt. Now fuck off!"

I can't remember this fuckers name, but I had met him somewhere else, a year earlier. He was learning to play guitar, and somehow, I wound up at his house. He was sat strumming away, with a "Kiss" plectrum. My jaw hit the floor, and all of a sudden I was the best fucking mate he'd ever had.

Me. "That plectrum. It's a Kiss plectrum isn't it?"

Lad. "Yeah, but I'm not bothered about them."

Me. "Can I have it?"

Lad. "No."

Me. "Well why do you want the fucking thing?"

Lad. "I don't. Somebody gave it to me."

It had Gene Simmons signature on the reverse, and I needed it badly. Fucking hell, this was fantastic. Probably a remnant left over from the "Love Gun" tour. My last link to 1978. I couldn't miss it, could I?" As soon as he knew it was what I wanted, he reached for some kind of sharp instrument, and scraped Gene Simmons name off the fucking thing, before turning it over, and chiselling out the "Kiss" logo. I fucking hate virgins.

After a sphincter twitching cancellation, the tour was re-scheduled from June, to September 1980, by which time you could get no fucking sense out of me whatsoever. Looking back, to get caught up in the emotions of something so intense, while so young, was as scary as it was exhilarating. Whatever those native New Yorkers had, it felt like it was delivered personally to me, on my very own frequency, day and night. The result being relatively innocuous, in that I grew my hair and wound up playing in a band. But what if there had been no Kiss, what if music had missed me completely? Adolescent fervour demands an outlet, and I wouldn't have been surprised if I'd have wound up in a house in Waco, Texas, with David Koresh saying,

"There you go Ginger, here's fifty cents, go and get us a box of matches."

I'm not a journalist, I'm not even a proper writer, so I don't want to even try and describe how I felt, the first time I saw Kiss, because you might not get the full effect of what I mean in my interpretation. Geoff Barton said everything about the gig, when his review appeared in "Sounds." He is a professional, and I couldn't add anything to what he said. He had all the similes, metaphors and superlatives covered, which he delivered with all the passion of a proud father.

# CHAPTER TWELVE

*"Eruption"*

My sweaty face slid down the coach window, which was steamed up with the condensation produced by fifty two hairy arsed rockers, as we sang "Love Gun." I clung to Stanley's plectrum and Eric's drumstick, while the Vulture's watched out of the corner of their eyes, waiting for me to drift off to sleep. No fucking chance. I'm just glad I didn't catch the "Firehouse" helmet; it would have been like the O.K. Corral on that coach.

The very next morning, I filled in the classified ad section in "Sounds", and started looking for a band. After the previous night's events, it was time to get serious. This turned out to be one of the best moves I have ever made, not because I became successful, my anonymity will vouch for that. No, the adverts brought me something far greater. They linked me up with Glyn and Rob, who are still my best friends to this day. Although I met them at different times, they are equal pains in the arse, equally as funny and probably equal weights now, the fat cunts.

Rob had a band called "Sam Thunder", who got a deal with an independent label, and released a couple of singles, and a picture disc album, and boy didn't we fucking know it. Swaggering round "Jilly's" with their dole money, cadging drinks off girls, while handing out free badges to anybody that would take one. Howard Johnson gave them a bit of a "kicking" when he reviewed the album in "Kerrang", which was a bit unfair, because they were an "English" band, out there doing it. Up to this point, they had received some good press, from a few enthusiastic sources. Trust the English scribes to stick their fucking hobnail boots in. They supported Lee Aaron at the "Marquee" in the early eighties, and also played with Terraplane, Girlschool and Shy, if I remember correctly. They also learnt Lee Aaron's songs, and came on again as her backing band after playing as her support earlier. Rob's "Sam Thunder" picture disc ended up being made into a clock. When I saw it, I said.

"Why have they put your eyes on the fingers of the clock? It doesn't make sense."

"They haven't."

"Well, it fucking looks like they have, you cock eyed twat."

Rob saw my ad in "Sounds", and invited me for an audition with "Sam Thunder." Now, if he's got a vodka, which is most of the time, he will take twice as long to explain, in great detail, how I turned up to the audition in a duffle coat. Yes, a twat I will admit, and not even a bitter winters' night can excuse me. However, it doesn't stop there. Underneath the hood lurked Benny Hill's "Ginger Tompkins" perm, and a pair of Mossad night vision goggles, cunningly disguised as a pair of Aviator spectacles. Well, after that fucking performance, it was straight back to my bedroom for me, and quite rightly so. One nil to cunty bollocks.

Fat cunts, thin cunts, tall cunts, short cunts, daft cunts, I met them all. They phoned, I answered, and before I knew it, I was hauling my Marshall into a musty smelling rehearsal room, coming face to face with lads who snarled at me across the dance floor at "Jillys", the "Banshee", or the "Phoenix." Manchester had a great rock scene, so you were guaranteed to recognise almost everybody you jammed with, but unfortunately, not before they had bullshitted for England, to get you to meet them in some shit hole in the city centre, where they backtracked on their stories about RCA and EMI.

One day, some lads invited me for an audition in a rehearsal room close to Piccadilly train station. They had a 4 x 12 speaker I could use, so they told me just to bring my Marshall amp and my guitar. I jumped onto the train with my guitar, my amp, and a bag containing my leads and effects pedals. Everything I owned was in my hands and over my shoulder in a bulky bag. Easy pickings, for any fucker that fancied some easy cash. "Close to Piccadilly", when you are walking carrying nothing, and "close to Piccadilly", when you are laden down with the fucking weight of the world, are two ends of the spectrum completely. I had no cash for a taxi, so I wobbled and weaved my spindly little frame down through Piccadilly.

It looked like I was in the final of "The World's Strongest Man", concentrating on carrying the biggest fucking weight you have ever seen, down a lonely road. Honestly, by the time I got there, it felt like I was carrying a fucking Volkswagen Beetle.

Obviously, by the time I got there, I wished it had been a Volkswagen Beetle, so I could have fucked off in it, and left the time wasters to themselves, the cheeky short haired twats.

Revolution Studios, Stockport, 1984. I turned up for an audition with a local band called Renegade. The singer was late, so we jammed along for well over an hour. Eventually, the door opened, and in walked the singer, Glyn Jones. The room fell silent as everybody stopped playing. The noise level soared again, as they started ranting at Glyn over his late appearance.

"Stop whingeing you set of soft cunts, or I'll give you something to whinge about."

Glyn was on top form, and over the years, has never strayed from his own brand of rhetoric. I liked him immediately.

We went for a beer afterwards, and found out we liked the same music. The reason he was late, was because he had been cutting down a tree. After hacking away for ages, the tree creaked and started to fall. I could tell that speed wasn't one of Glyn's attributes, but neither apparently, was calculating trajectory. As he ran, the tree twatted him in the middle of his head, splitting it open. He was late because he had been sat in the hospital, waiting to get stitched up. From the smell of his farts after eight pints of Bitter, I was wishing they'd have stitched his arse up as well.

Renegade, shmenegade. We weren't going to be seeing too much of the album charts, but it was all experience, and nothing can compensate for experience. You can sit in your bedroom all of your life, but there comes a time when you've got to bite the bullet, and just go for it. The heckles, the bum notes, the extra drink you shouldn't have had, the threat for looking at somebody's bird while you were playing, the bird who fancied you while you were playing, the broken strings, the broken down van, the P.A. that doesn't work, the guy in the band that you can't fucking stand. They're all there; it's just up to you when you decide to let them enter your life, because they will, regularly.

There was no love lost when the band split up. I had secured Glyn as a close friend, and despite constantly being called a cunt, with all the passion his body holds, we have just grown closer. We recorded a couple of songs together afterwards, with some other lads we knew, but after a while we both found new bands. This suited us both fine, as there was now double the nights out to be had, when we watched each others band. Now there's another thing that has never crossed my mind, and I can't remember too clearly how it came about. One minute, I was rehearsing with Glyn, making a demo tape, and the next thing he was in another band. Did he fuck me off for some reason? He must have done, because I just wouldn't have fucked him off. Not like that anyway. Remind me to ask him about selling me down the river, the Charlatan. There again, this was a time when I was "whoring" it with bands, so it could quite easily have been me that fucked him off. Either way, he's still at the end of the phone whenever I ring him, or at the neck of the fucking bottle when I pull the cork.

Rob played bass in Glyn's new band, along with another absolute diamond, Sean Clark. The band was called "Lanson", after the champagne, and it was Sean's baby. Sean was cut from the same beer soaked cloth as the rest of us, and was the most laid back dude around. Nothing ever got to this guy, and I can still picture his beaming smile and endless laughter. Girls found Sean totally endearing, and I've watched him pat three of their arses into the back of his car, laughing while they got comfy, as we wondered what to do with them. Luckily, he must have subscribed to "Gate crashing rock parties, where you don't know anyone, but you're gonna get fucked anyway" monthly, because he never let me down. I really don't know how he did it, because Rob sussed me out straight away. He says that I was, am, and always will be, a fucking Snake, because of my lascivious attitude to women. I have always found honesty a good ally, because you don't have to think about what you have said, and it has been known to work. Sean was just the same as me, but he managed to smooth it all over with a trowel full of "Terry Thomas" and "Leslie Phillips."

I don't think he tried any harder than me, but Sean knew where parties were happening, which girls were going to be there, whether their boyfriends were going, if the girls were staying over at the party, and he also knew which girls wanted to fuck which lads. Inside information on a fucking grand scale, for which I was grateful on more than a few occasions. Like the shoeshine boy from "Police Squad" he knew everything, and he had the transport to get us there. Sometimes he would ring midweek, just as I was ready to hit the sack for a much needed early night. Freshly tossed, and drifting off into a perfect natural slumber, the fucking phone would start.

The best thing about being single was that you knew it wasn't going to be your girlfriend, mithering for this that, and the other at 10pm. This particular night, Sean had found a place in Barnsley, that was open all night, and he promised me I would be in the place, supping a pint by 11pm. He'd got me just at the right decade. My morals, resolve, constitution, and ethics were at an all time low; so I supped that drink as the clock turned eleven, pale with fright at the speed of his driving. It was hard, because we were involved in a world that operated between midnight and the sun rising, even though we had to get up for work the next morning. Bed-sits, Halls of Residence, shared houses, car parks, dormitories, and hotels; I woke up everywhere, with a headache, and a girl I didn't recognise, on any given weeknight. It was great. Once he knew he had me as his co-pilot, Sean took free reign to include me in every club, bar and party, he could wedge his fucking foot in the door of. Top man.

Sean met a really pretty girl who lived in Manchester, but who was away at University. Like any red-blooded "chancer", he kept in touch with her while she was away, and sent her the odd tape of the music we loved. One Saturday, he decided to call round to her house, as she was gonna be home this particular day, even though he didn't know the time she would arrive. He knocked on the door, but there was no reply. As it was a big fucker of a house, he walked around the back of the place, to check if she was in the kitchen. As he approached the kitchen window, he looked in, to find the girl's mother, who was a babe by all accounts, getting rear ended over the kitchen table by her boyfriend. Sean didn't knock, and he managed to keep quiet as he watched the whole fucking spectacle. I bought the man a big fucking drink on hearing that particular tale. Obviously, he never divulged the address, because I'd have been stood in the back garden, camouflaged as a tree for months on end.

# CHAPTER THIRTEEN

*"So Here's To You Mrs Robinson"*

Saturday's have always been special. When you are young, it's because you are not at school, there's football on TV, and it's not Sunday. Sunday, especially a Sunday in the Seventies, was fucking torture. The country ground to a halt, streets were deserted, all of the shops were shut, and the only thing on telly was religion. Boring, Anglican shite. Where were the TV Evangelists when we needed them? Everybody knew they were thieving, philandering, lying twats, but at least there was a bit of showmanship involved, as they tried to rob you blind with their "Hotline to God", toll free donation number.

Or, what about some Black Gospel music? People with no reason to believe whatsoever, after the atrocities inflicted upon them over the centuries, but who stand proud, and sing out loud. They believed; I could see that. No, what we got was Anglicans, who didn't really believe, but who thought that they had better turn up at church, just in case there is something afterwards.

As you get older, Saturday's just get better and better. The "Banshee" was our church, and there was always a full congregation. A sweaty, furnace of a club, packed to the rafters with Sinners, and it was fantastic. Pretty girls everywhere, who must have spent hours putting on next to nothing. Perfume and hairspray hung in the dense atmosphere, where sex was top of everybody's agenda. Maybe it was down to insecurity, or trying to project a cool image, or maybe a bit if both, but I never took full advantage of the situations that presented themselves. Don't get me wrong, I always had a full dance card, but there was space on the back for more.

Sean bought the drinks, and we were deep in conversation. His eyes fixed on two girls, stood talking together. He wasn't even listening to me. Without an "excuse me" or fuck all, he picked up his drink and walked over. He beckoned me over, and we were all introduced. The girls were sisters, and were from out of town. Of course they were. My "Sister" was tanned and looked like Catherine Zeta Jones... no really!!! So, I spent the next few hours telling every funny story I have ever heard, while plying her with Budweiser. She seemed to like me, so I nipped downstairs to the toilet, and stuck my old fella under the tap, to freshen it up, just in case. Well, if I'm nothing else, I'm a gentleman.

Father Time must have had his fucking running shoes on that night, because the next thing I knew, the girls had their coats on, saying they had to go for a taxi. Then my old friend "Reality" tapped me on the shoulder, and pointed out who was left to choose from, at ten minutes to two on a Sunday morning. Luckily, Sean was having none of it. He pushed through the crowd and caught up with the sisters.

"Hey, do you fancy coming back to mine for a drink?"

The girls huddled together, whispering and laughing.

"O.K." said the blonde.

Sean nudged me in the ribs and smiled. I nudged the brunette in the back and smiled. Back at his house, we drank some more. The girl I was with said she was tired, and asked Sean if she could go to bed. He told her that she could use his room. As she stood up, she turned to me.

"Are you coming?"

I was already at the top of the fucking stairs!

Sunday morning, I was woken by a gentle tapping on the door. I opened my eyes, to see the girl asleep on top of the covers, naked, and fantastic.

"Hold on Sean."

I lifted the quilt, and covered her immaculate body.

"It's O.K. now."

Sean stuck his head round the door.

"Morning."

His tone implied that he knew exactly what had happened.

"Morning. Hey Sean, is there any chance of..."

He jumped in and finished my sentence.

"What, me taking over? I thought you'd never ask."

"Breakfast actually."

He smiled and shut the door.

After a replay of the previous night's events, we joined Sean and the other sister downstairs.

We took them home, swapped numbers, and arranged to meet them again. We never did go out with them again, and I often wonder why I never pursued her further. Was it the wanderlust of a young man living his dream? No, my girlfriend would have fucking killed me! As soon as they left the car, I turned around.

"Sean, Sean."

I could hardly contain myself.

"Aw man, you fucking missed it. You were so close."

"What do you mean?"

"This morning, when you knocked on the door, she was laying on top of the bed, stark bollock naked, with her legs wide open. I'm sorry pal."

"Tony my friend. Underneath this mop of hair is the brain of a genius. When I went upstairs, I opened the door to see if you were awake. I was greeted with a vision of that goddess that will stay with me forever. I crept in, had a good fucking look, and then tiptoed out. I shut the door behind me, nipped in the bathroom for a quick wank, and then tapped gently on your door once I was done."

I couldn't breathe for laughing, that was fucking outrageous.

Sean introduced me to two huge breasted girls that he knew, and before I knew it, my mind was concocting all manner of depraved fantasies, with me in the thick of it all. They were both pretty, and a bit more "Hippy" than I was used to, but I was sure something was brewing, by the way their chests fought for my attention, as they giggled at my nervous attempts at humour. I was sure that I was only a boozy encounter away from every lad's dream, a threesome.

The green light came in the shape of a phone call, when one of them asked me over for a drink. I could hear the other girl laughing in the background, telling me to hurry up. Raw from the intense scrubbing, my arse was on fire. There was no place for a shitty arsehole in the 20th Century, just as there isn't in the 21st Century, and if you can't take care of that as a matter of courtesy, then you don't deserve to get laid. When I arrived, the girl's mother was sat on the settee, drinking Gin, where she remained all fucking evening. She was around forty, divorced, and all over me. I left carrying what I had arrived with, my master plan foiled. The next night the phone rang.

"Hello Tony, are you going out on Friday?"

It was the girl's Mother. I spluttered some kind of response, trying to ask about her daughter, while caught in this uncomfortable conversation. In the end, I thought she was just winding me up, so I was laughing and joking with her. Friday came, and I was stood at the bar, talking to Sean. Again, he wasn't taking the slightest bit of notice of me. His eyes concentrated on something in the distance, over my shoulder. He finally looked me in the eye, and raised his eyebrows.

Have you seen Meatloaf's video for "Deadringer?" Well, I turned round to find "Mother" checking out every guy in the "Phoenix", looking for yours truly. When she finally spied me, she gave me a dirty smile that said, "I'm coming to get you." I swigged my beer and gulped, as she strode across the room on a mission. She wore skin tight, faded jeans, a white lace top, and a black leather Biker's jacket. The young girls stared at her, and the lads parted like the fucking Israelites were on their way through. As I opened my mouth to say "hello", she grabbed the hair on the back of my head, and thrust her tongue down my throat. I couldn't move; she had me in a "Widowlock." She made it perfectly clear what she wanted, but if I started this carry-on at an early age, where was there left for me to go? Years later, full of bruises from kicking myself, I know that I missed the opportunity of a lifetime. She kept ringing for a few weeks, but in the end my sister-in-law, Helen, told her I had moved. Alright, alright, I know!

# CHAPTER FOURTEEN

*"I Woke Up In A Soho Doorway"*

To me, it was just as good if your attempts with the girls were in vain, as long as there was a humorous tale of woe involved. Nothing keeps you on your toes, like a sure fire plan going "tits up." As you swagger up to the plate, you pull your cap down to take the searing sun out of your eyes. A bit of showmanship as you juggle that fucking Baseball bat, and then pure concentration. The bat is somewhere over the back of your shoulder, wound so tight, it hurts. This fucker's going over the fence, you just know it. As you swing like Tarzan, the morning after his first night with Jane, you can sense something is wrong. In a split second, the ball is safely in the Catcher's mitt, and you're out. Yes, you were thrown a curve ball. Welcome to the wonderful world of Women. Sometimes they throw it intentionally. Other times "Mother Nature" or "Lady Luck" stick their fucking oar in.

Late '86 early '87, I joined a local band called "Circus", and they were almost the band for me. How fucking bad does that sound? Listen to little old Prima Donna here! No, I wasn't the best looking lad around, and by no means the best musician, so let me get that straight from the start. I had no ego whatsoever, and was quite self-effacing; so the choices I made came from my heart, and not from any overblown self publicity. When it was good it was a fucking scream, which was all I wanted, but when it was bad, well who wants bad, when all you want to do is play music? Bad shouldn't even be an option. When we should have been rehearsing, we were practising being interviewed on the radio, by the manager, who was a makeshift DJ for the night. If it wasn't that, it was working out how royalties would be divided between the songwriters. Well, by my reckoning, without a record deal, 50% of fuck all is fuck all.

86

The first time we played at the Marquee club, we were supporting Dumpy's Rusty Nuts, on a bitterly cold, freezing Saturday night, early in 1987. The place was sold out, and it might as well have been the middle of summer, it was that hot. To hammer a few chords together with a 4/4 beat, and get to the Marquee deserves some kind of recognition. There must have been something special going on. Any band can write a song, but this gig meant we were a hundred miles in front of them. At that point, I was proud of what we did, proud of each lad in the band, and desperate to get laid. The pubs, clubs, demo's and damp rehearsal rooms seemed to be paying off. Not paying off in a monetary sense, but that didn't matter.

We hadn't made any money up to this point; so to continue not making any money, but at the same time, advancing to the "Marquee" my friend, was considered a fucking result. I stood and stared at the empty stage, looking at the famous "Marquee" logo. It hadn't changed in decades. Chris Harris had a great black and white "Who" poster on his bedroom wall, with Pete Townsend "windmilling" the fuck out of his old Rickenbacker, with the "Marquee" sign right behind him. I decided there and then, that tonight, I was gonna throw a few of those fuckers into my performance. Not only that, but I'd written a lot of the songs we were gonna be playing, so I couldn't wait for our unveiling.

"Dumpy" was a top man, and he gave us close to an hour to acclimatise to the revered surroundings. I knew that all of the music hacks leaned against the bar, pissed out of their heads, searching for a new collection of similes to expound their "oh so clever University wit", but we weren't too bothered about fat, balding, unshagged, middle class, specky, drug addicts, this particular night. Not that they were there to see us anyway.

Rock and roll should only ever be considered an experience, in the exact moment that you experience it, by the individual who experiences it. Reviews of gigs that turn up two weeks, or a month later, to be honest, are fucking rubbish, unless of course, it was a Kiss gig. They pad out magazines, and I used to wonder what these fuckers were thinking of, while Steven Tyler was only twenty feet away. It's not like he comes over every other weekend. Just put your pen down, chill out, and swing that fucking huge arse around, inside those ill fitting Tesco jeans, and walk this way. No, not that way you fat cunt, this way.

Across the road on Wardour St, was the "St. Moritz" club, where we ended up after the gig. I met a lovely Canadian girl called Sandy, who had been in the "Marquee" earlier. She never said that she recognised me, and I never asked if she saw me. I didn't care, no other fucker knew me either. Sandy asked if I wanted to go to a party, but the lads wanted to get back to our accommodation and carry on drinking. Well, where did you expect me to go? I waved my middle finger at the rest of the lads, as they trudged through the icy sleet, in search of Crouch End. We followed them up the stairs into the Soho night, and jumped into a taxi. The party was being held by "The Alarm", and was in a hotel close by.

We sat in the bar area in the hotel, and had a few drinks. She sat opposite me in a leather chair, hitching her skirt up as she spoke. Casually, her skirt got higher and higher, until the stockings finished, and the skin of her thighs came into view. Don't know about you, but for me, it doesn't get much better. From here it can go two ways. Either it finishes here, and a cheeky glimpse is all you get, or, all fucking hell breaks loose, and the prize is yours.

"Do you want to get a room?" I spluttered.

"That would be nice." She breathed.

"Right then, I'll go and sort it out."

I stood up, and slowly finished my drink. I swaggered slowly out of the room, trying not to appear too eager. Once out of the door, I legged it down the corridor to the Reception desk.

"A room please, I'd like to book a double room."

"Sorry son, they're all taken."

"OK, I'll have a single then."

"Sorry, we're fully booked."

I explained my predicament in a far more romantic way than my mind saw it. The guy behind the desk seemed to empathise with me. He led me out of the hotel, and pointed down the street.

"That building with the lights on is a hotel, and I know that they have rooms available."

I shook his hand, punched the icy cold air, and set off down the street. The hotel was only about thirty yards away, but the bitter wind still managed to bring on a severe case of "Acorn Knob." As I approached the hotel, I could see that the lounge was lit by a couple of inviting red lamps. I climbed the steps, and entered the Reception area. The desk was empty, so I rang the bell. Nobody came, so I walked through to the lounge, and sat in a high backed leather chair, in front of a cosy fire, warming my bones. Somebody tapped me on the shoulder, and I jumped up out of the chair.

"Can I help you Sir?"

"Yes, I'd like to book a double room please."

"Certainly Sir, come this way."

As I walked through to the Reception, I noticed the Sun was shining.

"Hold on, what time is it?"

"Eight-thirty Sir."

"Fuck me, cancel that room."

Go on, laugh you bastard, everybody else did, for about six fucking months. I scratched my head, while walking down the same steps I had bounded up a few hours earlier, trying to find something positive I could take out of this catastrophe. Was there a lesson to be learned or a moral to the story perhaps? No, I just fucked up good and proper. Of course, when I met up with the rest of the lads, they loved it. It couldn't have been any better, had the girl brought along two of her mates. Nothing could beat the story they had just been told.

# CHAPTER FIFTEEN

*"We Can Be Heroes, Just For One Day"*

If I can get away with sitting on my arse, or lying in bed for an extra ten minutes, I will. I don't know a lad that won't. Wanking, fidgeting, tea drinking, toast eating, arse scratching, porn reading, quality time. See how I put arse scratching after the toast eating? Top fucking tip if ever there was one. If you think I'm generalising with a broad brush, then I'd like to introduce you to every lad I've ever known. I don't know if I'm lazy, or if it is an excellent example of "time" management, but I love it. So, to find myself up before the alarm, showered, hair sprayed and bangled, could only mean one thing, a gig.

The best thing about being in Circus was that we hardly ever played in Manchester. This has got nothing to do with Manchester itself, I love the fucking place. No, this was about pretending to be rock stars. This was about travelling to Pontypridd already pissed; this was about getting lost in Bournemouth; this was about running out of petrol in Bath; this was about pissing off a biker in Warrington, because his bird wanted to take me home; this was about ducking from glasses in Llanharan. This was about the first time I signed my name, yes, my name, on a big pair of flabby tits in Cardiff. This was about life.

We managed to play at a few decent sized venues, supporting bigger bands. We played with Budgie, the Tygers of Pan Tang, even the fucking Groundhogs. Me and Simon Johnson were the guitarists, and Circus was his band. He started it, he knew what he wanted to do, and he dreamed big, just the way I did. He wound a lot of people up, but I have always had a lot of time for Simon. He loves Ritchie Blackmore with a passion, and I like anybody who loves something with a passion, whether I like it or not. He was always game for a night out, wasn't afraid of shouting the odds with the ladies, and boy could that fucker light a mean fart.

Simon wasn't particular where girls were concerned. I've seen him with some stunners, and I've seen him with things that have two X chromosomes. Cheadle Hulme's answer to Gene Simmons. We treated every gig like it was the Manchester Apollo, until one night it was. Simon phoned me, and said we had got the gig supporting Vow Wow at the "Apollo".

Dumpy was also on the bill, and he had put in a good word for us, after our performance at The "Marquee." Vow Wow were Japanese, and had Neil Murray playing bass for them, so it looked like an episode of "Land of the Giants." Vow Wow used to be called Bow Wow, and supported Kiss on their Japanese tour in 1977. That was close enough for me. Me, supporting a band that had supported Kiss? In Manchester? On December 2nd 1987? Fucking fantastic.

On the day of the gig, we rolled up to the "Apollo" around dinner time, and dived into the Apsley Cottage, for a couple of looseners. You couldn't see our blue Transit van parked outside, because it was hidden behind two of those fucking huge "Transam Trucking" juggernauts that became so familiar over the years. There are pictures of us climbing all over these huge trailers, trying to make out like the gig wouldn't happen without us. For a few weeks beforehand, our name was plastered all over town on the Vow Wow posters, so my homecoming was going to be extra special… wasn't it?

The stage was like a football pitch; compared to anything else I had played on. Normally, two Marshall 4 x 12 speakers did the trick, but that particular night, I had to set them up in front of about a dozen Marshall 4 x 12 cabinets. Who says size doesn't matter? Then it hit me, like a bolt of the sharp stuff. I dragged my Marshall stack, and just added it on to the end of Vow Wow's back line. Fuck me; it looked like I had fourteen 4 x 12 cabinets.

During the sound check, I turned to Simon.

"Do you know that I'm standing on footprints left by Paul Stanley, Dave Lee Roth and Coverdale?"

I think he was lost in his own "Ritchie Blackmore" world at this point, because he was like a puddle with eyes, just the same as me. I tried to piss in every available toilet in the "Apollo" because I knew that Dave or Paul must have pissed in one of them. Every band I had ever seen in the "Apollo" flashed through my mind, again and again. Was I supposed to be on such hallowed ground, or was I "Chosen?" Didn't matter, because I knew that later that

91

evening, it was going to be me doing the "choosing." Young, tall, slim, single, long-haired, white "Explorer" playing, pussy lover. This particular evening was written in the stars. Only a fool would bet against me.

Later that evening, I saw a fool waving a big fucking wedge of cash around. Like every self-respecting rocker, I had a stalker. She turned up at the "Apollo", and like a true pro, she scared away every girl I looked at. Like any lad that likes a drink, I seemed to end up in certain situations that could have been avoided, if I had kept my mouth and my flies closed.

In one of my weaker moments, I found out that my stalker would let me "do" things to her, which, in hindsight, wasn't the best way of deterring her. She followed me around the country, to different gigs, threatening girls everywhere. The "Apollo" was no different. I can see now, that it was all calculated and premeditated. You see, she would leave me alone while I was sober, and let me get wasted with my friends. Sometimes I wouldn't even know she was out. She would watch me from deep in the shadows of a club, waiting for the right moment to make an appearance. I can't believe that it's taken me this long to figure it out. Now generally, I'm a shy type, always have been. She must have waited, watching, until I opened up, and mustered the courage to talk to a girl. This was her signal to make an appearance, put the fucking lot on a plate, and tell me there was more if I could finish what was there. On Thursday 3rd December 1987, I woke up next to her, which leads me to the question; "Which one of us was the saddest?"

I should have asked the fool counting his cash. Easily in the handful of the greatest experiences in my life so far, the "Apollo" also had a down side, which was entirely my own doing.

# CHAPTER SIXTEEN

*"Everybody's Working For The Weekend"*

The following Saturday we played at "Bogeys" in Cardiff. Kevin
Kane ran the place, and I got to know him over the years. "Bogeys"
was a regular gig on the rock circuit, and we were just one on a
conveyor belt of unsigned bands that played around the country,
winding up in "Bogeys" every four to six months. Now this was
fine if you were in a band, but spare a thought for the poor bastards
who lived in Cardiff, and had to go to "Bogeys" every week.

For a start, weekends are private, and can take a lot of
planning. After working all week, the least anybody can ask, is to
do what they want, with whoever they want, listening to whatever
they want. Rockers in Cardiff, and in numerous clubs around the
country, were more tolerant than others. You can sit at home all
week listening to "10,000 lovers" by TNT, or "Go for Soda" by
Kim Mitchell, or whatever, thinking "I'm gonna shake my booty to
this one when it's cranked up on Saturday night." Only to find that
your request is on a list, just a couple of pages shorter than a
fucking telephone directory, and guess what? The band is about to
come on for an hour and ten minutes.

Based on personal experience, I would say that the chances of
seeing a good, not great, unsigned band are about 20% at best. I
would go and watch anybody, just to see if there was anything I
could learn, or learn not to do, when playing. Watching a shite band
would inspire me just as much as watching a great band. Either I
was competing with what was around, or there was something to
aspire to. Now the girl who's stood at the DJ booth, itching to dance
to "Don't tell me you love me" by Nightranger, isn't looking at me
in a favourable light, especially as she can see her song is next on
the list. In these situations, you've got to remember, that just
because the club is full it doesn't mean that everybody has turned up
to see you. A point I failed to take on board every time. Well, if I've
grown my hair this fucking long, and locked myself away in my

93

bedroom and rehearsal rooms for years on end, then some fucker is having a piece of me.

A drunken girl was rubbing her crotch against me, as I stood having a beer at the bar, after we had played. "No Substitute" by Vinnie Vincent was on the video screen, and I hadn't seen the video before, so I gave him the attention she should have received. She was still there as the great chorus and ridiculous guitar solo faded out, so I finished my beer, and bought her a drink. Fucking hell, I might as well have bought her a diamond ring. She started kissing me, and dragged me off to the girl's toilets. As she opened the door, she stopped dead in her tracks. "Don't tell me you love me" blared out of the speakers, and she was off on to the dance floor in a flash.

Meanwhile, Simon turns up with a woman that looks like Barbara Cartland with long dark hair. It is obvious that this woman's mirror only reflects black and white, because her make up has been applied with all the subtlety of one of Willy Wonka's Umpa fucking lumpa's. If she saved her birthday cards, then the ones marked "40th" would have been yellowed and faded. And these were her good points. Anyway, when the other girl returns from the dance floor, it turns out these two are a double act, and me and Simon are tonight's invited audience.

The girl I was with was pretty, with long dark hair and a dirty laugh, and if that wasn't enough, she opened her bag to show me a spare pair of knickers.

"Sold, to the Gentleman starting to fill with blood."

I grabbed hold of Simon.

"I don't mind you watching, but there is no fucking way I'm swapping ends at half time."

I wouldn't normally mind, but this was all his own doing, and I wasn't gonna be the one to bail him out this time. As we stood there arguing, his girl caught me looking at her out of the corner of my eyes. She turned away, pretending to be shy, and then slowly turned her head back and smiled at me. Her teeth were like a fucking piano keyboard. A couple of whites then a black gap, and so on. I bet she could have whistled like a fucking pan pipe. Teeth like popcorn!

She reminded me of a crockery stall on a fairground at closing time. She wasn't all that bad, she paid for the taxi. Come to think of it, it was the only way I'd let her in the fucking thing. A grey cloud loomed over me, as I could see that Simon was now all over the girl I was with. Like I said, not a problem normally, but there was no way I was paying for his mistakes. Back at the hotel I side-footed my girl into the room, having regained control of the situation. Simon was getting impatient.

"Fucking shut it, and get in there."

I couldn't see Simon, but I heard his instructions from the corridor. She stumbled into the room behind us, looking like an early "Doctor Who" monster. As we tore each others clothes off and dived into the bed, the other girl started getting undressed. Simon stopped her in her tracks.

"Oh no, no fucking chance. You can fuck right off. I don't even want to see your body. Get that light off now."

A bit harsh I thought, but I was more concerned about her storming out, taking my flesh Harley Davidson with her. She said nothing, turned the light off and climbed into bed. Simon tried continually throughout the night to rearrange the flesh furniture, but he had no chance. I actually turned down the chance of watching girl on girl. Even I wasn't that desperate.

This kind of carry-on could only end one way, so I wasn't surprised when we both started scratching and itching at the same fucking time. There's a word I'd never seen before, Genito-Urinary Clinic. Sounds a bit scary doesn't it? I met Simon at the entrance. We were both dressed from head to foot in black, with hair like we were on a big night out. We turned a few heads as we strode into the reception area, like "rock and roll" whippets. Not a fucking scrap of fat between us, cracking jokes with the nurses. Well, to be honest, we were cracking the jokes, but the nurses knew we were there for one reason, which wouldn't impress any fucker really, would it? So, they smiled nervously, probably praying that we wouldn't lay a dirty, sleazy, unclean finger on them. It was only when they separated us that it dawned on me that this wasn't in fact, fun. There could be something seriously wrong, and it was no longer a laugh. A few seconds on my own to contemplate, had me dreading the fucking worst. Suddenly, I was sat outside a room on my own, in silence. Not only had the laughter gone, but every sound had disappeared at the same time. No birds tweeting outside, no cars, no people talking, no background noise, nothing.

I had found a blister on the end of my knob, which was fucking uncomfortable. Now, I sat outside that room, trying to find the words to say to the doctor. "Bell End" or "Helmet." They were the only words I knew to describe the area where I was experiencing the discomfort, but I couldn't possibly repeat those words to a complete stranger, could I? Obviously there is a technical term for that piece of your body, but I was fucked if I knew it. My only other option was to say nothing, drop my pants, and roll my fucking foreskin back, in front of a bloke I had never ever seen before. Fucking hell, my only choices were all based around my worst nightmares ever. The doctor was a total professional, who made me feel at ease straight away. So much so, that before I knew it, he had my jap's eye squeezed open, laughing away as he slipped a thin glass rod down the fucking thing to take a sample. Suddenly, a serving hatch opened in the wall, and a nurse poked her head through, telling me to come to the next room for a blood test once I had finished giving a swab.

The total fucking indignity of it all. Some bloke twisting a rod around inside my knob like he was mixing a "holiday" cocktail, and some "old bird" of a nurse chatting away through a hole in the wall, laughing at me as my eyes looked like two hard boiled eggs, as the rod went routing around inside my knob. Turned out I had an allergic reaction to some washing powder that my boxers had been washed in. Simon on the other hand, had contracted genital warts, for which he was given a tub of radioactive cream, a spatula, a pair of asbestos gloves, and a pair of goggles, just to apply the shit to himself. That night, I went out and painted the town red, while Simon stayed in and painted his knob red.

# CHAPTER SEVENTEEN

*"Meet The New Boss, Same As The Old Boss"*

There are two things I will always remember about Ches, the guy that managed Circus. Firstly, his wife and her mate measured my knob once, backstage at King George's Hall in Blackburn. We had supported the Tygers of Pan Tang, and I was sat having a beer on my own, while the others were running riot at the bar. The girls came in to the dressing room and opened a beer each. One of them picked up a ruler, which was lying around.

"Hey Tony, do you think you can match up to this?"

"I'll be fucking lucky."

"Well how big is yours?"

"All I can tell you is that I've seen plenty bigger, and I've seen plenty smaller, but on its day, I've never seen one harder."

They fell about laughing, like an X-rated Benny Hill show, and before you could say "I hope this ends in a threesome", one of them had hold of my old fella, while the other rested the ruler against it.

"Fuck off, you've got to measure it from underneath, it's bigger from there." I pleaded.

One of them moved the ruler underneath, as I squinted to read it.

"There you go, look at that, it's fucking massive." I shouted.

"Those are centimetres." They replied in unison.

"Aah fuck it. I don't suppose that while both of you are down there, I could have a…"

"No," they snapped.

"Well I didn't fucking start it. What am I supposed to think? Shut the door on your way out girls."

The second thing about Ches is… well, I can't actually think of it at the minute.

Oh yeah, here goes. We had been gigging for months, and were getting some great reviews. There was no real hierarchy in the band, but everybody knew what was expected of themselves, and we were growing. Quickly as friends, slightly slower musically, but still growing.

Adrian Netherwood was Simon's cousin, and played keyboards. Practical joker, who didn't believe that women possessed the word "No" in their vocabulary. One night, we played this gig in South Wales somewhere. We sat at the bar afterwards, and Adrian perched himself next to a woman who was obviously older than us, but bearing in mind what year it was, she may have only been around thirty. Anyway, she looked like she could handle herself. Adrian waded in, bought her a drink, and pulled up a stool. I'll never forget this one, he said;

"Anyway love, do you come here often?"

"I own the place dickhead."

Doesn't get any fucking better, does it? It didn't matter. From what I remember, I'm sure he helped her into the back of the van, for some kind of appointment with the "doctor."

Pete Ball, the second keyboard player in my time in Circus. Muso, who talked about complex time signatures and chords I'd never heard of. Fill him with Cider, and he turned into a football hooligan. Pete made you feel good, because if you played an idea to him, he gave it the correct musical term, and outlined the benefits of that particular melody. He also let you know how fucking clever you were, if that melody possessed anything remotely quirky in its conception, thus lifting your spirit to that of some kind of master, even if you had ripped the idea off your favourite band that very morning. Last time I spoke to him, he was "scoring" music for corporate videos, the clever twat.

Pete Tuatara, singer. Long haired muscular Maori. Big Kiss fan who, like me, was in it for the girls. I first met him when had his head stuck in a wash basin, trying to soothe the pain from facial burns, after trying the old "Gene Simmons" fire-breathing trick. One of the most polite people I have ever met and the obvious choice for PR work, if we ever got signed. That was of course, unless you ever crossed the lad, or pissed him off. I liked Pete because he liked going "head to head" with anybody, over anything. Sometimes I was on my own against Simon over various ideas, but I knew that if I mentioned whatever it was, to Pete, in passing, then he would tip the fucking boat right over. Drank a full bottle of Pernod one night, before we played a gig at "Edwards No 8" club in

Birmingham, the fucking animal.

One night we were travelling back from a gig, and we stopped at a service station for something to eat. The place was empty, apart from a few wide-boys that were prowling around, looking for easy prey, either to rob, or give a bit of a kicking to. Anyway, we were sat eating, when these three lads came over, and gathered around Alex, who, although not small, was probably the smallest out of the lot of us. This wanker started accusing Alex of staring at him, and giving him the V sign, and the inquisitive chap went on to ask if Alex was looking for trouble. He wasn't, but Pete was. Pete jumped up, and started swinging like a fucking maniac. He connected with two of the fuckers, and knocked them sprawling across the tables, never to be seen again. The other twat could have made it to the 1988 Olympics according to my stopwatch.

Adrian Dorsett, drums. This guy lived for the music. If we weren't rehearsing, he'd be on the phone to me, throwing ideas at me, waiting for a response, like an eager panting pup. A bear of a guy, with a heart of gold. Ade had a fucking huge double-bass drum kit that took up over half of the rehearsal room. Consequently, the rest of us were jammed in like the "Shadows", with our guitars pointing at the ceiling, because there was no room left to pose in. Charming. I liked Ade, because like me, he was naive. Like me, he thought that everything would fall into place, matter of fact, and we would be huge. Ade's favourite rock star? Well then, that would be a certain Paul Stanley, of Queens, New York, seeing as you're asking.

Alex Rigby, bass. Quietest out of the bunch, but again, had his mind set on one thing, and one thing only, the prosperity of the band. Sorry, did I say quiet? Well, that was only until you filled the fucker with beer. I've seen him surpass everybody, in terms of rock and roll excess, but that's not for me to tell. He held me in some kind of strange fascination, because he saw Kiss at Madison Square Garden on the Love Gun tour of 77-78. Consequently, he had to relay the experience to me on a regular basis, poor twat.

Simon Johnson. You're already familiar with his genital tomfoolery. Great guitar player, with some of the associated demons. Tortured soul, still searching for some inner peace, which will ultimately be his downfall. Only because, if he finds peace, his fire, his passion, will die, and the Simon I love will be lost forever. When the working class of Burnage mix with the middle class of

99

Cheadle Hulme, then there will always be sparks, but we could put these aside, so we could get things done. Anyway, I was too fucking feisty to be shoved down the pecking order just because of class. I had a dream, I had a plan, and I had an idea to get what I wanted. It may not have been the right idea, but it was all in place, ready for anybody to listen to, who thought they could assist in my quest. Simon fit the bill because he was a "sayer" first, and then a "doer." The fact that he was both of these things drew me to him immediately. Being just one of them doesn't really get you anywhere, but if you can have enough self-belief to make people listen to what you've got to say, then you are halfway there.

Like I said earlier, fate, odds, and statistics also have to rear their ugly heads somewhere down the line as well, so it ain't always a smooth ride. He had an agenda that resembled mine, and we sat and talked for hours when we weren't playing, trying to hammer some cohesion into our dreams. I didn't mind in the slightest that it was left to me and him, because at the end of the day somebody had to grab the torch, and I knew we were both ready. Simon will argue to the death, for something he believes in, and if he believes in you, then you will have a great ally. 100% isn't enough for this guy, and even though we didn't go all the way, he gained my respect and friendship from day one.

The phone rang one Saturday morning, early in 1988, after a particularly heavy Friday night at "Maximes" in Wigan. Manchester was a "Saturday" night out, but Wigan, fuck me, Wigan was the best Friday night out in the Twentieth century. Alright Nottingham, I can hear you. Call it a draw. I couldn't ignore it any longer, so I picked up the phone, expecting my stalker.

It was Ches.

"I'm just phoning to let you know, that I've been sat up all night talking with Simon, and I've just sacked Ade."

Adrian was our drummer, and friend. He didn't deserve this. I was fucking livid.

"At least have the balls to say it to his face," I croaked.

"He's not the right drummer, he's holding us back."

"In that case, sack the fucking lot of us. That's a cunts trick that you have just pulled. You know you've probably broken that lad's heart? Anyway, what the fuck has it got to do with you, and why wasn't any other fucker consulted?"

Ade lived for the band as much as anybody, certainly more

than me, and I wasn't going to let this lie. Like most managers, Ches was a failed musician. I'm not saying that he wasn't any good, but his band did fuck all, so he booked a few gigs for us, hired a few vans, and invented a job title for himself. I think he panicked, because anybody can rent a van or send a tape to a club, trying to get a gig, so it wouldn't be long before one of us was going to say "Hold on, I can phone a club. I can rent a van. Will you all pay my phone bill?" Maybe, he thought he had to make a big managerial decision, to justify his position, and show he was in charge. You see, there was no real gap between Ade's talents, and the rest of us. I can easily recognise the difference between over-enthusiasm and ineptitude. Something a girl pointed out to me in her bedroom once. That's why I couldn't understand why he singled out the drummer. Anyway, unbeknownst to Ches, from the moment he put the phone down, I had also left the band.

The next time Ches phoned me, he asked me to go to a meeting at his house. He said that Ade was going to be there, and it might get a bit hairy. Well I had nothing to hide, so I wasn't scared. I took a bag full of beer and sat round the table drinking, while the lads tried to crack jokes, waiting for Ade to turn up. The laughter was uneasy and unnatural. You could tell by the atmosphere, that times had been better. Ade turned up, and sat on the vacant chair. Ches shuffled around uneasy, twitching and stuttering, as he tried to present his defence. Ade stood up, and the room fell silent. He quietly, but menacingly, called everyone a cunt, right to their face. This man was hurting. He said that he was leaving, and if he ever saw anyone of us outside this room, he would beat the shit out of them. I stood up from my chair.

"Fuck this, I'm off as well. I'm not party to any of this. I'm not having decisions made for me, not concerning a friend."

There was a bit of a "Come on, let's talk about it" outburst, but I had made my mind up. Anyway, I know damn well that I'm not that important. I wasn't that hard to replace, and it was just as easy to carry on without me. I left the house, following Ade down the path. We didn't speak, and went our separate ways. I was walking down the road, when Ade's car screeched to a halt. As he wound his window down, I could hear his bellowing laughter.

"Nice one pal. Get in."

I got in the car and he drove off.

"Where are you going?"

"Just take me to the pub Ade."

We sat in the pub all day, weighing up what had gone wrong, when a couple of weeks earlier we were starting to hit a bit of a "groove" between us all. Again, I had found a great set of lads. Not a cunt between them, and it showed by the amount of time we spent together when we weren't rehearsing. I didn't think it was time for a change, but forces were at work, that set off a chain of events that nobody had expected a couple of days earlier. Anyway, we sat and talked and drank for fucking hours. Ade bundled me into his car, and took me home. He dragged me to my door, found my key and let me in. As I lay on the floor, he said; "Tony, I forgot to tell you, I've already found another band."

"Fucking cheers. That'll be just me without a band then, will it?"

The next day I phoned Glyn, and explained what had happened.

"Shit hot, it's about time you fucked them off. Let's sort something out."

Glyn was working with Rob Naylor, who was putting a band together, called A.O.K. Glyn and Rob were in Lanson together, but Glyn said he wasn't going to sing, he was going to manage the new band. Now from what I knew, Glyn couldn't manage three fucking Weetabix, so this was going to be a laugh. He turned up at my house, with a tape containing three songs. Rob knew Tony Mills, from Shy, and he sang on the demo. It was right down my street. Andy Chemney played drums. He had been in Rob's previous band, Sam Thunder. Everybody had heard of Andy, because he was, and still is, a fantastic drummer. He looked like Rick Springfield, and drank like Dusty Springfield. A great looking lad that didn't have to try and compensate for a fucking ugly boat race by trying to grow his hair to cover it. Steve Kenny was already on board, playing away in his turquoise cowboy boots. Steve Ferguson, aka "Fugsy", played guitar in Sam Thunder, but played keyboards in A.O.K. Although, by the time I joined the band, he had emigrated to Canada with his wife. I listened to the songs, and turned to Glyn.

"Let me get this right. You've not got a keyboard player or a singer. You've only got three songs, and you've got a pisshead for a manager."

"That's about it." said Glyn.

"Then deal me the fuck in."

# CHAPTER EIGHTEEN

### *"Say, Say, Say, What You Want"*

I've just sat and read what I've written so far, and asked myself, "Would I buy this?" Well, to be honest, yes, I would. Then again, what other possible verdict could I offer? The validity of my argument lies in the Arts. You see, I hate Shakespeare, I never got a degree in English, let alone a fucking A level, and I write like I speak, but there is something that burns inside me, that compels me to tell my story. So, what I see as barriers, haven't got in the way of me writing this. Me? I love words, I speak them all day long, just like Keats, Byron and Shakespeare; but unlike them, I live in a world of educated people who can read and write, no problem, so everybody I know is a modern day Shelley or Shakespeare. They were lucky in some respects, because coming to me with a "Thee" this, and a "Thou" that, would have got them a boot up their arse.

To me, art is something I cannot do. Michelangelo's Sistine chapel, Da Vinci's "Last Supper", that crying Spanish girl, my Mum had in the Seventies, the Van Halen logo. You get my drift? All of a sudden, art became accessible and open to interpretation, 20th Century style. Art became "pop", as the artists themselves fought to be on chat shows and in "celebrity" magazines, dressed in their designer clothes and unpronounceable sunglasses. People bunged sheep into formaldehyde, or arranged a stack of bricks in a rectangle. Voila. While the Emperor was blushing, searching for his pants, I spied my opening, and in I sneaked. So, as these people offer up everyday objects as art, I offer this as contemporary writing. A million miles away from the classics, I can't deny, but at least I got off my arse and had a go. Hold on, I'm sat on my arse while I'm writing this. What the fuck am I talking about? Anyway, by the time this procession of clowns have been rumbled, this book will hopefully be out on the streets, and people will be slagging me off left right and centre. Too fucking late my friend. Join the queue.

You never know, this book may even be at least one person's favourite book ever. Yeah right.

There is one thing however, that may stop people reading this book, and that is the language. I can't apologise, and I can't change anything, because every "Fuck", "Cunt", "Wanker", "Twat" and "Bastard" is intentional. To me this isn't bad language, it's all in the dictionary, and is precise and direct. I could use a hundred words, and never summon up the venom inside, when somebody is being an absolute twat. However, throw "Twat" into the shortest of sentences, and you know what they are like straight away.

Besides, there is going to come a point, when I have to tell the lads that my story is about to be published as a book, or, more likely, that I have printed them a copy each, of how I perceived things at the time, after every Publisher in the land has told me to go fuck myself. When I started, all I wanted to do was to set this story out like I had actually spoken about it, with my friends. I wanted this to be personal, just like I had talked it through, with Andy, Steve, Noel, Glyn, Fugsy, and Rob. However, to make it personal, I have to write it just like we spoke to each other on a daily basis. To make this sound "real" to any of the lads, I have to include the "Industrial", Northern, foul, entertaining, comedic language we all employed. What fires me onwards, to continue in this "Seaside postcard" style, are the six faces I can see staring at me, if I didn't swear throughout this whole tale. If I kept it "clean", the lot of them would be on my case, saying, "Why didn't you write it like we spoke it? You had one chance to get this story right, and you've gone and fucking blown it." Well, I've written this just like we talked it, to keep the moaning fuckers off my back.

To me, by including swearing at every twist and turn, negates the bad language, by taking away any shock you may feel, because I never set out to shock anybody when I started writing this fucking thing. If it is in from the start to the finish, then it is just part of the story. To leave it out altogether, and then just include it at specific points in the story, would be to sensationalise what I have experienced. To include it from the very beginning, is to include you in my world from the very start, inviting you to live it with me for real, not just when I want you to jump in and "feel" it for the odd paragraph here and there. I want to touch you far deeper than that. You must have sussed that by now. I want you to know what it felt like when that rug was pulled from underneath me, just as much as when I fucked a girl on that very same rug. I want you to know what it feels like, when all you can do is hold your hands up and shout "Aaaah for fuck's sake." However, something tells me you already know. It's got nothing to do with a lack of education or laziness, it's about honesty, truth and life. Now fuck off.

# CHAPTER NINETEEN

*"If The Kids Are United"*

Two litres of vodka, a case of beer, a few bottles of wine, and a large bag of crisps. Was somebody having a party? No, this was my first night together with my new band mates. Glyn and Rob picked me up, and we headed for Andy's flat in Salford. It was a cool place, with a gym on the ground floor, and a separate room with a hot tub. Apparently, what swung Andy's decision to buy the place was that he fucked a girl in the hot tub, when he went to view it. That's my boy!

I'd known Rob for a few years, but we'd never opened up properly. This was our chance. We loved the same music, girls, beer, vodka, long hair, laughing, moaning, and rock clubs. He turned up wearing an A.O.K. T-Shirt, even though there wasn't a proper band at this stage. After years in Sam Thunder, he was still as enthusiastic as the day he started playing, and without a doubt, was the catalyst for the band. I should have pointed out then, that he should have opted for the "Large" and not the "Medium" A.O.K. T-Shirt, but it's a bit late now. Like fuck it is. Like me, he laughs at his own jokes, but if you're funny, who gives a fuck. The battle began early on, to see who could be the funniest, and I've cried time after time as we battled it out. If you're interested, I won. Oh, here we fucking go!

Rob married early, and snapped up one of the babes on the Manchester rock scene, his wife Christine. You know when you see a great looking girl, and you think, "Well she must be a right arrogant cow", for no other reason whatsoever, other than she looks great? Well Christine wasn't. She loved to dance, loved to drink, loved to laugh, and loved to party. Bearing in mind, this was 1988, it took me another five years to meet a girl of my own, with something so special, that it made my heart go boom bang a bang, continually, but it was worth the wait. In fact, I'd have waited fifty years, just to experience a fraction of the love that I found.

Rob had the best of both worlds. He could travel the country, gigging and ligging, and then go home to the girl of his dreams. Beneath the drunken gobshite that is Rob Naylor, is a man that never strayed, not once. A man, who, if he knows you are on his side, will fight the fucking Romans to save you. A man, who, if you are down on your luck, will move the Earth to help you. A man, slight by nature, but who will take the whole fucking weight of the world off your shoulders, while he tortures himself for an answer to your problems. A man that absolutely loves a night out, providing that his best mates are there. Not only have they got to be there, but they have got to be having the best night of their lives. Then, and only then, can he settle down, and start to relax. I've never told him, but I should have told him years ago, that he's a hero of mine. I've known him for close on twenty years, and I found out early on, that he was a cross between "Boney M" and "Billy Idol." Yeah, that's right, fucking "Bone Idle."

Steve Kenny turned up late, dressed like he was going on a photo shoot. Leather jacket, faded jeans, and a shirt open to his waist. Massive hair and a dozen Budweisers under his arm. Start as you mean to go on my friend. This was tantamount to spraying his rock and roll territory, letting me know that this was "Top Cat's" alley. I mentioned to him that he looked shit-hot, and we never looked back. All of us had been in bands before, so we kind of skipped a few bases, and rightly or wrongly, decided we were going to aim a great deal higher from the very start.

There's nothing quite like throwing up in front of your band, to test their candour, tolerance, and acceptance. Kenny was first in, with the "Matey" arm and the "Get it up son" routine. Andy was next, offering to make tea, and suggesting I should go outside for some fresh air. Maybe as a show of concern, but probably more fucking likely to save his flat from a gallon of beer, mixed with everything I had consumed in the last twenty-four hours. "Fucking soft cunt" fought to be heard through Rob's laughter, but I heard it. Glyn finished off with: "If I knew this was going to happen, I'd have drove right past your house, you soft cunt. Fucking hell, you look ugly when you are being sick." A lovely cup of tea later, normality had been resumed, and we got down to business.

Singer, keyboard player, songs, rehearsal room, gigs, demo-tape, publicity, and groupies. Things we desperately needed, some more desperately than others. We rented a rehearsal room in an old mill in Ancoats. A shitty old damp toilet of a place, but we were desperate to get going, and this was high on our list of "Wants." Noel Fraser was the singer in another local band called Strutz, and again, was on our shopping list. A great looking lad, with a chiselled jaw, and a big voice. We invited him to rehearse, and we wrote some songs. Pete Ball was next. After I left Circus, I kept in touch with Pete. He was always curious about what I was up to. I invited him down to find out for himself, and he jumped ship, the fucking "blaggard" of a Pirate. Although they never accused me outright, I'm sure the lads left in Circus thought I was a complete cunt. Within weeks of me leaving, I'd also poached the keyboard player. I remained friends with them, and I'm sure this was only because they were all fully aware that the house of cards only folded, when "Ches" made that phone call to me, that Saturday morning, leaving every one of us to try and salvage what was left from the rubble.

We made a demo, took some photos, wrote a biography, and booked some gigs. Then we sat in a room, like a million other bands, with a list of magazines, journalists, and record companies, writing envelopes to every one of them, while listening to our own demo, again and again. I absolutely loved this time in the band. The excitement, the belief, and the total unknown. This was where dreamers dreamed, and I was tucked up nicely, thank you. Glyn pestered and pestered people, until they would talk to him, just to get him off the phone. By the time we did our first gig, we were featured in "Kerrang" magazine's "Melodic Rock Special." During the 1988 "Children in Need" appeal, Glyn phoned up and spoke to Bruno Brooks, the Radio 1 DJ, who presented part of the show. Glyn pledged a wedge of cash, if Bruno would play one of our songs on his radio show. Brooks sweated, but there was no turning back. Glyn had him cornered, and unless he was prepared to go back on his word, then we were on the fucking radio. Radio 1 if you don't mind. The very next week, we went national.

I thought, in fact we all thought, that this charade would help us to the hallowed "Top of the Pops" studio, even though that was the beginning of the end as far as we were concerned. This was down to our inexperience, because I always thought about the rock and roll path going as follows. Unknown, unsigned, gigs, press, bigger gigs, signed, album, gigs, second album, U.S. tour, sold out U.K. tour, third album, hit single, Top of the Pops, dropped, cabaret, buy a pub and fill it with pictures of yourself, petrol pump attendant, brothel visitor, death.

We played at Edward's No 8 club in Birmingham on a Sunday night during the summer. It was a good night. Warm, sunny, a healthy crowd, no stalker, and even the unbelievably free flowing M6 offered its approval. Although we were on a massive learning curve, we were progressing quickly. Judging by my success with the ladies, we weren't on the verge of stardom, but I could wait. On the way home, we stopped at the motorway services for a drink. We sat around talking, when Noel dropped the bombshell.

"I'm sorry lads, but I'm leaving."

We were all stunned.

"Why. What is it, what's wrong?" I asked.

Noel had been offered a job in a band in London. They had management and a publishing deal, and must have seemed the better bet. Like a gaggle of fuckwits, we sat around, let our heads go down, and accepted it. We should have fought for him, let him know how right he was for us, and made him see the "bigger" picture. Either that or we should have booted him the length and breadth of the service station, the cheeky cunt. "Management deal", "Publishing deal", big words that I knew were meant to impress me, but I didn't have a clue what they meant. Management? Does that mean that this other band had one of their mates working tirelessly on their behalf for fuck all? Well Glyn was already doing that for us. Publishing? Well, I didn't have a fucking clue what this meant. Nobody did, not even Noel, but it sounded impressive. I kinda knew what a record deal was. Simple, you made records, but I never quite "got" what a publishing deal was. I still don't have a fucking clue. Were we so wrong in our vision and conviction? Had Noel recognised a weakness that was gonna hold us back? Was he so fucking right for doing this? Was he instantly in a league above us, because of the choices he had made? Do you know what fucking killed me about it? I couldn't dislike the guy, none of us could. He was one of us. He was such a belting lad that I didn't want him to fail for one fucking second, even though it meant worldwide success for some other fuckers. I was prepared to accept that, all because of my respect for the man.

# CHAPTER TWENTY

*"Knock three Times"*

I thought I was done with auditions, I really did. Strangers, in strange rooms, playing strange songs, with strange fucking haircuts, but at least people had to impress me now. The sweaty-palmed, clammy-arsed, dry-throated, staring at the floor, note-missing, song-forgetting, shoe, was on the other foot. Our collective foot to be precise, and it wasn't scared of hoofing time-wasters right back out on to the street, for their fucking audacity. I don't know what it was about us, but time-wasters would sit at home, eating toast, and scratching their nuts, while reading "Kerrang", or wherever our adverts popped up.

"Hmmm, Manchester. I could be there in four hours. I've got nothing on this weekend, so I'll go and see how long it takes until I'm rumbled."

So, Glyn would get a phone call from somebody professing to be the next David Coverdale, with knobs on. Oh how we rejoiced. This, finding a singer lark was a fucking doddle. We went and got shit faced, because we knew that our Saviour was on the early train on Saturday from Cardiff, no, Bournemouth, no, Oxford, no, York, no, London. Picca fucking dilly, it's only a train station, but I thought it had a personal vendetta against me, as it spewed out hopeless twat after hopeless twat, for us to feed and water, before fucking them off, right back from whence they came.

It was a bit of a laugh to start with, well, the very first time maybe. After that, the mood changed, and we had to be cruel, just to save precious time. When singers phoned, Glyn made a point of asking;

"Are you a time waster?"

I could respect a "Yes" answer. We had nipped it in the bud early, thus saving our time, but also allowing "Walter Mitty", a chance to reflect on his mistake, enabling him to avoid the initial pitfalls when applying for the Deep Purple, or Iron Maiden job later.

It was the "No, not me" replies, that stung us every fucking time. Our greatest asset when dealing with these situations was Glyn's Armadillo hide. He delivered some classic lines. Some subtle, some wrapped around a brick. Here's a sample.

"I thought you told me on the phone, that you weren't a cunt."

"What time is your train home?"

"When I said you had to have long hair, I meant all over your head."

"Well that was fucking rubbish."

"You're fatter than me, you fat cunt."

"Aren't you that wanker that goes in the "Banshee?"

"Hey, nice tooth."

One Saturday, we auditioned a lad that looked like one of the fucking "Chuckle" brothers. He didn't smile, had no social skills, and was about five feet tall, with a pencil thin moustache. Rob grabbed my arm.

"Who the fuck does he think we are... Sparks?"

Glyn soon brought the sorry ordeal to an end.

"When I said we wanted a singer for a rock band, which part of the advert do you think applied to you? Because let me tell you, a singer or a rocker, you are not."

The lad fumbled in his pocket, and pulled out a "Fidel Castro" sized cigar. He lit it, and let out a huge plume of smoke before he spoke.

"Look lads" he said.

Before he could say another word, Glyn jumped in.

"Hold on, hold on. You can fuck right off with that cigar and all. You're sat puffing on that fucking thing like you have sang your heart out, and blown us away. You're a fucking time-waster aren't you? You've slipped through the net, and you've fucking had us over, haven't you? Why have you turned up? You know you can't sing, don't you? Now do me a favour, and fuck off."

Desperate for beer, good music and beautiful girls, we waded into the "Banshee" after another delusional day. What, with the fella off the "Pringles" tub, turning up for an audition, we needed to get a little crazy. Malcolm owned the "Banshee" with Diane, and we hung out at the bar, chatting with him regularly. He was also involved in "Jilly's" in some capacity, which was another fantastic Manchester rock club, where we all went from the late seventies onwards. While we were all talking, he would regularly pull out his glowing lighter, and secretly hold it under somebody's arse, while the laughter got louder. There was a surprise in store for some poor unsuspecting fucker, as they laughed at an "in" joke. I can't remember if I could smell the burning before I felt the pain, but I dropped my drink either way. He ruined two pairs of my jeans this way, but I couldn't grumble. He saved me hundreds of pounds over the years, with free entry and free drinks.

Later, I met a small brunette, who was no taller than five feet, but she had these huge breasts, long hair, and glossy lipstick, painstakingly applied like a top-class whore. Standing at six feet two, I had to "lean in" to make myself heard, but "heard" I was, and things moved up a gear. She finished her drink, grabbed my hand, and led me to the Ladies toilets. Eager to consolidate our relationship, she locked the cubicle door, and removed her top. She had massive tits, and a great tanned body. I was still wearing about 25% of my clothes at this point, which may seem a tad excessive, bearing in mind what was about to happen. However, this only actually consisted of my cowboy boots, scarves and bangles. Yes I know, I've just seen the same mental picture. Cunt.

I braced myself, for something akin to the top ten roller coaster rides in the World, all rolled in to one, when I heard a voice.

"Tony, is that you?"

The voice was angry, high pitched, female, and was coming from the next cubicle. I recognised it immediately, it was my fucking stalker. I said nothing, and she stormed out. I was just about to… aaah you know exactly what I was just about to do, when there was a loud banging on the door. Three, big knuckled, ominous, neanderthal knocks.

"Open the door."

"I'm on the toilet." The girl shouted.

"Open the fucking door." He wasn't going away.

I opened the door, and recognised the guy immediately. It was one of the Bouncers. My stalker had stitched me up, good and proper.

"Fucking hell, not you again," he said.

"I'm sorry Dave. It's Saturday night for fuck's sake."

"You know I'm going to have to throw you out, don't you?"

"Come on Dave, I live for this place. What would I do then?"

"What do you mean Again?" said the girl.

I was fucked. I'd lost the girl, but more importantly, I was on the verge of losing everything. After much pleading, he let me stay. I went back to the bar, nuzzled in between Rob and Glyn, and grabbed my drink.

"Fucking hell, that was quick", said Glyn.

"Fucking rubbish," piped up Rob.

"You're in my band now. I don't know what your last band was like, but I won't tolerate any "hair triggers" in my band, not when you are single. This is the worst kind of publicity we could have. Now get back in there, or fucking resign."

They laughed, as they continued to take the piss. I argued vehemently, but this just gave them more ammunition, to store away for a rainy day. Like Dick Dastardly, I was always in the lead, but never won a fucking race.

The very next night, I was sat listening to music, drinking bottle after bottle of beer. Slouched low on the settee, I was extremely comfortable, and very drunk. My neck was resting on the back of the settee, and as I stared at the ceiling, my mind wandered. The weekend didn't exactly go to plan, what, with the singer, and the toilet escapade, but these were just minor blips. They weren't exactly a cause for concern. A quiet Sunday night, recharging my batteries for the week ahead, which began in earnest, on Wednesday, at the "Banshee", was just what I needed. I looked down, to reach for another beer, and there was my stalker, in between my legs, on her knees, hard at work. My jeans had been slung across the room, twenty minutes earlier.

See? I'm a fucking idiot. I should have opened a shop, where people could come in, choose a piece of cane, and then whittle it down into a personalised rod, which could then be used for stripping flesh from their own backs. All you need to know, is that she made a phone call, offered me everything I didn't get on Saturday night…plus V.A.T. and then picked me up. Fuck it, we're only here once. Then again, I said that last time. She put the Kiss "Exposed" video on, and turned to face the T.V. on her hands and knees. I climbed on board, and watched the video over her shoulder. Before "Who wants to be Lonely" had finished, I was curled up in my foetal sleeping position. She wasn't happy; it was the first song on the video. That'll fucking teach her.

# CHAPTER TWENTY ONE

*"Pussy Cat, Pussy Cat, Where Have Your Been?"*

Glyn called, and said that he was going to London the following Saturday, to see a singer that he thought might be good for us. Rob was up for the trip, so, if I didn't go I was a soft cunt. His words not mine. If you take Glyn's word at face value, it sounds like a great day out, with the potential to be fruitful. If you read between the lines, this is carnage waiting to happen. Three lads with a boot full of beer and vodka, none of whom could say no when the others were still fucking drinking. Because there was three of us, two would always gang up against the other one. It didn't matter which two, but from my experience, it's always better to be one of the two. Basically, if you are the "one", then you are fucked, both through alcohol, and through the abuse you endured, from the minute you said "I've had enough lads."

Glyn Jones is an organiser. He's good at it, and I don't know why, but he enjoys it. So, the phone call organising the trip went like this.

Glyn; "Alright? Look, I'll pick you up at Seven o'clock, on Saturday morning."

Me; "Hold on, we're going to Wigan on Friday night, I'll be fucked."

Glyn; "No Tony, you'll be tired. You can't get laid for love nor money at the minute. Remember?"

Me; "Fuck off, you know what I mean."

Glyn; "Well if I can get up, you can get up, you lazy twat."

Me; "Have you told Rob, because he won't be happy?"

Glyn; "Well, that "Steptoe" faced twat wouldn't be happy if I personally carried the fucker all the way there in a sedan chair, so he can fuck off and all."

Me; "Seven o'clock? Come on, we'll be there for Ten o'clock. That's twelve hours before the gig starts."

Glyn; "No, we'll stop for breakfast, then buy a few porn mags at the services. We can waste an hour reading them. We'll have a bit of a sightseeing trip around London, and then check in at the hotel for Midday. Then we'll jump on a tube, grab a pizza, then head for the "peep" shows. We'll spend the afternoon in Soho staring at oiled up pussies, in between diving in and out of pubs. Back to the hotel at teatime. Quick shower, quick wank, quick litre of vodka, and then out for some food, then straight into the pubs. Roll up at the "Stick of Rock" at half past eight, and if you can still remember your name by then, I'll buy the rest of your fucking beer all night."

Me; "Seven o'clock it is then."

The singer was billed as a solo artist, even though he had a band with him. He had received a few good reviews in the press, and he turned out to be a brilliant singer, with a great bluesy rasp to his voice. Afterwards, Glyn introduced himself to the guy's manager, and explained that we were looking for a singer. The singer's manager was sat on a stool at the bar, and appeared to be nursing a broken foot. There was a pair of crutches leaning against the bar next to him. Glyn handed him a card, and asked him to call. He took Glyn's card, and without saying a word, tore it up, and let it fall to the floor. Glyn handed him another one, and spoke into his ear;

"Look, here's another card. If you rip this one up, I'm going to take your crutch and stick it right up your arse. Go on, try me you cunt."

Hey, guess what? Yep, back to Manchester without a singer. Fuck all. Didn't matter, I had a fucking scream, we all did. Then again, I remember sitting on the pavement, as the sun was rising, with chips and gravy in my fucking hair, unable to stand up because of the amount of beer I'd supped. I know we jumped in a taxi after the gig, and went to the "St. Moritz" club, and we ended up in an all night take-away in Finsbury Park, skint, fucked, drunk and puking. So, how does that translate into a great memory? I must be fucking puddled. Oh yeah, I hadn't shit my pants, that's it. Funny, but you can do practically anything to me and I will take it all in my stride, and I will laugh out loud at your ingenious attempts to bring me to my knees. I'll even add whatever humour I can muster, to assist in your quest to assassinate my character, time after time, but you fucking dare follow through in my presence, and that's it. I'll tie a plank to the tallest skyscraper, and have you walking off the end of the fucking thing before you can blink, you dirty, slack-arsed twat.

It's nothing personal; I can't stand the smell of my own shite, so to offer me yours unexpectedly, will only ever get one fucking response from me, no matter how much I like you. To be honest, where shit was concerned, I had joined a band of "Gentlemen", so that was never a problem. No matter how drunk we got, I can honestly say that I was never woken the next morning by the smell of my mates' shite, but more importantly, I never woke any of my mates, with the smell of mine. Something we can all be proud of.

# CHAPTER TWENTY TWO

*"Ooh, I Hear Laughter In The Rain"*

If I wasn't playing music, having sex, or wanking, then my next choice would be laughing. Well, listening to music was up there as well, but a good fucking belly laugh is hard to beat. A great, natural laugh, that finds its own motion and propels itself to its own conclusion over several minutes, is one of the finest things on the planet. Forced laughter does have its uses though. It identifies wankers. People with some kind of agenda, who, for one reason or another, want to be recognised. Hey, if it's funny, laugh your cock off, but if it's not funny, don't insult me by forcing on me, what you think I want to hear. I always thought girls would be the biggest culprits, especially in crowds. You know... "Look at me, ain't I something else?", but most of the time it was lads. They might have been trying to get the girl, they might have been trying to hang with a certain crowd, but it grated on me something fucking awful. For me, laughter is as hard to do as tears, and it takes a lot for me to give either, but when I do, I do.

Comedy kept my band alive through the low times of being stranded without a singer. Laughter saved us. Rob crowned himself, "The King of Comedy", and I agree wholeheartedly. He's got a sharp mind, and an even sharper tongue, but his comedy "back up" was his "Highland Games, best of show, Championship "Haggis" scrotum. Bollocks like Mickey Mouse's ears. I can't remember exactly when it began, but all of a sudden, naked mates became part of the caper. I've been startled in my sleep several times, only to jump up into Rob's hairy arse squatting over my face, while the rest of the lads sat around me, trying to rouse me from my slumber.

"See that lads, he's gay. What are you doing, sticking your face up my arse?"

Everybody laughed, as Rob skated around the fact that he had been crouched over me until I woke up. Another time, I woke up to find Rob leaning over me, with his knob perfectly balanced on my nose, like the fucking bridge over the River Kwai.

"What is it with you Tony, are you gay? If this fucking carries on, I'll sack you. That's your final warning you fucking weirdo."

In that split second, when you wake up and don't know where you are, it can be very disconcerting to find a wrinkly, gnarly, musty, ugly, anaemic, overly seasoned, Anglo Saxon penis, resting on the only part of your fucking anatomy that can recognise smells.

"Lord Stilton of Stiltonshire announces his arrival."

I wouldn't mind, but fifteen minutes after I passed out, everybody was asleep. It's not as if the rest of them partied until dawn. If only I could hang on that bit longer, I would get a peaceful night. I tried getting up later, and drinking less, but nothing worked.

Travelling back from one of our early gigs, I was sat in the front of the van with Steve and Glyn. Rob was in the back, with the amps and the rest of the gear. Everybody was knackered, and the van was silent as we sped down the country lane. After a while, Rob piped up;

"Hey lads."

We turned around to find Rob stretched across the speaker cabinets, delicately balanced, with fuck all on. He looked like a Victorian nude on a chaise longue.

"What's going on, you ponces? Stop looking at me. I'll sack the fucking lot of you, and that includes you, Mr Jones."

Glyn slammed his foot on the brakes, and Rob flew into the back of our seats like the naked crime fighter of Gotham city. "Blam." "Thwack." "Swoosh." I turned the Van Halen tape down, and peered into the back of the van. Jesus, Rob's body had taken a right hammering, it was fucked. Add to that the injuries he had just sustained, and it was a write off. Glyn stopped the van, and Rob staggered to his knees clutching his head. Glyn seemed concerned.

"Are you OK Rob?"

"Yeah, I'll be OK."

"Right then."

Glyn jumped on the accelerator, and roared off. Rob rolled backwards, and disappeared from sight amongst the equipment. We could just about make out his groans beneath our laughter. As he was making all kinds of threats, Glyn turned Van Halen up to full volume, and we disappeared into the night.

Back at rehearsals, Pete the keyboard player said he was leaving. Once a decision like this has been made, just let it go.

Don't fight it, don't try to make it right, don't pander to anybody, just regroup and move on. Remember, a chain is only as strong as its weake… oh do me a fucking favour. Pete helped us out when we needed it most, and we parted as friends. Steve Ferguson was our final keyboard player. He played guitar in Sam Thunder, and was totally versatile. He married a Canadian girl, but moved back to England, when things didn't work out. Back in Manchester he had no job, but more importantly, no band. He turned up to rehearsals with a Korg M1 and a crate of beer. Perfect. From the start he was engrossed in our social pursuits. This man didn't know when to stop.

"If it's wet, drink it. If it's dry, smoke it, and if it moves, fuck it." That was Steve.

"Fugsy", as he was known, turned up at rehearsals one night, wincing, and was obviously in some kind of pain. He was desperately trying to scratch his back through his white shirt. As he turned around, I noticed five or six burn marks on the back of his shirt.

"Fucking hell Fugsy, what are those?"

"Well, I was driving along having a fag, with the window down. When I finished, I flicked the fag out of the window, but the wind blew the fucking thing back in. It went straight down my shirt collar, and got trapped in between my back and the fucking car seat. It was burning like a bastard, so I started banging my back into the seat, trying to put the fucking thing out, while swerving all over the road."

Saturday, we were back at Piccadilly station, waiting for the train from Bournemouth. Fugsy was covered in calamine lotion, as we awaited the arrival of another singer. A big strapping Italian looking chap with long brown hair, called Tim, was about to bail us out, and lead the Crusade, like Godfroi de fucking Bouillion. He said that he sounded like Joe Lynn Turner, and lived in a tree. Mad for sure, but if he could sing, I had just the tree for him. Turned out, he sounded like Anthea Turner. We gave him some plant food, and fucked him off back home on the "Seaside Special." Jerusalem would have to wait.

Honestly, it was like the fucking "Gong Show" sometimes. I don't want to dwell on the fact that it took us so long to find a singer, because it makes me so fucking angry. Week in, week out, Glyn would receive around half a dozen tapes from, I was going to say singers, but these weren't singers. In the end, we invited a couple of the worst ones, just for a laugh. In the middle of this madness, we got a tape from a lad in York called Simon, who had an amazing voice. He came over to rehearse and blew us away. He didn't have the strongest image, but we agreed it was something we could work on. We had a meeting, and decided to offer him the job.

Glyn phoned me the following night.

Me; "Have you phoned Simon?"

Glyn; "No, I can't."

Me; "Why?"

Glyn; "I've just received another tape today, and I think it's the one."

Me; "What?"

Glyn; "He sounds like Coverdale, and he's got hair down to his fucking waist. I can't phone Simon until we've heard this lad."

His name was Tony, and he lived in Oxford. He came up the next Saturday, and got the job. I knew it was gonna be a test, because he got hit by a car on his first night in Manchester, while looking the wrong way, crossing Oxford Rd, a fucking one way street. We had a gig booked supporting Wrathchild at "Fagins" in Manchester, and we shifted loads of tickets. We booked into a studio in Macclesfield and recorded a demo, just to have his voice on tape. In hindsight, the songs were the worst we had recorded, but we needed to get our fucking skates on. Boredom strikes pretty early, when you are working in a recording studio. Pinball machines and porn mags have a limited shelf life, when it's all you've got to do, while waiting for the call to do your bit. Then you are subject to abuse all the way through, for not being quick enough, or wasting time, or for making that one mistake, while six knobs are being waved at you from behind the mixing desk. Then again, I bet "Toys in the Attic", "Diamond Dogs", and "Sheer Heart Attack", were all made this way.

When I was done, I sat on a chair next to a pile of cardboard boxes stacked on the floor. I opened a box, and found a load of T-Shirts, with the logos of various indie bands on them. It was 1989, and the world had gone "Madchester" crazy. This was mail order madness, Macclesfield style. I opened the T-Shirts, and dropped my pants. I must have rubbed between fifteen or twenty of the fucking things, up the crack of my sweaty arse. I only ever meant to do one, but before I knew it, the rest of the lads were goading me to carry on. My arsehole was red raw, from the dry cotton, ripping against my poor old sphincter. My shitter was in tatters. I felt like a fucking "Old Etonian" that had made it to the House of Lords. Yes, I did have a shower before I went to bed.

Problems, problems, problems. The week before the gig Tony went missing. He'd just upped and left, without a "kiss my arse", or fuck all. This wasn't going to look good. We had sold loads of tickets, and it looked like we were going to have to pull out. Pissed off? You could say so. This wasn't like cancelling one date of a two hundred date world tour. We hadn't played live for fucking ages, we needed this. We were angry, because we had opened up, trusted somebody, let them in, and paid the price.

Glyn was all set for getting three black balaclavas', and going and kidnapping the soft twat. Me and Rob managed to talk him out of it, mainly because we didn't want to spoil our hair. We drove down to Oxford with our back combed locks pressing against the roof of the car, like Marge Simpson and her doppelganger. We persuaded him to come back up for the gig, but we all knew it was a temporary arrangement. The gig was packed out, and we went down really well. It was fucking scary really, because "Wrathchild" looked like every dodgy bird I had ever fucked.

I went to the bar afterwards, and found Glyn talking to a guitarist from another local band. Now these people never usually bothered with us. We all knew each other, but everybody kept everybody else at arm's length. To be honest, I couldn't give a shit about what anybody else was doing; I had too much to worry about. They were all two-faced cunts anyway, desperate to stick the fucking knife in whenever they could. Jealous fuckers, the lot of them, and that was the problem. Not because we were famous. Not because we were great musically. Not because we had that elusive deal. No, what we had, was a fucking brilliant crowd that turned out every week. Because we laughed all night until our cheeks ached. Because we took over the bar area every time we went in the place, be it the "Banshee", "Jilly's", the "Phoenix", or later, "Rockworld." Because we looked cool. Because we drank until we were no longer cool. Because we had a crowd of girls with us that bordered on "Porn Star" quality. That's what pissed the other bands off. Lovers, fighters, losers, chancers, romancers, dancers, filchers, jokers, charmers, drinkers, dreamers. This was my crowd. This was where I belonged.

Anyway, I walked over to Glyn, to find out what was going on. Glyn scratched his chin while supping his beer, as the guy gave his verdict on the nights performance. As I approached, Glyn leant into his ear, and began his response.

"For a start, your fucking breath stinks. Your eyes are on the piss, and you've got a perm that barely reaches your fucking collar. You are without doubt an ugly cunt, and to top it all, you wear cowboy boots outside your jeans. You stand on your own every week. You've got no mates, and the only girls I've ever seen you with are fucking pigs. Your band is a widdly diddly pile of shite, and you are all a set of cunts. Now fuck off... Oh, yeah, by the way, Tony's fucked your girlfriend."

As he walked off, Glyn threw his demo tape back at him. It bounced off his head, and smashed on the floor.

"Fucking hell Glyn, nice one."

"Cunt", said Glyn.

They didn't understand. We didn't want to be their friends, they were our enemies. Their success meant our failure. We wished the plagues of Egypt on these fuckers, nothing more, nothing less. We were relieved, because we could now tell Tony to go home, and carry on doing whatever it was that drew him back to his hometown. All of a sudden we weren't that desperate. The gig was finished, and he had kept his word, and turned up. We could finally relax our arseholes, so that they could all return to that "Goldfish's mouth" shape. The furrowed brows went simultaneously.

Noel was back in town. He came to watch us and have a drink with us at the bar. Things hadn't worked out for him in London, and he was in the process of moving back up to Manchester. We explained what had happened with Tony, and before I could finish my vodka chaser, he was back in the band. What could we do but celebrate? After far too many drinks, I put on my beer goggles, and spied a beauty. Once again, I was bundled into a taxi, on my way to a "Close Encounter of the Furred Kind." It was just like the old saying, "I went to bed with Bo Derek, and woke up with Bo Diddley."

Dick Dastardly's wheel had come off again.

# CHAPTER TWENTY THREE

*"The Hills Are Alive…"*

Noel Fraser. Singing, songwriting, guitar-playing, keyboard-playing, acrobatic, demolition derby driving, masturbating, narcoleptic. It was great having him back. He could grab an idea by the scruff of its neck, sprinkle a bit of his magic over it, put it in the oven for twenty minutes on gas mark 6, and then pull out something very fucking special indeed. So, he had something about him that contained the ability to make a simple idea sound amazing. I thought I was biased because he was the singer in my band, but it is a quality he has retained to this very fucking day, when I need no excuse at all to champion the man. He has a great gift with melodies and harmonies, but not 1 in 6 gradients. He was out walking one day, when he tripped and fell over a rock. He had his hands in his pockets, so he tumbled down the full fucking hillside, rolling through sheep shit, and bouncing off rocks, until a dry stone wall saved him from the main road. I think he finished his performance with a triple fucking salchow. Straight sixes from the judges. He didn't make rehearsals for a couple of weeks. By the way, the wall was a fucking write off by all accounts.

Noel loved tinkering with cars, and he spent hours customising total heaps of shit into shitty heaps. Fat tyres and deep red velvet on the seats, made every car he ever had, look like the "Munsters" half-coffin, half-dragster. After a photo session one wet Sunday, Noel rushed off early, while the rest of us surveyed the contact sheets for an amazing photo. Not of the band mind you, we each searched quietly for a great picture of ourselves. Narcissism was alive and well in my band, and in my view, was very healthy. After all, it could only make the band look better as a whole, and that was the point of it all, wasn't it?

Noel came running back into the studio, soaked to the bone, and out of breath.

"What is it mate?" said Andy.

"I was just driving around the roundabout outside the "Apollo", when my front fucking wheel fell off."

He had forgotten to tighten his wheel nuts the day before, and they had worked loose. We jumped into Glyns car still wearing our stage gear, looking like dandy AA men. As we stood in the pissing rain lifting Noel's car, our mighty "album cover" hairstyles, took several buckets of Manchester's finest.

Noel is probably on a par with me when it comes to drinking. He loves it, but it creeps up on him, and by the time it has said "Boo", he's fucked. Sometimes though, he had a unique built-in defence system that bypassed the vomiting and falling over. He fell asleep. Obviously, we took advantage of this by drawing on him, emptying six tins of shaving foam on him, and leaving him in various states of undress, wrapped around lampposts in quaint market towns across the country. Then, when he didn't wake up, we had to carry him around, like that fucking corpse in "Weekend at Bernie's."

Summer came, and we booked about five gigs close together, and tried to convince ourselves it was a tour. Laughable really, but our spirits were always high, and what else could it be but a fucking scream? London, Cardiff, Cirencester, Gloucester, and somewhere else. Swindon I think. We played at the "Royal Standard" in Walthamstow on the Friday, and then made our way over to the west of the country. Glyn booked us into two caravans in Cirencester for five days. It was pretty central for the gigs, so we used it as a base, and travelled back to the caravans after each gig. Not exactly Led Zep's "Starship", the Boeing jet they used to fly in and out of the same U.S. city, to try and keep some semblance to their crazy lives while on tour. But then again, nobody nicked a quarter of a million pounds off us.

We hired a PA system and took it with us. This was carefully packed in the van, next to a barbecue, TV, video, CD player, crates of beer, bottles of spirits, porn mags, gas lamps, bags and bags of food, charcoal, firewood and a football. Then there were the instruments and amps, and everybody's clothes and toiletries for five days. Oh, and toilet rolls, the most valuable commodity known to man. "To shit, or not to shit? That, my friend, is the question." As long as I had my Andrex double strength with me, I was dropping loads, like a bomber over Dresden, after we declined the offer to join that fucking Aryan race carry-on. Some kind of inferiority

124

complex, if you ask me, that went back to Martin Luther and beyond, and manifested itself in twats like Wagner. In fact, Luther and Wagner weren't fucking worthy of wiping my arse. See? I've gone and done it again with my language, but maybe now you understand exactly what I mean. And no, I'm not a Jew, but if I was, I'd be proud to be one.

The caravans were in a field the size of six football pitches, behind a farm. There were only two more caravans in the field, and they were probably a quarter of a mile away from us. Glyn had the kitty, and decided to go get some more food and vodka, and fucked off into Swindon to the shops. People were getting stir-crazy, so they all dived in the van, just for a change of scenery. There was enough beer in the fridge, so I crashed out on the grass with an ice cold bottle. Fugsy stayed with me, as he was fixing something on the PA system, which by now, was set up in the field, pumping out "Last of the Runaways." Fugsy used to go into a "Technotrance" which could last for hours. If he had enough fags and beer, he'd be gone all bastard day. There was another world, of soldering irons, wires, and circuit boards, which was alien to me. He swigged at his beer, while scratching his head, trying to catch a tan in his boxer shorts. The lazy summer afternoon was alive with the smells and sounds of the countryside. I could see for fucking miles, and there wasn't a soul around, besides me and Fugsy. This was the England that you read about in poems. Well, if you took the fucking council house scum out of the picture it was. I don't know if I'd been asleep for thirty minutes, or thirty seconds, when a female voice woke me up.

"Hello."

I opened my eyes, to find a woman looking down at me. She said she was staying in one of the other caravans. She was probably around thirty five, wearing a summer dress, and had a school teacher's hairstyle. Innocent enough, but she also had her sunglasses perched on her head, with that "Jackie Onassis", "I'm the dirtiest Woman on the planet" look.

"Are you on holiday?"

Fucking nosey, I thought.

"No."

"Well what are you doing?"

"We're a band."

My eyes closed.

"That must be nice."

"Yeah."

"How long are you here for?"

"Only five days."

"Err… what's your name?"

"What?"

"No, not you, your band. What are you called?"

What the fuck was going on? Was she after me? Did she have an axe? Why was she interested? I opened my eyes. Although she was talking to me, she was looking at Fugsy. I sat up, and saw him hard at work, with his soldering iron smoking away. His boxer shorts were stuck up his arse, and his knob and bollocks were dangling out of the side in the sunshine. She had obviously spotted the ten minute freeview.

"Hold on, you're looking at my mates knob."

"No… no… I'm n…

Before she could finish, I shouted out;

"Fugsy, Fugsy, she's looking at your knob."

She went bright red, and ran off. Now if I'd have played it cool, I'm sure we could have had some red hot porno situation going on, for which I apologise Fugsy. We laughed briefly, but Fugsy was soon back in his "Technotrance." I handed him a fresh beer, and he threw his fag on the floor, and stamped on it. He started screaming, and hopping around like Rumple fucking Stiltskin. He had forgotten that he had no shoes on.

There was a shower block opposite the caravan, and you would have thought that somebody was giving away twenty pound notes inside the fucking thing. A tiny concrete hut in the middle of nowhere that always had a queue outside it. Cleanliness was something not always associated with rockers, but a myth nonetheless, especially in this fucking neck of the woods. The reason? Wanking, pure and simple. Twenty pence, for ten minutes of hot, soapy, foamy, "It's mine, so I'll wash it as fast as I like", fun. The farm was isolated, so every time we went into the village, everybody made sure that they stocked up on twenty pence pieces. Sometimes, people fucked up, and were offering to buy a twenty pence piece for a pound. I could have made a fortune, but I shared. No, not the shower, my twenty pence's, for fuck's sake. I don't know why the shower block didn't figure in the top ten Cotswold attractions that year. Fucking "spud juice" everywhere. We checked

126

each other's feet as we left the shower block. Webbing between the toes meant that you had stepped in your mates stringy bits, either by side footing them down the plug hole unsuccessfully, or, by thrashing around after losing control completely, highlighting the fact that you were no doubt a complete fucking animal. One morning, I was in the queue behind Rob. Ten minutes later he stumbled out, waving another twenty pence piece, and rejoined the queue. Another morning he couldn't be bothered waiting, so he climbed into a field of hay, flopped onto his back, and started the phenomenon known as crop circles. Wanker.

Andy supplied a lot of the music for our jaunts, and like me, tried to keep up to date with what was happening with other bands. He introduced us to loads of new bands, some of whom left their mark, and some of whom hit the post and went out for a goal kick. However, once we were drunk, we always ended up listening to ""Stargazer", "Still in love with You", "Only you can rock Me", "Good lovin' gone Bad", "Back in the Saddle", "Highway to Hell", "Walking in the shadow of the Blues", "Now I'm Here", and other classics.

Andy had a great quest for knowledge, and always had a book in his hand. He loves Egypt and its mysteries, and he is mesmerised by the Pyramids.

"What are you reading this week Andy, "Footwear of the Pharaohs?"

When he went on holiday, he just packed a rucksack, and fucked off. Every now and again, I think civilisation gets on his tits, and he needs to lose himself for a while. Borneo, India, Vietnam, white water rafting down the Zambezi, Butlins in Skegness. He did it all. Don't get me wrong, scratch his skin and you'll hear "Back in Black" scream from his soul, but Andy has always had a "Dave Lee Roth" string to his bow. I liked Andy because he was the unpredictable one out of us all. I liked him, because although he was into the band and his rock music 100%, he also had another parallel mind, which was full of questions, yearnings and endless possibilities. I often imagined the "Kerrang" interview.

"Hey Tony, that was a great sold out tour."

"Yeah, thanks."

"So, what are your plans?"

"Well, new record by the autumn, then back on the road."

After an hour, the interview would wind down and end with a

couple of laughs.

"Well it's been great to see you all, but where's Andy?"

"Funny you should ask. He's sat on a mountain ledge in Tibet, dressed in a white fucking sheet, saying the word "Hom" for two bastard weeks."

He told me a story once that he had been paddling up a river somewhere for days on end. Don't fucking ask me where, but it was either in Africa, Asia, or South America. Anyway, besides the few people in the kayak, and the guide, he hadn't seen anybody for days and days. The guide stopped in the densest, thickest, most overgrown piece of the planet you have ever encountered, and ran off into the bush. He brought some villagers to meet the tourists, and they were all welcomed into the tiny village, a fucking million miles away from anywhere. Andy was greeted by some guy that was selling some deep fried locusts, or some shit like that. Next, some guy offered him the biggest fucking bag of weed he had ever seen, in return for his old, battered "Nike" trainers. He swapped the trainers quicker than Linford Christie could have run in the fucking things, as he crunched the locusts. Stoned and dry throated, he stumbled into the centre of the village, gasping like he had been crawling through the Sahara for a week and a half. He couldn't believe his eyes. In the middle of nowhere, in the middle of the planet, was a bright red, glowing, buzzing, "Coke" machine. He rolled a big spliff, and cracked open an ice cold "Coke." Of course, if I'd have been there, the damned thing would have been out of order. Indiana Jones with a fucking drum kit, that lad was.

Remember Andy's flat? That's right, the one with the blob of jizz, floating in the hot tub. Well, he had a housewarming party, and invited everybody. As I went in, the first thing that hit me was the smell of fresh paint and new carpets. We supped some fucking beer that night. We ended up sat in a circle on the floor playing cards, concentrating hard, just to make out the numbers on the fucking things. Andy started sniffing loudly.

Andy; "Can you smell burning?"

Rob; "No."

Andy; "That's funny. I could have sworn."

Me; "I can."

Glyn; "Shut up you cunts, and deal me a card."

Steve; "Buuuuuuuuuuuuuuurrrrrrrrrrp."

Andy; "No, I can definitely sm… Oh, for fuck's sake Fugsy."

128

Fugsy was slouched with an outstretched arm, struggling to support his body. In his hand was a fag that, due to the amount of alcohol he had consumed, was pointing down resting on Andy's new carpet. There was a brown smouldering hole, with a ring of glowing red ashes around the edge.

Andy; "What are you doing? I've only just moved into the fucking place. Put the fucking thing out will you. Right, outside if you want a fag."

A few minutes later, I went into the kitchen for another beer. Fugsy followed me in, opened the kitchen widow, and lit a fag.

Me; "What are you doing?"

Fugsy; It's OK, the window's open. I can't do any damage in here."

Me; "He'll fucking kill you if he finds out, go outside."

Andy walked into the kitchen, and Fugsy threw his hands behind his back.

Andy; "Hey lads, I've just been saying to Rob....Hold on, what's that smell? Somebody's smoking. Fucking hell Fugsy, it's you."

Fugsy; "Is it fuck."

Andy; "It fucking is."

Andy pulled Fugsy away from the wall. He was standing too close to the wall, and his fag was resting against the wallpaper. The wallpaper was on fire, and turning to ashes, which floated gently to the floor. It was a while before Andy had another party.

# CHAPTER TWENTY FOUR

*"Room Service"*

Summer, along with our tour, ended. I couldn't find fault with it, but we needed to get out far more than we were doing. Glyn managed to get us a gig supporting "Dare", at the "Marquee." They were signed to A&M, and were promoting their first album, and didn't we fucking know it. To be fair, we liked Vinnie Burns, the guitar player. He used to come out in Manchester and get wasted with us. He loved all the trappings that came with being a professional, but he was down to earth, and loved a drink and a laugh. Just a genuine guy, who could play the shit out of his Les Paul. Darren Wharton was the singer, and he was in Thin Lizzy for about thirty seconds longer than I was. He played keyboards in Lizzy, but actually thought he was Phil Lynott. Now Lynott was a rogue, a poet, a fighter, a drinker, a romancer, a hero, a star. Wharton played the piano. See, this is beginning to sound like jealousy; but I can smell a twat, wrapped in tinfoil. Anyway, I got on great with Vinnie, and I also had a lot of time for Greg, the drummer, and I liked a lot of their songs; so try again.

You know from the very second that you meet somebody, if there is something not quite right about them, don't you? It's not a particular gift. I think most people give credence to their first impressions. You won't find "Suffering Fools" in the "Hobbies" section on most peoples' CVs. Now for somebody to look me up and down while holding a fucking briefcase, sporting Kevin Keegan's 1974 FA Cup Final hairdo, trying to pass themselves off as "Rock and Roll" is a non starter in my book. This happened while we were stood around in the "Marquee", trying to get a sound check. Me, Rob and Glyn sniggered, and looked at each other.

Me; "Cunt."

Glyn; "Cunt."

Rob; "Cunt."

Apart from Vinnie, the rest of his band sat around nice and

quiet, scared to laugh, fart or shit, waiting for their next instruction. Glyn wolf-whistled as Wharton walked off. Steve Kenny joined in, and our fate was sealed, tour-wise. We managed to get a short sound check, and then went for a beer with Vinnie. He said that Wharton had gone to do an interview, and wouldn't be back until just before they were due to go on stage. A coach travelled down from Manchester, full of friends, girlfriends, wives, and dare I say it, fans. When we went out on stage, I recognised every face in the first five or six rows, including Vinnie, who was punching the air. Afterwards, we sat in the changing room, ripping into our rider, which was a dustbin full of beer in ice. We couldn't believe it. If this wasn't making it, what was? We were busy taking the piss out of each other, when Wharton stuck his head round the dressing room door.

"Hey guys, I just wanna say. Caught the show, you were great."

Rob was out of the blocks like Ben Johnson.

"Fuck off you cunt, you weren't even there. Go on, get out you wanker."

He shut the door. We were a tightly knit band of friends, and we could spot these clowns a mile off. Occasionally, we met bands with the same outlook as us, but not very often. Mostly, they were caught up in one-upmanship, and pecking order, whereas, we didn't care as long as we all had a beer afterwards, and we didn't have to go home the same night. Music was our soul vehicle, and "Fun" was the destination.

We stayed at the Holiday Inn in Marble Arch, and made our way there after the gig. "Dare" were also there, so the bar area was busy, even though each band stayed at opposite ends of the bar. Apart from Vinnie that is, who was sat telling us about his exploits while on tour supporting "Europe." Paul Heaton, the singer from "The Beautiful South" was sat having a drink, so we invited him to join us. I looked around the table. There was a multi-million record selling artist, a guitar player from one of A&M's new acts, and us. And you know what? I didn't feel out of place. We held our own, and we had them in stitches. I could do this. I felt like "Yosser Hughes".

"Go on, gizza job; go on, I can do that, go on, gizza job."

Paul Heaton was a gentleman, and even excused himself when he went to the toilet. A few minutes later, me and Rob went for a leak. We stood talking in the empty toilet, when a voice shouted out;

"Rob, is that you?"

It was Paul Heaton inside a cubicle. Rob acknowledged him.

"Do me a favour, there's no paper in here. Will you pass me a roll from the next cubicle?"

Rob grabbed a toilet roll, and held it under the gap at the bottom of the door. As Paul's hand appeared, he pulled the toilet roll away. He put the toilet roll back under the door, but as soon as he saw the hand again, he pulled it away. Rob suddenly broke into song.

"Are you ready, are you ready?"

He was singing "Caravan of Love", which was a hit for "The Housemartins", the band Paul Heaton was in before "The Beautiful South."

Comedy that. You see, it doesn't have to be arty farty. Keep it simple and funny. When he finally came out of the toilet, Paul Heaton said to Rob;

"I'm gonna write a song about you."

I never knew he wrote "Wide eyed and Legless."

When I returned to the bar, I glided through the crowd, and sat down in between two young ladies, who had put that little bit too much lipstick on. My conversation couldn't have been that riveting, because I was blatantly pissed. However, the next thing I remember, I was getting into the lift with one of the girls, on the way to my room. Result. I remember falling on to the bed with her. Then, the next time I opened my eyes, she was gone. I had been asleep for an hour. Drat, and double drat. I turned over, and went back to sleep.

I woke in the darkness; sweating, convinced that somebody else was in the room. For a split second, I couldn't remember where I was. Disorientated and drunk, not a good combination. Before I could turn the light on, I was hit by a bucketful of ice cold water. The light went on, and the lads were stood at the end of the bed, howling with laughter. Rob had an empty bucket in his hand. My bed was pissed wet through, and I was shivering. I grabbed the bucket, and everybody ran for cover. I came out of the bathroom like "Captain America", and launched the contents of the bucket over Glyn and Rob. Mike Harris shouted at me to join him in some kind of resistance, but I'm sure he hit me with a "sucker" punch as I ran past him. In fact, it may have well have been the fucking bucket he hit me with, come to think of it. A fight broke out for control of the bucket, so I emptied a vase, and ran back into the bathroom. Andy was filling the bath with cold water.

"You'll never lift that fucker mate." I said.

Andy stripped off, jumped in the bath, and submerged himself. He surfaced a good twenty seconds later.

"At least none of you twats can get me now."

There was a loud knock at the door, somebody had obviously complained about us. Everybody froze, and the room fell silent. I was nearest to the door, so I opened it warily, expecting hotel security. As I peeked through the gap, a foot booted the door right open, and in waded Glyn, with the fire hose. He had taken it off its reel on the wall outside, and yanked it down the corridor. He had obviously fucked it up, because nothing was coming out of the nozzle, so I laughed in his cherub-like face. Then it hit me. "Whoooooooossssshhhhh" It nearly took my fucking fillings out. He barged past me, soaking everybody in the room. Once he was satisfied, he turned to hose off. He wound the hose back into the corridor, and Rob shouted;

"Hey Glyn, fancy a race Fatty?"

"Yeah, I'll beat you, you streak of piss."

They both stripped off, and I started the race. They had to run down the corridor, to the lift and back. The two wobbly white arses set off, as I sang the "Chariots of Fire" music. It was neck and neck as they approached the lift. More like fucking "Turkey's" neck, come to think of it. The lift doors opened, and out stepped "Dare."

"Oh fuck off" shouted Glyn.

They had obviously disapproved. The race continued, but I couldn't tell you who won, because I locked the door. After a few minutes hammering, I let them in. Noel's clothes were slung out of the window, onto Edgware Rd, so he made a pair of makeshift pants out of a shower cap, with two holes punched through for his legs. He found his clothes in the gutter the next morning, but they were fucked. He looked like the Artful Dodger, when he put them on.

I don't exactly know what point I'm trying to make here. You're probably thinking,

"That's not very wild."

Well it wasn't. It was all part of male bonding, and having a laugh, that's all. We weren't Guns 'n' Roses. We didn't want to be. We weren't dangerous, but I've never known a band that is, including Guns 'n' Roses. It's all piss and wind. Serial killers are dangerous. Rapists are dangerous. Armed robbers are dangerous. Not the four guys over there, with a couple of Fenders, a drum kit and a piano. Take Oasis. Many a time, I've seen a picture of Liam squaring up to a six stone weakling, laden down with cameras, or a drunken seventeen year old student. What you don't see, just out of shot, are Gallagher's two eighteen stone heavies, making sure that no one tears his head clean off his shoulders. And he relies on that. The best one though, was when Jason Kay started pushing that photographer around, because he had his "posse" with him. The photographer said "Fuck you" and then proceeded to leather the space cowboy, ten gallon hat and all. They used to call him the "White" Stevie Wonder. Well, he didn't see that photographer's fist coming, did he? You can imagine his minders, once he'd gone home can't you. I bet they sat round a table with a few beers and laughed their cocks off. I used to like the guy, but from that second on....

# CHAPTER TWENTY FIVE

*"Are You Ready... Are You Ready?"*

"How much? That's fucking scandalous, you robbing twat."

What was it? The bill after a night in a strip club? My basketful of goodies from the "hair products" shelf at "Boots?" Rob's leather cowboy boots, with silver tips on the toes and the heels, he bought in Hollywood? Andy's repair bill after his party? No, it was the toll bridge across the River Severn into Wales. Glyn handed over the money grudgingly. That's another thing about Glyn. He can't just do something, anything, without causing a fucking fuss. If there's the slightest whiff of injustice or exploitation in the air, he takes it as a personal affront, whether it concerns him or not. He's then hanging out of the window, shouting at the cars behind.

"Turn round, don't fucking pay it. It's a rip off. You don't even get a fluffy dragon."

We were back in Cardiff, but not for a gig this time. We were booked into a recording studio for a week, at the tail end of November 1990. Kevin Kane was going to help produce the demo, along with Glyn and the rest of us. A guy called Tony Etoria owned the studio, and he also turned out to be a great help. He had a single in the charts in 1977, called "I can prove It." Now I love "irony." Well guess what? The recording studio was called "Famous" studios, so I'll leave it at that. By the way, fucking caravans again. The difference being this time, when we set off from Manchester, we were wrapped up in layers of clothes, trying to keep warm. Summer was as far away in our past, as the next one was as close. Huge slabs of catering packs of bacon were unloaded from the van, like some kind of vacuum packed corpse at a cannibal's barbecue. It was so reassuring to know that we were going to be able to eat regularly during our stay in the middle of nowhere. Then came the tins of beans, followed by the eggs. Forty-eight of the fucking things, on two big square trays, looking like a miniature army of

"70's" football hooligans. Packs of sausages, tins of tomatoes, fucking everything from brown sauce and bread, right down to the salt and pepper pots. The way Glyn operates is this. He would just say to everybody;

"Give me thirty quid each, and I will guarantee that you will be able to eat and drink as much as you can all week, without spending any more money. Shit house paper included."

Big talk, but we had all been there before, so we chucked our cash at the man. One night, we were sweating a bit, because when we returned to the caravan, there was no food to eat. Nothing was being cooked, and the lack of smell of anything edible was causing concern. We all poured some big fucking vodkas, put some music on, turned the porn on, and got cosy in the piping hot caravan, as "Fugsy" rolled a "three skinner." Maybe we were gonna eat a bit later. After all, it had been a long day, one of those days when every fucker had their hands full. Tempers were starting to fray, and stomachs were starting to rumble, and "Jonesy" was starting to get some shit for it. The timing was perfect, because as soon as the tantrums broke out, there was a loud knock on the flimsy caravan door. Glyn opened the door, and in strode a pizza delivery guy, bowing at his fucking knees under the weight of pizzas and garlic bread. Fandiddlyfuckingtastic. The guy had a quick toke on "Fugsy's" masterpiece, and zigzagged down the drive on his moped, while munching on a piece of his next fucking delivery.

One day, me and Steve were in the studio, working against the clock, but we managed to get most of the guitar parts down. When you are without a record deal, and you are funding the recording yourself, there is no leeway for artistic license or spontaneity whatsoever. You have to know your parts perfectly before you go in the studio. There is no fucking lounging around or savouring moments to be done at all, and because of this, a lot of bands sound sterile, limp, and unproductive. In these circumstances, the studio is not a place of enjoyment. It is simply a place that exists in between the ideas taking place in your heads, and that idea being made available for people to listen to. I nearly said "available to buy", but to be honest, all we ever did was send the tapes out to record companies and magazines. The majority of the rest we gave away. I don't want to try and kid you or myself, that there was a legion of fans waiting for our next output, with baited breath.

So, as you can see, the less cash you spent recording the

fucking thing, the better, because you were on a hiding to nothing from the very start. There is no fun involved, because you can't relax, you can't experiment, and at the end of the day, no fucker else is paying for this apart from yourselves. There is no time for legendary tales to take form, because there is no time for anything else other than getting your fucking heads down, purely as a cost cutting exercise. I read about bands that would test out different guitar amps for days at a time, just to get the right sound. Other bands would decorate the studio, just to create an ambience in keeping with their mood. Some bands had an endless stream of girls coming in and out of the studio, fucking everybody in sight, including each other. You don't understand how much I wished that would have happened. Just once.

We came from a world of cold grey steel with dull skies, where money wasn't something to be disrespected. Mistakes cost money, and not necessarily your own. Remember, this fucker of a bill was going to be split seven ways, and the pressure was on if you didn't know your parts inside out, after your mates went in and breezed through, first take. All of a sudden, click tracks and headphones became the norm, and everybody realised they had been playing out of time for years. Not out of time so as you would recognise it, but just enough for the metronome to wave its middle finger at you. I loved the fact that we were always close, but never spot on. That was the essence of rock and roll wasn't it? Tight but loose? A bit like one of my old fucking birds.

Noel was next on with his vocals, and from what I remember, he was booked in to work through the night. He had slept in late, and only turned up in the evening. So, he benefited from a full English breakfast, a few beers at lunch with a pizza, a cosy caravan, his acoustic guitar, a porn film, more beer, pasta for tea with a glass of wine, all of the porn mags, countless spliffs, a few games of cards, an afternoon nap, more beer and a couple of wanks, spread out over the day. I'm telling you now, I wouldn't have bothered turning up at the studio. I'd have gone straight to bed. Either that, or the nearest fucking club. That man is a professional. If I was the singer, every fucking song would have been an instrumental. Noel was cool, because he worked out melodies and harmonies, and had them "nailed" in his memory before we were even aware of what was going on. He turned up on many occasions, sang his bollocks off, told the engineer exactly how he expected to hear it, and blew my fucking mind in the process.

Me and Steve jumped in a taxi, and headed back to the farm, where the caravan was situated. It was a freezing cold, damp, foggy, miserable night, and as we sped down the dark lanes, we passed a pub, about a quarter of a mile from the caravan. We jumped out, and dived in the pub. We sat by the fire thawing out slowly. My toes uncurled slowly, so they pressed back into that fucking impossible, painful, point, in the front of my cowboy boots. My problem was that, without any shoes on, my feet looked like two fucking meat and potato pies, so you can imagine the fucking pain I endured when I tried to get them in my tiny sado-masochistic boots. Fucking torture. Steve, on the other hand, could slip his fuckers on and off no problem, so I guess his feet looked like a couple of "Dairylea" cheese triangles. Well they smelt like the fucking things anyway. It was strange to find a pub without "Fugsy" inside, but at least he wouldn't be there begging for a lock in. So we could return to the caravan at a decent hour.

The local brewery was called "Brains", and one of the beer pumps had a plate on the front, saying "Brains S.A."

"What does S.A stand for?" I asked.

"Skull Attack" said the barman.

"Right then, two "Skull Attacks" please.

"You'd better go easy with these boyo, because they will fuck you up good and proper."

"Yeah, yeah."

I didn't pay any attention, and we sat talking and drinking for a couple of hours. When we got up to leave, we didn't have a fucking working leg between us. As soon as I got outside, my stomach decided it was going to make its own way back to the caravan without me, so out that bastard jumped. Steve's bloodshot eyes were spinning around his head, like the cherries on a one armed bandit, and he was talking to a menu board. We held each other's hand, like two doddering, incontinent, geriatrics, and tried to get across the road. We got down on our knees, and crawled across the road, just to try and avoid falling over and lying there until a truck ran over us. We reached the entrance to the farm, but that's where the night ended for me. I woke up the next morning, lying on a bed in the caravan, covered from head to toe in shite, but I don't remember that last three-hundred yards. Then again, I don't think I remembered the last three-hundred days.

I had just split up with a long-term girlfriend, but I got no sympathy from these fuckers. I didn't expect any, but these were my closest pals who I spent most of my time with. A simple "You alright?" would have been sufficient, but no, they fucking crucified me. If you've stayed with me this far into the story, you are obviously interested, so I will tell you that she fired me off, and I was stinging a bit. Glyn and Rob would regularly explain in great detail, what some lad was probably doing to her, right at that very moment. Not only that, but what she was doing in return, and how she was loving it, and how much better than me, he was. I couldn't let them see that I was stinging, or else it would have gotten worse, so I feigned a smile. Maybe I should have been used to it by now, because I could never seem to settle with a girl. It didn't seem to be that hard, because all of the other lads had found some great girls, and that's all I wanted, but I was always the architect of my own downfall, time after time.

The next night, we finished early at the studio, and stayed in the caravan, eating and drinking, as the wind howled outside. Like a fat Patrick Moore, Glyn had obviously been studying the night sky, and decided that it was going to be fucking cold. Something nobody else had considered. Besides the usual stuff, Glyn had packed a calor gas heater and two electric heaters in the van. Now without these, it would have been a miserable week, but Glyn had the foresight to weigh up the situation, and turn the caravan into a cosy "Wank Cabin." It was bitter outside, but because of Glyn we were able to waltz about in vests, T-Shirts, and shorts, like a "soft" Anthrax. Glyn had sorted it, so that we could come away from the studio, and rather than having to sit there in jumpers and coats, with a pair of gloves on with a fucking headache from your freezing ears, you could relax, have a laugh, and bask in the warmth of a roasting hot caravan. Fucking marvellous. I was watching telly, and the rest of the lads were huddled around the tiny table, playing cards. It was strangely quiet, apart from the muffled giggles, which escalated into crying laughter.

"What is it?" I said.

"Show him Rob, go on," Steve was begging him.

"I can't."

"Come on Rob, show me," I said.

"Rob's been doing an impression of you", said Glyn.

"But it's like Marcel Marceau", said Andy.

139

"Fucking Marcel Arseau, if Rob's got anything to do with it," I chirped.

Rob agreed, and I squeezed on to the seat. Everybody cracked open a new beer simultaneously, and watched for my reaction. Rob smiled and hugged an imaginary girl, then took a huge toke on what "Fugsy" had been constructing for the last ten minutes. He pretended to kiss her, while rubbing his hands up and down her back. After reaching her bottom, he leaned back, silently laughing at a remark she had made. While she was laughing, there was a quick stroke of her "giggle pin" through her jeans with his middle finger, and he was fucking laughing. He kissed her again, and started massaging her breasts. He slowly opened her blouse, and removed it from her shoulders. The expert manoeuvre, of unhooking a bra with one hand followed, and the spoils were his. He massaged her breasts, and lifted one up to his mouth. All of a sudden, his hands clasped together, and he fell to his knees. He searched around, but she was gone. He held up his hands, in a "What happened?" gesture. The rest of the lads were crying again. Rob finally spoke.

"That's you that is, you soft cunt. Now get me a beer."

What could I say?

"Budweiser alright Rob?"

Luckily, for me, I met a lovely young Welsh girl who possessed some great healing qualities, especially where matters of the heart were concerned. I was a bit wary at first, being so emotionally raw and what have you; but there was a softness in her voice, when mixed with the "universal" black stockings and suspenders that girls seem to know when to wear, that snapped me out of any self-pity I was wallowing in. She installed a temporary route from my brain to my groin, bypassing my heart completely. We both knew that it wasn't permanent. Nobody was looking for "permanent", but it would do for now.

We left Cardiff with a four track demo, consisting of "Two Souls", "Loving the Danger", "Sarah", and "Stormy Weather." Four songs I can guarantee that you have never heard, but they are out there. I'm not one to blow my own trumpet, but you listen to "Two Souls", and tell me it shouldn't have been a hit. You can't. Anybody who likes rock, that has heard the song, loves it. I still can't fucking understand why it slipped through the net, into oblivion. You were the one that I believed in.

After banging our heads against walls for what seemed like

ages, a few doors started opening for us. Glyn was invited down to Chrysalis Records, for a meeting with Chris Briggs and Spencer Wells. I don't know if he was any relation, but the guy that invented forceps was called Spencer Wells. Hold on, how the fuck do I know that? Anyway, Chrysalis. "Strangers in the Night", one of my favourite albums ever. That'd do for me. I practised my signature and had more highlights put in my hair, waiting for the phone call, and the "Kerrang" double page spread.

Next thing, Glyn got a letter from Warner Chappell, saying that they were interested in the band. They are a publishing company, and despite not knowing what the fuck a publishing company does, I was dreaming already. The head of A & R was a woman called Gina Walters, and she wanted to see us live. We arranged a gig at "Rockworld" and invited every record label and publishing company we could think of. One night, Glyn turned up at rehearsals, with his answer phone under his arm. He plugged it in, and sat us down.

"Listen to this fucker, lads."

There were eight or nine messages from different companies, all saying they would like to come and see us, all leaving their ticket requirements.

"Fucking hell Glyn. Is this it?" I said.

"I don't know, but if anyone deserves it, we do."

We listened to the messages again and again, then decided that we needed to be in a pub, drinking. So, we packed up, and fucked off. I don't think my first four pints touched the sides. All of a sudden, in the last two weeks, we had received more interest than in the last three years. A deal? A record? Interviews? A tour bus? Parties? Theatres? Arenas? You couldn't shut us up. Then the big light came on in my head.

"Girls… girls," I spluttered.

Amidst the excitement, I'd almost forgotten. A record deal would not only give me the chance to live the life I had dreamed of for years, but it would also allow me to wallow in my favourite pastime…Girls. Two, three, four? How many could I manage in a day, or all at once? I wasn't sure, but I knew I was ready. There was a list of fantasies I still needed to work my way through, but I could tell that the two babes dressed as nurses were a damn sight nearer than they were yesterday. I wasn't the only fucker, don't get me wrong, everybody was pussy mad, but I was the only poor bastard

141

that wasn't getting a slice of it every night. We talked for hours, and not once did anybody mention money. Naive? Probably, but I'd like to think that money wasn't the motive for our existence. Anyway, there was far too much to contemplate, without even considering boring old money.

Pete Dutton booked the bands at "Rockworld", and he was a good friend of the band. Again, he was enthusiastic about us, and we all had a great laugh together. We always loved people that were bored. We were bored, and this meant that instead of just talking nonsense to people, you would actually get on with something, and create something humorous. Pete was the same. He was bored, and he didn't want to listen to rubbish all night, nobody did. Well maybe we did, but at least give us some original rubbish. Give us some nonsense that would make us laugh or expand our mind in some way. At least make us think, you twats. Besides mischief, boredom can lead to some fucking fantastic doors being unlocked, be it in the mind, or some girls underwear. Glyn sorted out a date with Pete, no not a date, a date for the gig, for fuck's sake. Spring was round the corner, and we were booked to play in early April 1991. We checked the weather forecast, which showed a storm brewing over Seattle, but we didn't think anything of it. It couldn't possibly reach Manchester England, could it?

Chris Tetley helped promote the gig on his radio show, and he offered to review the gig on his music page in the Daily Sport. He put snippets about us in his music column, in the weeks leading up to the gig. At night, we were busy putting up posters, in any available free space we could find. Only, in Manchester, there is no "Free" space. I was with Glyn one day, when we passed one of our posters. It had a "Cancelled" sticker, right across it. Glyn stopped the car, jumped out, and peeled the sticker off.

"That's fucking strange. What's going on?"

"I don't know" he said.

We carried on driving, and spotted another poster with the same "Cancelled" sticker on it. Again, Glyn jumped out, and pulled it off. As we drove on, every poster we passed had the same sticker across it. We drove down to "Rockworld" and found Pete, who was always knocking about. We walked in, and he didn't look happy.

"Some blokes have been in here looking for you lot."

"Why?" We both said.

"You can't just put those fucking things up wherever you want."

"Well nobody told us. Anyway, we made sure that we only put them over posters of gigs that had already taken place."

"It doesn't matter Glyn, there's a way of doing things, and this isn't the right way."

"So what should we do now?"

"It doesn't matter, I've sorted it."

Totally oblivious to the gangland protocol, we enthusiastically pissed people off, unaware that we were doing any wrong. Pete paid for the posters, which at the time were ridiculously cheap, at something like twenty pence per poster. For this, you could guarantee that your posters were in a prime spot, wouldn't get torn down, and you could sleep easy at night.

I wouldn't mind, but I used to have a drink with one of the guys that ran the poster racket, called Charlie. He even brought me a huge poster into the "Banshee" one night, after the "Crazy Nights" album came out. One Sunday night I'd had a few beers with him in the "Phoenix", and we caught the bus home together. Any late bus in Manchester was always a fucking lottery as to whether it would kick off or not. Charlie wasn't as tall as me but he was always in the gym, so he looked like a "Transit" van, with long hair. There must have been a "wankers" convention in town somewhere, because when I got on the bus, the whistling and jeering started, which was fuck all to me, as it was the life I chose to live, and live the fucker I did. I found that the downside of being a slim wannabe rock god, with hair down to my waist, didn't go down too well with spotty necked "Aramis" wearing twats, all with the same shirts on. The upside of it all however, was that it gave me some fucking great friends, a great band, unbridled laughter, and of course, the girls. As I walked down the bus, a few malicious overtones crept in, as some big jealous virgins vented their spleens. Of course when Charlie got on right behind me, the fucking bus fell silent, as he asked me to point out the perpetrators. Some extremely dry gulps thudded up and down the eerily quiet bus, as sorrowful eyebrows pleaded with me not to spill the beans. I declined to pass the death sentence on a few pissed up lads, so I got a nod of respect from each one of them as they left the bus with a full set of teeth each.

Anyway, where was I? Oh yeah, we left "Rockworld", and Pete followed us outside. I turned to him.

"What is it with you Pete; don't you ever take a fucking break?"

"I'm only here because of you cunts."

"Why?"

"Well, as it was quiet, I thought I'd come down and put your name up on the sign outside."

"Cheers Pete, you're a fucking star my friend. The gig isn't for another two weeks. I've got to get laid on the back of this piece of genius marketing."

"Well Tony, there was a problem, but I've sorted it out."

"Eh, what's that then?"

"Oh, it's nothing really. I don't like heights, but you're here now, so I'll get the ladder, and you can put the fucking things up."

"Yeah, right. You can fuck right off and all. I fucking hate heights, so think again."

"Well, soft lad, you can either climb up this fucking ladder and put the letters up, or your name won't be appearing above this club."

"Hold on, if I hadn't called in this afternoon, you would have had to climb the ladder, and put the fucking letters up yourself."

"I know; it's fucking great isn't it?"

"Fuck off."

Pete positioned the ladders, and handed me a box full of red plastic letters, with magnets on the back of them. Now, you've got to bear in mind that this was "Oxford Road", which was always busy. People were always in a rush, going absolutely nowhere. Pete tried to steady the ladders, as I reluctantly began my ascent. Nobody seemed to care as they wrestled around Pete, banging into the ladders. I'm sure that he was shaking the fucking things extra hard, even when the slightest old aged pensioner faintly brushed against them. I looked down, and he was shaking them even when there was nobody near.

"Come on Tony, I haven't got all fucking day."

Pete started people watching, and I rummaged through the box of letters. I finished sticking the letters on the board above the club, and shouted down;

"Hey, Pete. What do you think?"

"Let's have a look."

He stood back, in the middle of the "Oxford Road" crowd, and read the sign. Bemused passers by read it with him.

"PETE IS A CUNT", it said.

Pete grabbed the ladders and shook them violently. I nearly fell off, I went white with fear.

"Alright... alright, for fuck's sake, stop shaking the fucking ladders... please."

I changed the letters and returned to terra firma, with our name jutting out proud and level with the upstairs windows of every double decker bus that passed by.

On the day of the gig, we turned up at "Rockworld" early in the afternoon. This was our day, so we spent ages getting the sound just right. Not acceptable, not just OK, but amazing. Chris Tetley turned up early, to listen to the sound check. No he didn't... no... no... he could get a sly drink at the bar, that's what drew him in so early. He brought a photographer with him from the "Daily Sport", who was busy checking his equipment. Once we were satisfied with the sound, we left the club and went for a drink, and then grabbed a pizza. We returned a couple of hours later, and the place was bursting. It was like a Saturday night. So many friends had turned up, but it was the people I didn't know that excited me, and there were hundreds of them. There were also the sceptics and the critics, but Glyn fucked them all off, long before the first note was played.

We made sure we wound these fuckers up at every opportunity. A few weeks before the gig we bombarded "Rockworld" with flyers, advertising the gig. We covered the fucking place in them so much, that I got sick of seeing the things. We stood at the bar watching all the local bands give them a cursory hateful glance, before screwing them up and then slinging them on the floor. It didn't matter, there would be a new set of flyers in place the next time they came into the club, and the time after that. "A.O.K. The best unsigned band in the U.K." We weren't, but we knew that by having this on the flyers, people would probably say "What? Well go on, prove it," and pay their money to see the band. Obviously, the other bands wouldn't have looked at it this way. They probably thought, "Oh yeah, you cheeky big-headed twats, well let's see you fall on your faces, you long haired fuckers." Either way, the place was fucking heaving.

In the dressing room, we went through our usual rituals. This consisted of Noel loosening up with some kind of "Julie Andrews" carry on. I think he changed the words to "Doe, Re, Me, Fah, So, Lah, Dildo. Meanwhile, your intrepid hero set to work with his hairspray and combs, in a vicious battle with Steve and Rob, for the biggest, fullest, highest, longest, coolest, hairiest, thickest, lady thrilling… hairdo. I nearly said "knob" then. No, hair, definitely hair. Do you know what I fucking loved about myself? Well, I knew that I would only ever be 50% of the musician I could have been, no matter what I did. Some lads wasted time while trying to improve themselves, even though they remained at 50% forever. Me? I knew I would only ever be 50%, whatever I did. The difference being, that I made up the other 50% with looks, attitude and desire. Not the ideal recipe for success, but at least you got 100% from me every fucking time.

Everybody adjusted their knobs for maximum comfort, and we were ready. Glyn fired us up, like pre-match boxers, while checking the amount of alcohol we had consumed. He wouldn't let anybody have more than two pints before a gig. There was plenty of time for drinking afterwards. I was just about to have my first drink, when Rob shouted;

"Glyn, Glyn. That's his third fucking pint; I've been watching him for fuck's sake. He's not taking this fucking seriously."

"Fuck off. I've not even had a drink yet."

Glyn marched over, snatched my drink off me, and downed it in one enormous gulp. He drew his forearm across his face to wipe his lips, and then burped in my face. Rob flipped me the "bird" as he finished his fourth drink. We all hugged each other, goading each other to be the best fucking rockers we could ever be. Steve Kenny winked at me and grabbed my shoulders and squeezed them without saying a word. His beaming grin said it all. Fugsy looked fucking angry. He was desperate to get out there and show his mates off. Noel took a deep breath. "Right then, let me at the fuckers."

Suddenly, the rumbling intro tape started. One last look in the mirror, and we were on.

There was a loud roar as we took to the stage. It was all systems go.

"Good Evening Manchester."

There is no feeling quite like playing to a full house, when everybody is there to see you, home town or not. We started with "Why can't love Survive?", which was a big, chest beating fucker of a song, and despite the "Marquee", always laid down the gauntlet, and kicked up the dust. A sure-fire hit, with a stomping infectious beat. When it ended, I knew there was going to be a massive roar, I just fucking knew it. I couldn't wait for the song to end. True enough, the fucking place erupted as we segued on, watching lycra tops full of perfect breasts, bounce approvingly, only an arms length in front of us. Rob shouted in my ear as we twisted and posed under the spotlights.

"Babe, blonde, two rows back, on the right."

I had to laugh, because usually there wasn't a third row. I peered into the dark to check her out. It was his wife, Christine. Nice one mate.

After the gig, the dressing room was packed with people who came in for a drink and a laugh. As usual, the clowning around had already begun, and everybody was a potential victim. Chris Tetley came over to me.

"Hi Rob; are you ready to do an interview?"

"I'm Tony, Rob's over there with Glyn and Noel."

"Sorry. Anyway Rob, are you ready?"

I couldn't fucking win. I felt like Rodney Trotter, having a conversation with Trigger. Tetley asked if there was any scandal, or sexual exploits he could include in his article. Of course there was.

"Tell him about that girl in Cardiff."

Rob had suddenly taken an interest.

"Fuck off."

I laughed.

Rob started to tell the story, as Tetley scribbled away. He was laughing as he wrote, and kept muttering, "Grrrrrreat."

Glyn was busy talking to Gina. She loved the gig, and told him she would try and get some money released for us to do a demo for Warner Chappell. What was wrong with the demo we had just done? I didn't understand. Maybe they wanted to make sure that we had more ideas inside us. We knew that rock music was a massive gamble, and she brought this point up with Glyn. It had nothing to do with the music. The music was massive, and it was easily outselling any other type of music. The fans are the best fans in the world. I know; I'm one of them. Dance music, for instance, doesn't cost much more than recording, pressing, and promotion. With a rock band, no matter how good you are, you need to tour, and this is a massive expense. The band, the crew, accommodation, food, advertising, transport, fuel. It all adds up. Unless you are selling records to counter-balance the deficit, the record company will be out of pocket. If you multiply this by the number of new hopefuls on the label, then the record company is losing shitloads of money. Add to this, the failure of any other types of music they have, and their profits are seriously affected. The money never did appear, but Gina was enthusiastic about us, and would always listen to anything we did. I don't know if it was due to the reasons above, or if we just weren't good enough. Hey, I'm big enough to admit it.

Rob was busy recounting the lewd story from Cardiff, and now had a captive audience. They fell about, as he exaggerated the actions in his comic routine. When he finished, he turned to me,

"Well, that's you fucked. Show that one to your mother."

We laughed as we made our way to the Koh I Noor for a few beers and a curry. On the way out, I noticed one of our flyers on the floor. I picked it up and looked at it and smiled. There was a big fucking footprint right across it. Kind of said it all really. I tucked it in my pocket, knowing the very page in my scrapbook where it was going to end up, footprint and all.

Glyn spoke to Chris Tetley the next day. Tetley confirmed that we would be in the following Wednesday's edition. On the Wednesday, Glyn picked me up on the way to rehearsal. Rob was sat in the van looking solemn, and Glyn lay across the steering wheel, clutching his sides, crying with laughter. He couldn't speak.

"Come on, what is it? Tell me lads."

Glyn handed me the "Daily Sport." He dried his eyes, and took a deep breath.

"Read that fucker."

I flicked through the paper, and found the music page. There was a two page spread on "Rockworld", with a great picture of Rob, posing like Rudy fucking Sarzo. The article about us was just below his picture. As I started to read, I noticed that something was wrong. Because of the problem with our names, Chris Tetley had used "Tony" when he should have used "Rob", and vice versa. So it looked like I had told the story about Rob. So now it was old "Robbie boy" up to no good in Cardiff. Now there were two of us sat crying in the van, while Rob sat in silence.

"No, that's you fucked. Show that one to your mother." I said.

"Never mind my mother. Christine will fucking kill me."

"Well, there's a free fucking lesson going here, isn't there? Gobshite."

"You'll tell Christine, won't you Glyn?"

It was definitely the wrong shoulder.

"You can fuck off. I'm with Tony. I'm loving it."

We got to rehearsals, and the rest of the lads had turned up with their own copy of the "Daily Sport", just in case he had missed it. We went to "Rockworld" after rehearsals, where Pete had laid out loads of copies of the newspaper all over the place. It was like a "Gentleman's" club, with people sat reading newspapers, tapping the ash off their fags, and swigging their vodka. Rob couldn't get away from his dexterous exploits.

When Rob finally got home, Christine was asleep. He went upstairs clutching the newspaper. He might as well get it out of the way. He woke her up, and nervously tried to explain the mix up, as she read the article.

"Ooh, that Tony Bell." She said.

She laughed, and turned the light off. Rob went downstairs, and removed the duvet he had laid on the settee, just in case. Maybe another night.

# CHAPTER TWENTY SIX

### *"It's Not Quite A Jaguar"*

Ford Fiestas, great cars. All mine needed was a handle on the back, and a blade underneath, and I could have mowed the fucking lawn with it. All the torque of a bastard Hornby train. Mike Harris is a bit tasty with a paintbrush, so I asked him to paint the Van Halen logo on the doors.

"Of course I will mate."

However, the look on his face said,

"Don't be a cunt Tony."

Mind you, I was twenty seven at the time.

She was a bit of a drama queen, what, with her stopping and starting, and folding her fucking arms while huffing and puffing, especially on the way to the "Highwayman" near Stoke, or "Rock City" in Nottingham, but we had some great times together. Condoms, toothpaste, tapes, and VO5 gel spray in the glove compartment, and my sleeping bag in the boot, along with a thick blanket. She had one of those heaters that you could never get right. Either it was chilly, or your fucking toenails were melting in your boots. However, she pumped out rock music like no other car before or since. Inside reeked of "Fahrenheit" after shave, and that wonderful "woman" smell, mixed with various perfumes, nestling deep in the fabric of the seats. If you looked closely, on a sunny day, you could just about make out the impression of a young lady's footprint on the left hand side back window. No, I wasn't fucking a one-legged rock chick. If you looked up, you could make out a "scuffed" heel mark on the roof of the fucking thing, where her other leg had been. Now I know that the amateur sleuths and detectives amongst you will immediately deduce from the evidence, that from the position of the footprints, there should also have been an imprint of my arse cheeks on the windscreen. Another girl fucked herself on the bulbous gear stick one night, while sorting me out at the same time. Like I said, great car.

I used to park my car at Stretford Sports Centre, around the corner from where I worked. "Aaah work" I hear you say. I knew you were wondering if this literary maverick actually got off his arse and did anything. Well, keeping it brief, I worked for the Inland Revenue, where I still continue to work. Shit job, shit pay, but I could spend my time drinking, wanking, and growing my hair. Some great people there help keep each other from going insane, while stopping the whole fucking country from dropping to its knees. No don't thank us; you just keep on fucking moaning about us at every opportunity. Cunts, the lot of you.

One Wednesday night I went to my car, and found a letter in a clear plastic bag, which had been placed underneath my wiper blade. I knew what it was. The sports centre was having a bit of a crackdown on people using the car park, but not using the facilities. This was a polite "Fuck off" notice. I picked it up, and sat in my car reading it. It was hand written, and didn't look official. The letter was from two girls, called Karen and Samantha. They said they were both nineteen, and went to the college next to the sports centre. They had noticed me a couple of weeks earlier, but were too shy to say hello.

"Fucking hell", I thought.

The letter turned into a blur, as my brain tried to keep up with my eyes. They had followed me to work one day, and asked the doorman who I was. He told them my name, and said I could always be found in the rock clubs in town. They started going to "Rockworld", and the letter said that I had spoken to one of them a few weeks earlier. It was no use. Try as I might, I couldn't picture this girl from the last few weeks out in town. They then described in great detail, what they wanted to do to me, and said they would wait by my car, at five o clock the next evening, if I was interested.

After a longer than normal shower, I got ready and waited for Glyn. Wednesdays were already great because we rehearsed, and then went into "Rockworld" and got totally fucked up, but this particular Wednesday was even better. I got in the van, and Rob was already moaning about what a shit day he'd had, and why weren't we gigging more often. Then Glyn fucking started. They were like a couple of "Panto" dames. I was dying to tell them about the letter, but the more they moaned, the better my letter got. I let their frustration build, as I tried to calculate the best moment to enlighten the pair of non letter receiving fuckwits. They were particularly vociferous this fine evening, so in I jumped. I couldn't contain myself any longer.

"Hey, guess what happened to me today?"

Rob; "Oh, here we fucking go. Don't tell me, you got laid at work."

Me; "No, it was nothing like that."

Glyn; "What, you beat your wanking at work record?"

Me; "Nope."

Rob; "Did they rumble you, and find out you were a skiving, lecherous, wanking, drain on their resources, and fuck you right off out of the building?"

Me; "Nearly."

Glyn; "You're fucking boring me now you cunt, so either tell me or fucking button it."

Me; "Look, I got a letter."

I pulled the letter out of my jacket.

Glyn; "What kind of fucking letter?"

Me; "It's from two nineteen year old girls, who I've never met before and they both want to fuck me."

Rob; "Fuck off, do you think we're daft? You've written that bastard yourself."

Me "Honestly, I haven't."

I started to read it out loud. Rob went quiet, and Glyn looked at me and raised his eyebrows in disbelief, as the sexual threats gained momentum.

Glyn; "Fucking hell, I want every detail, you jammy bastard."

I carried on reading, and Rob jumped in.

Rob; "Hold on. Is that letter from Karen and Samantha?"

Me; "Yes."

I was gobsmacked.

Rob; "No it's not. It's from me you daft cunt."

Rob was crying as he spoke. He had been working in Stretford earlier in the day, and passed the sports centre. He knew that I parked there, so he drove around until he found my car. It was then that he concocted his masterpiece. Glyn, by this time, was in his usual position, slumped over the steering wheel, crying, as the story unfolded. He had to stop the van, and the three of us couldn't speak for a good five minutes. This was the finest example of Rob's humour. He didn't tell Glyn about the letter, so Glyn was living the contents with me. His hopes were as high as mine, until Rob sledge-hammered the fucking lot. If he had told Glyn, he would have known the eventual outcome, and the fall that awaited me. Instead, he got the double whammy, with me. It was an incredible piece of comic brilliance. The twat.

# CHAPTER TWENTY SEVEN

*"In The Church Of The Poison Mind"*

Once we discovered "Rock City" in Nottingham, we saw it as some kind of fucking pilgrimage that took on a religious devotion. Lourdes, Mecca, Jerusalem, Medina, Hill Cumorah, Bethlehem, Nottingham. It worked for me and the boys, just as much as the Dome of the Rock, The Church of the Nativity, or the Wailing Wall, worked for others. Blasphemy? No, seeing as you're asking, it's not. Maybe if there was a God, but there isn't. A lot of scared, greedy people pin their hopes on the "Big Man", because they cannot accept that we are "Freaks" of the Universe, and when we die, it's the end. Finito. As Freud said, "Religion is an illusion."

"Fear?" Everybody is scared of dying, it's only natural, but fear only exists up to the point of death. If, by my reckoning, "Its all over, it's Full Time." The UEFA official may have held up a board, with a ridiculous extra five minutes plucked from nowhere, but there's no Sheringham and Solskjaer to bail you out at the last minute, then that is where it ends. No more fear, no more anything. If however, there is something afterwards, there is no need to be scared in the first place, because the life you have just lived is a microdot compared to what's in store for you. So, the fear has got to be based on the idea that there is nothing after you have checked out, and left an unholy mess in your room, despite what you may say to the contrary. If people truly believed in an afterlife, they wouldn't be bothered about death in the slightest, because everybody they have ever known and loved, will be with them again, forever.

"Greed?" Good old greed. One of the seven deadly sins, I believe. Well, this is fucking easy, this one. Let me get this right. Sunday, the most boring day of the week, when absolutely fuck all happens. Now then, if I get up early, and spend an hour in Church, before the pubs open, then you can guarantee me "Eternal Life?" "What, forever and ever and ever?" Sounds good, doesn't it? Go on then, I'll fucking take it. Can't you see, that religion is moulded, to fit in with what people want, without having to make one fucking concession?

God, and the concept of Heaven brings everything full circle, and lends itself to a satisfactory conclusion, after we slip off this mortal coil. People need the promise of something extra, just to help them get through this life, and stop them going mad. Like we fucking deserve something extra, after the way we have treated the planet, and every race, colour and creed on it. If we were judged on our track record, we should all burn in a fetid pit forever, never mind exist in a state of Nirvana. Do you honestly think you deserve to live forever? If you do, then you are an arrogant piece of shit, who obviously doesn't. See, if you think about it, these questions answer themselves. Conjecture and supposition. Two of the flimsiest words you can think of, but these are the basis of every religion, bar none.

Religion equals brainwashing, and here is the proof. Say there was a Muslim child, born to devoutly religious parents, and they gave him up for adoption. Now if a Christian family adopted that child, he would become a Christian, because of the indoctrination he was exposed to. If at the same time, a Jewish baby was adopted by a Muslim family, then that child would become a Muslim for the same reasons. If it is all you have known since birth, it becomes the "norm", and you absorb whatever views are fed to you on a daily basis. Similarly, the Christian baby adopted by a Jewish family, would become a Jew. This nonsense is passed down through families for centuries, like racial hatred and bigotry, which are inexorably linked to religion.

Also, think of the poor buggers that are born deaf, dumb and blind. They don't even know what they are, or that they are part of a bustling planet full of life. Somebody feeds them, changes them, and looks after them continually, because they are unable to do anything, in their world of nothingness. Do you think that they are aware of a God, or the concept of a God? Of course they're not, because they have never been exposed to communication with the fucking strange ideas of the twisted individuals that have been blessed with all five senses.

Anyway, what about the women in Nottingham? They outnumbered the men three to one apparently. Let me see, that's one... two... three... six big juicy titties all to myself. Come to

"Daddy." We waded into "Rock City" with massive hair, tight jeans, cowboy boots, bangles, and gleaming teeth. "Good evening Y'all."

Over the years, we developed various techniques, which would benefit us personally, over the course of a night, in any given rock club. Travelling to clubs was always a laugh, checking into hotels, and supping a rake of beer, before we went out. Meanwhile, underneath the hairspray and the pouting, brains were whirring frantically, calculating beer consumption, time available, and the number of people involved. If you were first to the bar, you could end up paying for ten or twelve drinks. Everybody was prepared for this, but on a good night, you could end up with everybody getting a round in, until it was back to you. People would be totally fucked up by this stage, and you knew you were on a fucking hiding to nothing. Nobody had twenty drinks, not ever, but they would fucking holler and scream for their eleventh. So, if you were, say, maybe, fifth or sixth in the round, you were pretty much guaranteed, that you would only have to buy one round. Anything after that and you're fucking laughing. Anything before that, and you were fucked.

Three distinct patterns developed, and I'm not ashamed to hold my hands up, and confess that I am "Guilty" to all three. Firstly, I would hold open the door, and let a dozen of my closest friends into the club before me, fighting their way to the bar, to buy me a drink. Secondly, and I was rumbled quite quickly here, I would bend down, and tie an imaginary shoelace, while my mates "fought" for my beer at the bar. I was soon fucking rumbled considering I only ever went out in my cowboy boots. Thirdly, on entering the club, I headed straight for the toilets for a piss, and to check my hair.

"Hey lads, can somebody get me a beer...? Cheers."

A shyster I will admit, but I was operating on "Fagin's" territory, and if you didn't play by the rules, some other fucker would have you over, with all three manoeuvres, and leave you high and dry, with no cash for a taxi. These people didn't give too much of a fuck at three o'clock in the morning.

One particularly magnificent Friday in Nottingham, I met a really pretty girl, who was on her own.

"Strange," I thought.

She was dressed in black from head to toe. It was so dark, that I couldn't see where she finished, and the club started. I soon fucking found out. She stuck her tongue down my throat, and dragged me towards the exit, threatening all sorts. I dug the heels of my cowboy boots into the carpet, but I slid across the floor like a shit Tug of War team. As I was dragged into the foyer, the light suddenly hit her. She was fucking massive. The alcohol and the shadows of the night had played a wicked trick on me. I tried to resist but it was futile. She was on a mission. She marched me to a multi-storey car park, to look for her car. It turned out to be a hoax, as she had come in a taxi with her mates. We walked up to an empty level, where she cornered me.

Unfortunately, through some manhandling of the "old fella", my "on" was fully "lobbed", so circumstances were beyond my control. As I rummaged under her dress, I reluctantly yanked at her knickers, wishing I was back in the club. I had to stop for a second, just to look at them once they were off. They were fucking huge. They looked like the sling from an old Roman catapult. Evel Kneivel would have had a fucking problem getting over this one. Sometimes, I fucking well disgusted myself I did. She lay on a ramp, in between two levels, and beckoned me, as she adjusted her dress. "Ribbed Tickler" in position, I climbed on. I almost started laughing, because if Glyn could have seen this fucking nonsense, he'd have dragged me off, given me a "dig" and then called the cops. All of a sudden, there was a screeching noise. A car was racing down, from the top of the car park. As it turned onto our ramp, it skidded to a halt. The driver must have thought he was about to hit the "A-Team's" van. I pulled up my jeans, and returned to my senses. Two security guards jumped out of the van, and told us to "Fuck Off."

"Thank you... thank you," I said. I started running, and didn't stop until I was in a taxi.

A night in Nottingham usually consisted of three cars, and between ten and twelve lads. The seven lads in the band, including Glyn, then Steve Walker, who operated the lights for us; Mike Harris, my old school friend and Kiss buddy; and Dan Price, just for starters. There was usually around another six or seven extra lads who would be up for the night out, but depending on who you could get to drive, it was a lottery as to who got left behind. It didn't matter, because I knew I would be strapped in the front of Glyn or Rob's car, or at the very least, driving myself.

Dan was a friend of Steve Kenny's, and played in a few bands

157

over the years. "The Walk", who had a publishing deal, "Sister Rose", and "In a Big Way", to name a few. I know, not a good fucking name between them. I was just thinking exactly the same. I could never work out if Dan was an amazing bass player, who was continually poached, or if he was fucking rubbish, and sacked without any reservation whatsoever. Oh yeah? Well fuck off and write your own book Dan, because in my book you're fucking rubbish. He should have taken up the bugle, because he's got lips like a fucking cod.

I liked Dan. He wore a black leather, cowboy boots; smoked Marlboro's, wore necklaces with musical notes on them, and looked the spitting image of "Slash." No, I don't mean a "Hall of Mirrors" version of "Slash", I mean "Slash", the man. His favourite rock star ever is Paul Stanley, followed by Dave Lee Roth, and David Coverdale, so we got on just fine. Even compared to me, he had an unhealthy interest in girls, which I took as a challenge. Looking at it from a "1988-1991" perspective, the time that "Guns 'n' Roses" were at their absolute pinnacle, Dan cleaned up, on the back of "Slash." Dan wound up playing the part of Paul Stanley in a Kiss tribute band called "Deuce." They were excellent, but hey, guess what? They fucked him off too. Well, spandex can only stretch so fucking far. It looked like Gene and Paul were both inside the same fucking leotard. Just like the rest of us, Dan's metabolism hit the brakes when he turned 30, and we all became cuddlier, slower, and took longer to wash, because there was so much more of us. However, it happened to us all at the same time, so it wasn't that big a deal.

Dan made a dream of mine come true, one cold night in Ashton. He asked me to introduce the Kiss band. Hiding behind a fucking huge American flag that covered the whole stage, I adopted my gruff Kiss Alive II voice.

"Allllllllllright Ashton. You wanted the best, you got the best. The hottest band in the World... Kiiiiiiiiiiiiisssssssssssssssss!!!!" Fucking fantastic.

Like any Paul Stanley worth his salt, Dan smashed a guitar to pieces at the end of the set, during "Rock and Roll all Nite." Unlike Stanley, Dan didn't have an endless supply of cheap electric guitars he could smash to pieces and then sling into the adoring crowd. Dan had one old guitar that had one very loose screw holding the neck on to the body. Obviously, to get the full Kiss effect, he had to smash the fucking thing and launch it into the crowd. However, if he did this, then there would be no guitar for the next gig. A problem that never ever crossed Paul Stanley's mind, but one I could tell, was causing Dan great concern as he puffed on his Marlboro, leaving a thick lipstick mark around the filter, as he searched for an answer to his problem. A smile broke out on his face, as the machinery of his mind clunked and whirred up the answer. The answer was indeed simple.

"Hey Tony, you stand right at the front. When I get to the end of "Rock and Roll all Nite", get ready. I'll give the guitar a quick fucking whack, and then I'll sling it to you. Keep hold of it for a while, and then give it back to me later."

"Yeah, nice one mate, just make sure I've finished my fucking pint first."

Now then, the thing that you have to understand about Kiss is that their fans really are the best, and if Kiss are not playing themselves, they will turn out in their droves to pay homage to a band that cares enough to pay tribute to the real thing. Anyway, cut to the scene at the end of "Rock and Roll all Nite", as I am hemmed in at the front of the stage, wedged tight, as the low stage is digging into my shins. All of a sudden, the guitar is slung my way, and a hoard of drunken Kiss fans jump on my back, fighting for the cheapest fucking guitar in the shop, which I might add, has never been on the same continent as Paul Stanley, let alone been touched by the man. My shins nearly snapped against the stage, as some fat sweaty fucker in a "Lick it Up" T-Shirt jumped on my back. I turned around and swung at the twat with the neck of the guitar. Too much back lift in the swing gave the fat cunt a split second to rethink the situation, and he dived backwards avoiding an Ace Frehley makeover. After ten minutes of this fucking carry on, I managed to find Dan, and handed the two bits of guitar back to him, vowing never to do this again. I looked like a cat that had just run through a "dog pound."

Dan is Jewish, and is one of the reasons I instantly warmed to them. He knows fuck all about the pentateuch, the carnage at Masada, or the "Burma Road." There is nothing sinister about him. He doesn't dream of a "New World Order." He puts bacon on his Bagels, for fucks sake. "Reform Judaism" apparently. The only things that ever mattered to him, was girls and music. Period. He is a velvet jacket wearing, red wine swilling, piano in the dining room, cigar smoking, foreskin missing, aftershave reeking, high backed leather chaired, "Still of the Night" humming, stuffed olive eating, lah di dah, diamond.

One night, his band were double booked, at a gig in Bury. I can't remember which fucking band, because like I said, he was poached/fucked off monthly. Anyway, it was a Friday night, but this particular Friday, was the "Children in Need" appeal. His band decided to drive down to Manchester, and do a spot of busking, to raise some cash instead. They set up their gear on Oxford Road, and "blagged" some free electricity from "Amigo's", a Mexican restaurant, who were happy to oblige. Anyway, they started playing, and a crowd began gathering, which increased by the minute. They had a pavement full of cash, which, luckily, they could take across the street, to the BBC, whose offices were opposite.

As the cash rolled in, Dan spotted a familiar figure coming out of the BBC, crossing the road towards them. It was Mick Hucknall, with a delectable young filly. The crowd noticed the "Bonnie Langford" look-alike, and fell silent. Dan spotted his opportunity in the silence, and called out;

"Hey Mick, any chance of a quick song for "Children in Need? Beatles, Rod Stewart, you name it."

"Fuck off" came the reply.

"Too fucking tight to mention, then?" shouted Dan.

Although this book was initially started in September 2001, this is the third time it has been written, and now and again, it gets on top of me, as to when, where, and what, exactly happened. Part of the delay has been because I've been sat wracking my brains, trying to remember chronology, names, places, faces, and if I was single at the time. Then, after passing my own quality control test, I'm left with the decision of whether I should mention names, who will never be heard of again, or if I could possibly disengage myself from the story completely, and tell it in the style of the "Third Person." Well it was me, and I stand or fall by the life I have led so far. Then there is the question of where do I fit, in all of this? Is anybody really bothered about anything I have done with my life, when you can buy a book about Elvis or the Beatles, for a fiver? Success is an attractive, powerful, addictive stimulant, which leaves me out on a limb when you think about it. "Tony who?" It could be the title of this fucking thing couldn't it? What drove me is that nobody wanted to succeed more than me, and I don't care who they are. They might be sat in a castle, unable to make a dent in their amassed wealth, but they only ever wanted it as much as me, and not one fucking dream more.

Another thing that has played on my mind is the sexual angle of the book. I didn't want it to turn out like some sleazy, glossy, porn magazine, without the pictures. You know, just the letters page. We're all grown up, and I credit you, yes you, with the intelligence, that every caper involved a knob and a pussy. I don't need to tell you what they look like. We've all seen them before, and when it boils down to it, sex, as long as you are getting it, is pretty much the same. Far more important than the sex, is trying to get across the sense of humour we had, or the closeness we felt, that came from seven lads who fucking loved each others company. If I'd have looked closer at the time, I would have noticed that we were far too comfortable, to be hungry enough, to do anything to set the World on fire. So, we all paid the price for being great friends.

It could be worse; I could have been the bass player in Bon Jovi, or, even worse, the latest bass player in Bon Jovi. Alec whatsisname, was dispensed with in the early "Nineties" only to be replaced by Hugh whatsisname, who to date, has not had his mush on one fucking album cover or video. That's not a mate Hugh, that's a twat. You should try www.wakeupandsmellthecoffee.com. Then again, he has been provided with the greatest "Out clause" ever.

"What? No it's not me playing on that pile of shite. Well you go and fucking prove that it's me, because you won't find me on the album cover or video. Now fucking shift, unless you want a Ferrari on your foot."

Perhaps he got it just right. Clever man.

Getting back to Nottingham, it summed up a perfect time in my life, when there wasn't really anything to worry about besides getting drunk, getting laid, and getting the sixth round of beer. One night, we were queuing to get in, and I was standing with Rob, behind a blonde goddess, who was wearing "Stars & Stripes" Hot Pants, and white, stiletto, knee length boots. She turned around and smiled at both of us.

"Aren't you two in A.O.K?"

Recognition, we were famous. We both spluttered into our tins of "Stella", and Rob managed to acknowledge her. I prowled around the place all fucking night, but her boyfriend didn't let go, not once. It was getting late, so I mingled, and met a couple of pretty, impressionable, young dames, who had been liberated, by the wine and the beer. Earlier in the evening, the lads had made pacts with each other, so that nobody would get left behind, and we could all get back to the hotel bar, and have a few more drinks before crashing out.

"Look Rob, don't leave here without me. Even if I'm with a girl, just drag me out, and back to the hotel. I'm fucking sick and tired of wandering around town centres, where I don't know where I am."

"Alright soft lad, but remember this, when you're telling me to fuck off later, because I can tell you now, you have no intention of getting in a cab with me, no matter what you say now."

Sure enough, I was ruing the very words I had spoken, as he came to get me at kicking out time. The girls asked me to stay, but after much heated deliberation, I was given a "peck" on the cheek by each of them, and I shrugged my way out of the club behind Rob. I knew he was right, but they had both seemed so up for it. My name and the word "threesome" were destined to never be in the same sentence. It was something I was just going to have to deal with.

We got back to the hotel bar, and Glyn was handing out "Elephant" beers to everybody. I slumped into a chair with my "radioactive" pizza I had purchased somewhere between "Rock City, and the hotel. I could barely hold the box, it was that fucking hot, never mind the pizza inside it. The bar fell quiet, as various fast foods were destroyed, and beers were guzzled. The door to the bar opened, and in walked the two girls from "Rock City." I had told them where I was staying, and they had decided to come for a drink. I bought them a drink, and then nestled in between them, as I returned to my seat. Outside the dim lights of the club, they were both foxes, and I could tell by the lad's reactions, that I had weaved a bit of my "Burnage" magic. Usually, there would be derisory comments, which reached the usual crescendo of "Fuck Off" aimed at some unsuspecting female, but tonight there was a whiff of respect in the air. I was so busy puffing my chest out, and slapping "high fives" that I didn't notice that the pair of them had eaten my fucking pizza.

As I eased my way to the finishing line of the " Nottingham Threesome" Handicap, I noticed a hurdle right in front of the finishing line. It was Rob. We were sharing a room together, and

162

there was nowhere else for me to go. Now, as you know, he is a great, great, mate of mine, but he unfortunately enjoys lifting my bonnet, and throwing the biggest fucking spanner he can find, right into my "works." Time and time again, I am supposed to accept his paper-thin excuse that it is all in the name of "laughter." One of his eyes was shut, so I knew I was in with a shout.

Me "Rob... Robbie... Robbie. Come on, wake up you cunt."

Rob "gnnnfrruppt... wha... fuck... psssssh... cunt... fuck... vodka."

Me. Hey matey, any chance of you getting in with Glyn and Steve tonight?"

Rob. "Fikken... twet... hhhrrrrrr, pssssssten, kent... ffffffhhhhhhhhhh"

Me. "So, is that OK?"

Rob. "Uuuuugggh... twat."

Me. "Cheers mate."

I asked the girls if they wanted to come to my room for a drink, and they both agreed. The bar fell silent as the three of us stood up, and then the lads started to whistle and jeer, as I bade them all a good evening. Once inside the room, the three of us fell on the bed laughing. I don't think they were as nervous as me, but it didn't show if they were. For one split second, I saw a vision of myself, tied to a bed, with all of my cash nicked, along with one of my shoes, so the journey home would have been that much more degrading, but I fucked it off, sharpish.

If you are as old as me, you will remember that old poster from the "'70's", of the alphabet, spelled out in cartoon sexual positions, with all kinds of set ups forming the letters. Well this was the night I had planned, since I first saw that poster. From what I could gather, "X", "Y" and "Z", would cause the most problems, but if I could get anywhere near "W", then I would forfeit the last three, in the name of "chafing."

I kicked off my cowboy boots, as the girls lay each side of me on the bed. The laughing stopped, and they both started kissing me, and rubbing up against me. "Frotting", if you're after the technical term. Butterflies fluttered around my stomach, while I desperately tried to hold in a fart. With the wind under control, I started to kiss both of them, while massaging their breasts. Fucking hell, this was it, what I had dreamed of for so long. An unhealthy addiction that had reached boiling point, and had come about so nonchalantly, so matter of fact. A fucking "Polaroid" moment if ever there was one. Did I need to jettison some fuel early on, to give myself some leeway for an emergency, or did I try and keep a full load, knowing that this was a long haul flight? I did not have a fucking clue. In fact, I didn't have anything that remotely resembled a clue. One of the girls lifted her skirt up to her waist, and was far less inhibited than the other. Amidst the quiet groans, my "Adams Apple" thudded against my throat, as I tried to keep breathing. I had one hand up a skirt and the other hand on a bare, tanned, firm, excited, breast, as my tongue slipped between two, overly lipsticked mouths. Their perfume filled my nostrils, as I tore at my jeans. I had one leg out of my jeans, when somebody started kicking the door frantically.

"Tony… Tony… quick, open the door."

It was Rob's voice. He sounded agitated, and all I could think of, was that a fight had broken out in the bar.

"Hold on pal, I won't be a second."

I pulled my jeans back on, and opened the door.

"What is it mate… what's happened?"

Rob had by now, re-mastered the English language.

"Funny you should ask, "Cunty." I've paid twenty five quid to sleep in this room, but you expect me to shoe horn myself in between Steve and Jonesy. They will be farting and snoring all night, and I won't get a wink of sleep, so you can fuck off, I'm sleeping here."

I understood his logic, but if I'd have had a gun, I'd have shot him, with every bullet in the fucking thing.

I turned around, to find the girls fixing their dresses, sitting looking sheepishly on the edge of the bed. I pleaded with Rob, but he was having none of it. We used to piss each other off, when we knew somebody was on their back foot, ready to snap, by saying the word "No", for about thirty seconds, extremely loud. Rob drowned out my feeble pleading.

"Nooooooooooooooooooooooooooooooooooooooooooooooooooo ooooooooooooooooooooooo!"

The girls decided it would be better if they left, so the "pecks" were handed out again, and they left me with Lazarus, who had come back from the dead, and the bar. His drunken corpse lay where the girls had been, and he was laughing. I flicked through the Yellow Pages, for a 24 hour "Dial a Hammer" service, but I couldn't find one. He was fucking lucky that night.

What had happened? Ten minutes earlier, I was a 20th Century Caligula, but now I was stuck with a drunken fucking lump on my bed, where the girls had been. I dragged him on to the floor.

"You're not sleeping on my bed, you cunt. Fuck off, get on your own bed."

He wasn't listening, he wasn't awake. A few minutes passed, and he grunted and climbed on to his bed, where he lay, snoring and farting all night.

**"Maybe I'll write a book someday."**

*"Yeah, I'm the drummer. Wanna make something of it!"*

*Andy Chemney. Don't be fooled by the cool exterior.*

*"Where did it all go wrong?"*

*"That ain't no Beethoven, Fugsy's playing!"*

*Glyn Jones. "And we let him manage our band."*

*"Sing it to 'em Noel."*

*"Who turned the lights out?"*

*Noel Fraser. "He's just spotted a KFC bargain bucket!"*

*Rob Naylor. "And he told me he wasn't Glam!"*

*Rockworld 1991*

*"How much hair do you want?"*

*Steve Kenny… "Rock God". The poster.*

*Tenerife… my third day without sleep!"*

*"Tossers!"*

# CHAPTER TWENTY EIGHT

*"Parklife"*

With major record labels hot on our tail, and proofreaders at the top magazines, scrambling for the correct spelling of our name, we decided to lay waste to the country, so that nobody could ignore us. Any inkling of doubt that the record companies may have had, would be short lived, as they folded cheques into paper planes, and launched them at us. Oh fucking yeah???

The next foothold on the "Edmund Hilary" climb to the top was Workington, followed by Bradford "Rio's", then an outdoor gig at Heaton Park in Manchester, and then a right fucking trek up to Aberdeen, but there were young ladies in Tartan mini skirts and high heels to consider. On the map, it looked nearer to Norway than England, but if we were out to conquer the World, this was a Sunday morning stroll for the paper.

Workington is kind of in the Lake District, but on the coast. Now I know that fuck all happens there, because we were big news for the afternoon. We played at a place called "Monroe's Bar" and it was full of rockers who loved their music. We had a half page feature in the local paper, and the rockers were out in force to check out the "handsome, hairy, young bastards" daring to step on their turf. They turned out to be fine, and sat drinking with us for ages, eager to talk about music, and help us load the gear in and out of the van. More than a certain Mr. Naylor and Mr. Kenny did all fucking night.

Some bloke made a half-hearted attempt to give me his girlfriend for the night, but I could tell that he didn't mean it. It was like some kind of grateful gesture because we had actually bothered to travel all the way there, just to play for them. I don't know if he tried this trick on every fucking band that passed through, but I ended up giving him a load of free tapes, a couple of T-Shirts and some promo photographs. It was humbling, because we weren't anything special; we were just doing what we loved. It wasn't like

Van Halen had flown their full rig into Workington for the night. We had an agenda that consisted of "beer" and "fun", which luckily, we were able to pursue while playing music together, under the dusky shadows of different town or city skylines. You're beginning to get it slowly, aren't you?

Every girl in the place had a swarm of lads around them, so I wandered off to find something to eat. We had gone down really well, and loads of the crowd stayed behind for a few beers. I found a take-away, and joined the queue. Some of the people from the club were in the shop, and we spoke for a while. I shouted my order for pie, chips and gravy and handed over my cash. After a few sweaty hugs and high fives from the rockers, I grabbed my order, and made my way back to "Monroe's". I opened my supper under a streetlight, and noticed something familiar. It was my fucking face on the newspaper around my chip carton. We were already yesterday's news. Fucking charming.

We drove back to Manchester the same night, and dropped Andy off at his flat. We parked across the road, directly in front of Andy's window, although it was around thirty yards away. Andy had a flat mate called Steve, and we could see that he was still up, watching TV. Glyn turned the engine off, and as we sat in the darkness, Rob said.

"Jonesy, give me your phone."

Glyn handed Rob the phone, and he dialled Andy's number. We watched Steve stand up and walk across the room. As he bent down to pick up the phone, Rob stopped the call. His timing was perfect, for once that fucking evening. Anyway, Steve sat down again, and continued watching TV. Rob phoned again, but just before Steve could pick the phone up, Rob cut him off. Steve stood by the phone for a while, expecting the phone to ring again. When it didn't he sat down again. As soon as his arse touched the seat, Rob tapped the last digit of the phone number, and it rang again. Up Steve flew, but no matter how quick he was, that darn phone kept cutting off just before he reached it. We were crying in Glyn's steamed up van.

In the end, Steve just ignored the phone, and it kept ringing and ringing and ringing. He couldn't take any more, so he flew out of his chair and dropped to his knees, as he dived for the phone. Guess what? Yep, too late. In the end he was jumping up and down like Basil Fawlty, next to the phone when he missed the call yet again. When we could take no more, we took our tear-soaked puffy eyes out of the van and into Andy's flat. Steve opened the door, looking particularly flustered and unkempt. Andy greeted him.

"Hi Steve. Have I had any calls?"

Andy tried to explain everything, as our laughter drowned him out. Steve slammed the door and went to bed.

Bradford 'Rio's' passed me by for some reason. I do not remember one fucking thing about the night, which is a pity, because I had some great nights there. Did we support somebody? Were we the only band on? I haven't got a fucking clue, which is strange for me, as I am renowned for my "Train spotter" like, anal retention of absolutely rubbish facts and dates, relating to the band. I don't know if I was pissed or what, but I don't remember going, playing, or coming home. Fucking strange.

I had two particular fantastic nights in "Rio's", both for entirely different reasons, and not a fucking female to boot. Firstly, a gang of us went to see Glen Hughes play there. Some kind of rock icon, who I thought I would never get the chance to see. Me, Andy, and Rob were fired up for this fucker alright. Amazing voice and he looked "not English." You know, he had a kind of "Californian" glow to him. Glen Hughes? Of course you know him. "Burn", Deep Purple. Coverdale takes the song, and sings the bollocks out of it. It's fucking amazing, but hold on, what's this? While you're pouring yourself a "Crippler" of vodka, to rejoice in the magnificence of "Sir" David's voice, there's a tap on your shoulder at the end of the chorus as "Hughesy" comes steaming in with that fantastic vocal, that takes it to another level. "Burn" is where Paul Stanley got "I stole your Love" from. Well, my fucking thumbs are up.

Anyway, after leaving "Purple" he released an album with guitarist Pat Thrall, in 1981, called Hughes/Thrall, which was an absolute classic; and it was the threat of anything being played from this album, that yanked us across the Pennines. The place was packed, and so it should have been. We supped beer, and whistled like cunts, as we beckoned our man to come and play "Look in your Eye", "Who will you run To" or "Muscle and Blood." The lights dimmed, and the band took to the stage. This was a "Houston" moment. You know, everybody's tense, as the countdown begins. The riff from "Burn" came scorching out of the speakers, as the band threw their shapes. I don't know if you've been to "Rio's", but there is a set of stairs at the side of the stage, leading up to the dressing room. Anyway, a spotlight hit the top of the stairs and out popped Glen Hughes in a gold lamé coat, with the whitest home perm I have ever seen. He belted down the stairs screaming at the top of his voice, like a fucking scalded cat. I looked at Rob, and he looked at me. We were both expressionless, as he skipped about, pointing into the confused crowd. Our smiles widened, as we were overwhelmed by the moment. Then the laughter started. I couldn't fucking speak, and Rob was doubled over in tears. We gasped for breath simultaneously, as we tried to clear the tears from our eyes. One of the lads with us was Mark Alger, who owns Z Records. He turned around and said, in his broad Scouse accent,

"Toe, Rob. Fockken brilliant, or what lar?"

Mark was fucking loving it, but he had missed the comedy completely. This set us off again, and I dropped my drink. We finally calmed down, only to be asked to join in a rendition of the "Lords Prayer", for Tommy Bolin. Now we were laughing as a few hundred people chanted the "Lord's Prayer", in all seriousness, like a bad "Hammer" horror film from the early '70's. I think we got "Coast to Coast" from the Hughes/Thrall album, which was originally recorded by his old band "Trapeze", and I left "Rio's" with the same feeling I left the "Apollo" with, after seeing Billy Connolly. I love "Burn", I always will, but for me, it has now been reduced to the fucking "Birdie" song, by the very man that made me love it so much in the first place.

And so began the unexpected emergence of "Comedy" gigs, where we weren't supposed to laugh, but things were so fucking ridiculous, we stood jammed in the middle of massive crowds, laughing our cocks off, at people we had paid good money to see. The more somebody snarled and preened, the louder we laughed. I loved a good song, I still do, but to hear a great song and have a fucking good laugh at it was something else.

The pinnacle of my comedy gigs came at "Donington" in 1996, when Kiss put the make up back on for their reunion tour, and stomped all over the world again. Eighteen years had passed since our paths first crossed, and I was no longer the wide eyed, pussy starved, short haired, ginger fuckwit, they relieved of his cash, daily. I'm not knocking the show or their songs, but I watched four men, fast approaching fifty, in lycra outfits, with wigs on, trying to give me back a bit of my youth. Well, nice try, but my youth has gone, along with theirs, and sometimes it's better to move on, and be left with the memories that you treasure so dearly. Ace is a junkie. Peter Criss is a poor, poor drummer, who I endured in my youth, just because he was Peter Criss, but not any more. Besides, I'd been spoilt by Eric's ferocity. Gene stood there in silence with his arms folded, for what seemed like an eternity, as the crowd screamed his name. He was probably trying to count the crowd, and work out how much cash he'd made that night. Paul Stanley. My hero. Kiss isn't his cash cow; Kiss is his "air." Kiss is how Stanley breathes, Kiss is who Stanley is in love with, and I have nothing but respect for the man. Be it the guy who changed my world when he was twenty six, or the "Dude" who could still reach the high notes in "Strutter" and "Love Gun", almost twenty years later. He is the best front man I have ever seen bar none. He "saved" the night for me. I never saw Freddie, but even if I had, for me, there is only one guy.

Now, I'm gonna bore the living daylights out of you for a while here, as I list my top five Paul Stanley moments. Not in any particular order, but I'm gonna mention them nonetheless. He deserves a special mention, because to me, he is the true fucking essence of a rock star, and besides, it's my fucking book. So, you can go and get a brew, grab a beer, or wank yourself to a pulp, while I indulge myself. Alternatively, you may be ready to compare your top five "Stanley" moments with mine. You may indeed be thinking, "Why only five, there are hundreds of the fuckers?" Well, you know that, and I know that, but those fuckwits out there don't know that, do they? Anyway…

"I was made for loving You." After the second chorus, he repeats the phrase "I can't get enough", three times. He's singing falsetto, and each time, he pushes himself to the max, and gets higher and higher. By the third time, not only does he reach that fucker of a note, it is perfectly in tune, and I've got my "disco" flares on, carrying a tin of paint, just like John Travolta in "Saturday Night Fever." Pure "Studio 54." Fucking marvellous. I also love it, because I think part of him wrote it just to piss Gene off. Stanley must have known that he had a monster hit on his hands, so he knew that he was gonna have the scariest, most evil, blood spitting, fire breathing persona in rock, singing a chorus consisting of the words "I was made for loving you baby. You were made for loving me." Then again, go and listen to it live, it's as heavy as fuck.

185

"100,000 Years" from Kiss Alive. Good song spoiled by a drum solo. Anyway, "Stanley" raps over the last few minutes of the drum solo. The song is over twelve minutes long, so you can forgive him for remembering what day he started singing the fucking thing, never mind what key it's in. Anyway, "Stanley" leads the instruments back into the song, and not vice versa. If the music came in first, he would have had a chance to "pitch" himself, and have a slim chance of coming in, in tune. Oh, no, this clever fucker doesn't need that. His "pitch" is so perfect, that he doesn't need the "assistance" of his band mates to help him. He comes in "bang" in tune. You probably don't appreciate how fucking difficult that is, so just take it from me, he's good. No, he's the best.

The "Firehouse" helmet. Now don't get me wrong, because I love women, and I am not in the slightest bit gay, but Jenna Jameson wouldn't look as good as "Stanley" looks in that Fireman's hat. Come on, I mean, who could A) come up with the idea of wearing a Fireman's hat in the first place, and B) look so cool in the thing, once they had put the fucker on?

Kiss Alive II. Not any song in particular, but the start of the album. "You wanted the best… you got the best…" You can tell it's gonna be something special. The riff of "Detroit" starts and the explosions commence, as the plectrums are scraped up and down the "low" strings of the guitars. Then, you get "Stanley" screaming, "Whoooah, hello" in the middle of it all, in an ersatz "Texan" drawl. You can tell from those two words that he is fucking loving it. He's on top of the world. He was twenty five years old when this fucking gem was recorded. A hell of a lot was asked of the man, as they were rocketed to mega stardom, but he took it all in his stride. Nobody was made for it more than him. Nobody.

Conviction. I mentioned this word "generally" before, but I have never seen this much "drive" in an individual before. It's like he knew what he meant to me, and he wasn't gonna let me down, not once. Maybe you felt it too. Who else was gonna put the star on for me? Who was gonna pout like there was no tomorrow? Who else was gonna wear the short black jacket with stars down each arm? Who was gonna wear the "Love Gun" boots, with the chains down the front of them, every fucking night, without fail? Which fucker on this planet of ours was gonna come up with a "whore" of a guitar called the "Iceman" in jet black, and churn out my favourite tunes on it? When that wasn't enough, he rolled out an "Iceman" with a shattered mirror on the front of it for fucks sake.

Garters? No, garters only looked good on women, surely? Well think again my friend. "Stanley" had every base covered. If you were straight, you went and bought your girl a garter, because if they looked this good on a lad, then you were fucking laughing. If you were gay, hey, there was something new to try. If you were a virgin like me, you just prayed that you would meet a girl shortly. It was either that, or go buy a garter, and start wanking with the fucking thing on. Thank fuck I met a girl. He was like the coolest kid in the class, who everybody wanted to be. To top it all, he could pick up a guitar and knock out some great "romantic" songs, all with a great melody. Paul Stanley, yeah, let's fucking hear it for the man. Thank you my friend. It's like I've known you all my life. It might just be me, but I "Sure know Something."

Oh, just before I leave this section, I've got to mention Stanley's solo album. It should have been the Kiss album before "Dynasty." Not a duff song on the fucker, it was brilliant. From "Tonight you belong to Me", which was strong, powerful, heavy, romantic, dramatic, melodic and downright fucking awesome, with an absolute "beast" of a riff, right through to "Goodbye" it was fantastic. We were given a guided tour of his state of mind, trying to deal with the mega stardom we had thrust upon him, when he was just a lad, when all he wanted was a bit of normality. He was twenty-six, I was fifteen, and this album was a personal message from him to me. He told me what I wanted from life, what to expect from life, and how it would probably turn out. He told me how to deal with it, how it wouldn't always go according to plan, and how sometimes I wouldn't have a fucking say in the matter whatsoever.

"In a dream, a long time ago."

Fucking tell me about it.

What did piss me off, was when the press started calling the 1980's L.A. bands, Kiss copies. What, you mean Vince Neil? He talked a good fight, but he sounded like a fucking bee trapped inside a tumbler. Fucking rubbish. Stanley, never ever, dropped a note live, and I bet he has got at least a three octave range, possibly four. Now, you mix that in with a black star, a shit hot hairstyle, and a pair of shoulders that would have helped Samson out, and you have the reason why I set out on this rocky path in the first place. If there is a God, I'll give you 1000-1 that he's got a black star on his right eye. Now fuck off while I listen to "Alive II."

Anyway, at this point, I've just heard the pot call the kettle "Black." Why? Well, the other end of the spectrum involved me and Rob watching "Warrant", one non-descript evening at "Rio's." Written off by almost everybody, and wrongly I might add, lumped in with the consistently shite "Poison." We'd seen "Warrant" a couple of years earlier, supporting Dave Lee Roth, and we now happily handed over our cash, just to hear "Uncle Tom's Cabin." The crowd was sparse, and we reckoned we'd bought ourselves a Turkey this particular night. Expecting another night of our new found comedy, we mingled in the middle of the crowd. Well, they started with "Machine Gun", and wiped the fucking smile off our faces. Pronto. Something had changed; they had James Kottak on drums, who pinned everything together like the skin of a ship. This was tight. A fantastic night out, was rounded off by Jani Lane and the keyboard player duetting on "Bohemian Rhapsody", with just the piano for accompaniment. We got back, and nobody would believe how good "Warrant" were, not a fucking soul. This was during a week when I also saw "Jimmy Barnes", "Skin", and "Crown of Thorns", all within seven days. Ah well, as "Meatloaf" nearly said, "Two out of four ain't Bad."

And so to Heaton Park. Tennis courts, used condoms, pets corner, mountains of dog shit, a boating lake, pickpockets, over priced Hot Dogs and Ice Creams, burnt-out cars, and me in all my glory, churning it out in the summer sunshine, on one of Grover Jackson's finest. Well, one of his cheapest actually. It was a Charvel, with a bolt on neck, but it still cost me the best part of seven hundred quid, the robbing twat. There was no chance of playing "Donington", so this became our own "Donington." The gig was organised by Reebok, and was to raise money for one of the local children's hospitals. Booth Hall or Pendlebury, I can't remember which one.

There were six bands on the bill, but we were the only rock band. The stage was made out of two, forty foot long trailers laying end to end, with a big PA system and lights thrown in. Sounds a bit ropey I know, but it looked quite impressive. We turned up, and the first thing we did, was put up the massive backdrop we had made. It consisted of three huge pieces of black material, each bearing a letter of the name of the band. A bit of fabric and a splash of paint doesn't sound very good I know, but you've got to remember that Steve Kenny designed the logo, and took complete control with the making of the backdrop. Consequently, it turned out fucking amazing, and gave us a sharp professional edge. I might have cut the cloth for the fucking thing, I can't remember. Rob might have gone and bought the white fabric paint. I dunno. Fugsy may not have had a drink the night before, because he knew he had to have a steady painting hand the very next day. Andy and Noel may have paid for the thing, but I doubt it. In fact, I think Fugsy must have painted the "A", because it had fag burns in it. Whatever happened, and wherever each of us fitted in, we sat in silence, tongues hanging from our mouths, as we created the best back drop in England. Well, Iron Maiden might have something to say about that, as might Leppard, Zeppelin, the Stones, the Who, and Thin Lizzy, but it was a great backdrop either way.

Now because the backdrop came in three pieces, we could put them as close together, or as far apart as we wanted, depending on the size of the stage we were playing on. Glyn jumped up on the back of the trailers, and paced out a good sized area in the middle of the stage, then shouted us up, to help put the backdrop in the primest of positions. There was a good gap between each letter, so when you stood back and had a good fucking gander, it looked really cool.

A crowd started to gather around Glyn, so I walked over to see what the fuss was about. It turned out that these were members of the other bands, and they were all objecting at having to play in front of our backdrop. Glyn was in no mood for diplomacy.

"Fuck off, it's staying up. Phone the Police."

"Phone the Police", is a corker of a saying we invented, to shut people up when they were pissing us off. It is a fantastic put down, for which there is no reply. It means, "I don't give a shit what you think, now fuck off", but with fewer words. We used it regularly between ourselves, and it was guaranteed to stop any argument dead in its tracks. You had to wait for your moment. It took timing. If you went too soon, it had no effect, but the more you riled the other person you could see it looming in the distance. It then became a battle of wits as you pushed each other further with slicing insults, praying that the other had forgotten all about the saying. Then... "Boom", you threw the fucker in, and it was all over. You stood victorious over a broken man, resplendent in your glory.

"Bastard, I was just about to say that." I protested.

"Too fucking late my friend, I've won." Rob glugged his beer.

We waited for the next opportunity to present itself, determined to fuck the other one off.

The stage had a proper festival style railing between the stage and the crowd, which was only around ten or twelve people deep, as the majority of the big crowd chilled out on the grass, wherever there wasn't a dog turd. Pete Dutton came and mixed the sound for us, but when he turned up, he looked like he'd seen a ghost. I asked him what was wrong, as he darted around, with wild eyes.

"What is it Pete, are you on fucking speed or something?"

"I fucking wish. I've still got last night's takings from "Rockworld" in the boot of my car. There's a few fucking grand in there. If my car gets nicked, I'm fucked."

"Well look on the bright side, it's a fucking shed. So nobody's gonna be interested in that piece of junk."

"What do you mean, you cheeky cunt?"

"Come on Pete, it's fucked."

"Well so is yours."

"That's not the point is it? Yours has got an all expenses paid holiday in the boot, for the fucking retards that might nick it, but like I say, you're safe, because it's a fucking heap."

"Right, yeah, fucking idiots. They'll be looking out for posh motors, the dumb fuckers."

"Anyway Pete, how much money did you take off us lot last night? You must do a fucking roaring trade out of us. Surely you could let us drink for free all night, now and again."

"It's not all fucking profit Tony. Don't forget the overheads."

"What!!!!! The carpet is like a piece of fucking hardboard, it's been down that long. If you don't keep moving, you get stuck to the fucking thing. There are no lights on in the place, so your electricity bill must be fuck all. There's never any paper in the shithouse, and the girls are crouched over, pissing in our sinks. Hold on, I've fucking strayed on to the good points there."

Malc, from the "Banshee" turned up in his RS Cosworth, with his gold and his suntan, looking like some kind of Costa Del Sol criminal, where, not surprisingly, he had some property. He didn't even roll his windows up, never mind lock his car. You could tell that he knew nothing was going to happen to it. There was a time during the late Eighties and early Nineties, when clubs were getting smashed up in Manchester, right around the time when the "Hacienda" was at its peak. I asked him one night, if he thought it would happen to the "Banshee."

"Don't worry, it's not gonna happen."

He obviously had his finger on the pulse of what was happening at the core of Manchester nightlife.

After every band had played, the organiser told the bands that there was an extra half hour of playing time, but it was up to us to sort it out between ourselves. The guys from the other bands started to gather members from each band, to have a quick discussion to resolve the situation amicably, possibly with a "Short straw" competition, but in this case, the shortest straw won. Glyn came over to me.

"Quick, get your fucking guitar on, and get playing."

"What?"

"Fucking hurry up you cunt. Quick, all of you, on now. What the fuck are you waiting for? Pete's already at the mixing desk."

"What about…"

"Fuck them, soft cunts."

While the other bands handed out the fags, as a show of solidarity, we drowned out their niceties, with a cacophony of rock, for another thirty minutes. I saw them remonstrating with Glyn, but I couldn't hear them, because of our sonic resonance. I saw Glyn bellowing "fuck off" into a crowd of faces as I pouted at a camera aimed at me from the front row. We finished again, and went to the backstage area. I was last off the stage, and I passed Glyn as I headed for a beer.

"Well go and phone the fucking Police. Go on you cunt, phone the Police."

Glyn was in discussion with the manager of one of the bands who didn't have the foresight he had, and was probably getting a load of shit for it, off his own band. Doc McGhee would have had a fight on his hands that afternoon. Glyn is not a nasty man, but if you push him, he will push you back. Some managers are weak people, who allow themselves to get pushed around, and consequently, their bands lose out. The thing with Glyn was, he wasn't a professional manager, it wasn't his "job", just like the rest of us. It wasn't our "jobs." It wasn't that you were taking liberties with his band; you were taking liberties with his friends.

I left Glyn to it, and wandered over to the lads. I heard Rob's voice above everybody else.

"Now then, who wants to see some magic?"

191

Like a fucked Ali Bongo, he picked a young girl who was standing around. His claim was that he could walk away, while she picked a member of the crowd to touch a beer bottle. Upon his return, he would be able to identify the person who touched the bottle. Big talk indeed, for somebody who was now slurring his words. He stumbled out of sight around the corner of a truck, while the girl picked somebody to touch the bottle. Rob's piss got gradually louder as it splashed in the puddle he had quickly formed, somewhere around the back of the truck. He returned a couple of minutes later, with wet cowboy boots.

"Right then love, did you pick somebody to touch the bottle?"

"Yes."

"And did they touch it?"

"Yes."

"Right then, let's get this fucking show on the road."

He threw a fag in the air, caught it in his mouth, and then lit it. Now this is where we differ. Although I loved being on stage, I could only do it if the rest of the band were with me. I'll say it again, but I really am a shy type of chap. Rob loves a bit of attention, and he was back on stage here. He's not a big-headed twat or anything like that, but he knows he can entertain people, and if he's on form, he is in a league of his own. Despite leaving school with less qualifications than a fucking seven year old Victorian chimney sweep, he is sharp, witty, knowledgeable, ironic, truthful, intelligent, opinionated, respectful, friendly, well, to a fucking point, fiercely loyal, and faithful to the death.

Rob picked up the bottle, and inspected it. He closed one eye and peered down the neck, as if there was a clue inside the bottle. He never just said, "It's you", and finished the trick. Oh no, there was a bit of fucking Vaudeville coming your way, whether you liked it or not. He sniffed the neck, and closed his eyes. Then he lifted the bottle up to his face and lay it against his temple, as the silent crowd waited for a response from him.

"No, it's not working, come on, fucking concentrate, the lot of you."

He wasn't happy. He put the bottle down, and rubbed his chin.

"This is fucking hard. Somebody's not concentrating."

He crouched down, and looked through the bottle at different angles.

"Yes it's coming…"

Our hearts rose.

"It's... it's... Andy... No. no. Come on Andy, you're trying too hard."

This was "Down on the end of the Pier" stuff. The girl looked at him in amazement, as he lifted his hands to the sky, while puffing on his Benson & Hedges with his eyes firmly shut. The crowd had grown, as Rob battled with his sixth sense for the answer. His eyes opened suddenly, and he smiled. He walked over to Noel, and tapped him on the shoulder.

"It's you my friend."

The girl was amazed. Of course it was Noel. The crowd demanded to know his secret, and clung to his words. He wouldn't divulge his secret, but he told us that his "Gift" had been passed down to him by an old Chinese man. The girl wanted to know more. Rob responded.

"I am a simple man of simple means. What you see is all I own. My face is my fortune."

I couldn't help it.

"I take it you're fucking skint then."

The young girl walked off, as we selected another victim. There was a stooge in this jape, and it was usually Steve Kenny. All Steve had to do was surreptitiously mimic the actions of the person who touched the bottle. If it was himself, he'd scratch his nose. It's as simple as that. I couldn't believe that so many people could be suckered in this way. We had a licence to print fun, and it wasn't counterfeit. My laughter soon stopped as my arse caught fire. Malc had got me with his fucking lighter again.

Well, we managed to get through three gigs without one fucking write up, review, or the slightest acknowledgement of our existence. Nothing, not a fucking bean. I wouldn't have minded if somebody had said we were complete shite, but to get absolutely nothing, to be ignored, was far worse. At least there was Aberdeen left to redeem ourselves. Fucking miles away, but I couldn't wait. Hey, guess what? Cancelled. Can't remember why, but we were gutted. It was always such a fucking let down when gigs were cancelled. We were all fired up to fuck, desperate to shake off the shackles of the mundane lives we led, and jump into our alter-egos, ready to push each other to the max, all in the name of fun. I'll tell you now, it fucking hurt when gigs were cancelled. Not just me neither, we all knew that a fucking fantastic night out had been scuppered for some paltry, piss poor, lame reason. Like I said, we weren't gigging week after week, so it was a right let down when we got the call. It didn't happen too often, but we were so fucking revved up for these things, that we went and took it out on the nearest beer pumps and pussies we could find. The "mother" of all let downs came when Glyn had been sorting out some gig with a promoter in Europe. At every rehearsal we all only had one question.

"Have you got any news Glyn?"

"Well, there might be an outdoor festival in Spain."

I raised my eyebrows, and turned and smiled at Noel. He looked at me, and he was totally fucking cross-eyed. Fucking hell, it was good news, but he was taking it a bit too far. It wasn't a fucking record deal. He eventually exhaled, and handed the spliff back to "Fugsy." Then he spoke.

"What did you say Glyn?"

Rob wasn't listening properly, as he had managed to pull his "child's blanket" of a scrotum, through a small hole in his jeans, while leaving his bollocks safely inside. Don't fucking ask me how or why, he just does these things, all right? Then again, wouldn't we all, if we could? It looked like one of those fucking flying squirrels had landed in his lap. Once he couldn't blink, he knew he couldn't get any more skin out, and he finally paid attention.

"Sorry Glyn, did you mention a gig?"

Glyn had been looking at ferry prices, temperature charts, voltage differences, freight costs, and strip clubs. However, at that very moment, he was staring at the glowing embers of that big fat fucking spliff, racing towards his lips, as it burnt like a bastard.

Rob; "Glyn, the gig for fuck's sake. What were you saying? And that fucking spliff as well. It's not a fucking Benson & Hedges. Pass it on you cunt."

Rob eased back into his seat and puffed on the spliff, as the ash floated down onto his bright pink exposed scrotum flesh. I should have left the band there and then. A few days later it all went pear-shaped, and we spent the summer, driving up and down England in warm rain, to some remarkably low-key gigs.

# CHAPTER TWENTY NINE

*"Living For The City"*

When things didn't go as planned, or when they did go as planned, we always wound up in our own backyard, drinking in celebration, or, more fucking often than not, in commiseration. It's changed now, but if you were a rocker in Manchester, in the Seventies, Eighties, or early Nineties, you would have had as much fun as anyone on Sunset Strip, or anywhere else on the planet. Sure, some people will say that they don't remember it like that, but there are boring fuckers the World over, who are scared to make friends, even under the most temperate of conditions.

You know that it only comes your way once, no matter what that "it" is, you desire so much. Whatever it is you are waiting for, it will come, but just the once. So, to be a rocker, when "rock" came to town, and not fucking revel in it at every opportunity, is your own fault, and I don't want to hear you whingeing about it two decades later. You didn't have to be in a band to scrape the bottom of the barrel marked "Depravity", that was a totally separate thing, but I will admit that it could be used to your advantage.

One of our favourite haunts was the "Salisbury" pub on Oxford Road, below the train station. I could hop on a train, and be at Oxford Road in ten minutes, and then straight down the steps, and into the "Salisbury." How fucking easy was that, when you fancied a pint in the thick of it all? It looked like the "Lost Boys" hangout, with black leathers, cool hair, and chiselled cheekbones everywhere. Bikers, rough arses and pretty boys, stepped aside to let each other pass by in the narrow channels between the tables. It wasn't so much a "respect" thing, it was just a place where you knew you could go and have a laugh, without any hassle. Some of the clientele did look intimidating, but this was a place you could just get a beer, talk bollocks all night, and feel safe. After all, it was the other "normal" pubs, where you were singled out for not fitting in, and where animosity simmered, because of people's complete ignorance, and fear of the unknown.

Saturday night, we tried to meet at the "Salisbury" around seven o'clock, to give us a mighty fine crack at getting legless. Too much, it was all over, and you could end up home early, and alone. Too little, and you were stood at the bar in the "Banshee" or "Rockworld" playing catch up, wasting time that could be better spent with girls. Get it just right, and you were beating your chest like King Kong, as you burst through the doors of the club, nodding at every fucker in sight. Now who started that fucking carry-on? Don't know, don't care, but I could nod like fuck when I was drunk. If you met a boring fucker that you vaguely knew, and the music was blaring out, as it always was, you could just nod at them. They nodded back and then you fucked off. Perfect, you didn't have to speak to them, and they probably thought it was a friendly gesture, like,

"Hey, it's too loud in here to start to chew the fat for half an hour. See you next time."

I'm sure I was nodded at in exactly the same context over the years.

Glyn knows what I can drink, and what I can't drink. So once we got in the "Salisbury" he made a point of trying to fuck me up as soon as possible, to end my night early, and all in the name of fun. It took me a while to learn, but I could only rely on myself to look out for me, as bets, threats and insults challenged your mettle. It wasn't just me, Glyn would happily pay for anybody's beer, just to see them throw in the towel, and have to jump in a taxi outside "Rockworld" on their way home, before the fucking night had even begun. I've waved at girls in the queue for the club, from my taxi window, as I've swallowed the sick back down my gullet, praying that I got to my bed before I threw the lot up, and was turfed out of the taxi in the wilderness.

One night we were in the "Salisbury", when Glyn started trying it on. It was early, and he was already talking about Tequila chasers with our beers. Now, you knew if Tequila made an appearance, you were on a slippery slope, and sooner or later, there would be casualties. Glyn has a great knack of coercing people into drinking far more than they should, and took great delight in pissing himself laughing as you lay in a heap on the floor. Steve, Rob and myself were quite happy with the beers we had.

Glyn; Right then, it's my round. I don't know about you three

196

soft cunts, but I'm having a Tequila chaser with my next beer. Anyone with me?"

Before anybody could answer, he grabbed a barmaid's attention.

"Four Tequilas and four beers, when you're ready."

Me; "Fuck off Glyn; I'm not ending up on my bastard knees again. It's only eight o'clock."

Glyn; "Steve, Rob, what about you two. Are you soft fuckers 'n' all?"

Rob tried to abstain, so Glyn leaned on him, by downing his Tequila in one.

Glyn; "Fuck me; that was fantastic Rob. Ice cold, and really smooth. Come on, you'll fucking love it."

I could hear Rob's mind whirring. He had been here many times before. We all had. He was weighing up the pro's and cons that lay ahead, but again, the joy of being drunk surpassed the retching agony of being drunk, and he necked his Tequila in one, and shouted up four more.

Steve; "Pass me that fucking Tequila, come on."

Glyn: "See that Tony, Steve Kenny is half your size, but he will drink you, yes, you, right under the fucking table we are sat around."

Of course, my fucking heckles went up, and Glyn had won without even thinking about it. Me and "Kenny" were pitched against each other in silent loggerheads, as "rock" blared in the background, painting the perfect "Soundscape" for the evening. Fugsy pulled the doors of the "Salisbury" open, and made his entrance, like "Clint" in "Pale Rider." I had a full pint, and two Tequilas, nestling by my side. "Fugsy" looked me straight in the eye, and weighed up the situation immediately. He picked up my double shot, and dispensed with them in about two seconds.

"I take it you didn't want those fuckers?"

"No, not really Fugsy, but keep your thieving hands off my bastard pint or your "Liberace" fingers will be slammed in the fucking door. And that means no wanking for a week or two."

Glyn had won, and we sat drinking Tequila chasers until we left for "Rockworld." We all stood up to leave, and must have looked like the fucking "Tracey" brothers at the "Thunderbirds" Christmas "do."

Now and again, I would catch a bus to the "Salisbury", which took about twenty minutes. Although it was slower than the train, it was far more interesting. I saw all kinds of people on the bus, heading into town for their own special night. Back then, "music" was your badge, and you wore it with pride. Rockers, Punks, New Romantics, Skins, Rastas, Rockabillies, Mods, Ska boys. We all had our own unique look, and were equally as proud.

I was just the same as the New Romantics, who got on the bus, eyeing up the passengers warily. They got off the bus on Oxford Road, rode the torrent of abuse, wiped the spit from the back of their head, and went in their club, for a fucking fantastic night. Apart from that shit on the back of the head, I experienced the same, we all did. We belonged to something far greater than people could understand, or wanted to understand, and it suited me fine. You had to go that extra mile for your music, it was our faith. True music fans could be spotted a mile off, as non believers and part-timers faded into the background of the grey urban landscape. This has all but died out now, as one music fan fades into the next. Hairstyles and clothes are identical, as risk and imagination are kept to a minimum. I grew up in a vibrant, exciting, colourful world. What about you? Ziggy Stardust just couldn't exist in the 21$^{st}$ Century, even though that's where he came from, and that is a fucking travesty.

I was lucky, because the biggest problem I encountered on the bus was trying to get up the stairs of a double decker in my cowboy boots. The stairs were like a spiral staircase, so they started as a small point on the left hand side, and gradually fanned out on the right hand side. There was no problem getting my right foot on a stair, but I was fucked if I could get my left foot on the stair. The problem was multiplied, because the bit of the left shoe I could get on the stair didn't contain any fucking foot in it. The point of the boot was so sharp that my toes were a taxi ride away from the end of my boot, so, I couldn't even get a monkey grip on the stairs with my toes. Regularly my left boot would curl up at the toes as it slipped from the stair, and my shin would crack on the stair below. The only way to avoid this was to turn my left foot in, so it was pointing at my right foot, as I climbed the stairs like John Merrick. Looking back, this probably explains why I never copped for any of the rock chicks on the bus.

I was sat with the lads recently, celebrating the importance of Oxford Road in our lives. It was easily the most important street in

Manchester, for us, and thousands of others. I don't know where "Oxford" comes in to it, because it certainly doesn't go there, but that's not the issue. My life, all of our lives, are intertwined with this two way, then one way street. The "Phoenix" was there, "Rockworld", "Jilly's" the "Banshee", and before that, "Henry's." Rob and Glyn both played their first ever gigs in "Henry's", but at different times. The "Salisbury" and "The Shady Lady", both great pubs, who welcomed rockers with open arms, and on loads of occasions, the "Stage Door", next to the "Palace" theatre. This place was full of "Luvvies" who called each other "Dhhharling" but it was also full of leggy dancers from the shows.

Then there were the music shops. "A1", "Barratts", "Johnny Roadhouse" and "Reno's." Me and Mike Harris spent our youth wandering in an out of the guitar shops every fucking week, for years on end. Like me, he is left-handed, and we just dreamed about being right-handed. Not that we had any cash mind you, but the only left-handed guitars you could buy in those days, looked like I had made the fucking things. I can still remember that our favourite guitar was a Gibson "Firebird" which they had in "A1" for ages. Wood finish with a white scratch plate, which had a fucking Eagle on it. So fucking American, it was unbelievable. It was identical to the one Paul Stanley used up to 1976, when Corky Stasiak, the Engineer on "Rock and Roll Over", snapped the fucking thing in half, because it was made out of one piece of wood. He knocked it off a guitar stand, but as it had no "give" in it, the fucking thing "gave." It could have been a lot worse though. It could have been my guitar. Stanley was loaded by this point, and probably had a new "Firebird" delivered the next day. Had it been my guitar, I would have had to nail four legs to the body, and use the fucking thing as a coffee table. Of course you remember, it's the guitar Stanley is playing on the cover of Kiss "Alive."

We had a rehearsal room in the arches under Oxford Rd railway station, next to "A1" for a while. "Yank's" record store was just off "Oxford Road." I don't know what went on there, but you could buy dirt cheap albums, and later CD's, but they all had a piece missing from the corner of the covers. Before McDonald's and KFC arrived, we only had "Angels" take away, and "The Oxford Road Chippy." They both opened until the early hours, and on several occasions I inspected the meals I had just bought, shortly after they were consumed. A pizza place opened on the corner, next to the

"Banshee", well not exactly next door. There was a "Barbers" next door to the "Banshee", but I never saw it open. I always thought that was weird, a fucking "Barbers" shop right next door to a club where nobody ever cut their hair. I first met Rob in "Jillys", "Fugsy" too. I met Steve, Andy and Noel in the "Banshee." I fell in love for the very first time in "Jilly's", and ended up falling in love almost every Saturday night in the "Banshee" and "Rockworld" years later. Well, for part of the night at least.

Oxford Road stops at the "Midland" hotel, and turns into "Peter Street", with the "Free Trade Hall" on the left hand side. It has now been turned into a hotel, but Kiss played there in 1976. I don't remember a thing, not an advert in the press, fuck all. I was probably too busy practising "wheelies" on my "Chopper." Two years later, they consumed me. Just past the "Free Trade Hall" was "Paperchain", the bookshop where I bought my American music magazines. Further down on the same side, was the "Gallery." This was a venue for bands, but I only went there a few times. From the University, to the junction of Deansgate, it was a fucking amazing experience, especially if you were a rocker.

I don't know how I would have turned out without "Oxford Road." Of course I would have still been a rocker, but "Oxford Road" gave me confidence, it confirmed what I believed in was right. There is a big old building on "Oxford Road", with a clock tower that has a green dome on top. It was the Refuge Insurance building, but again, is now a hotel. It avoided being bombed in the Second World War, because the Luftwaffe used it as a reference point, because of its distinctive green dome. We all come from somewhere, and I am proud to say that "Oxford Road" is my particular place. I didn't know it at the time, but this is where my spirit developed. Then again, there appears to have been no respect involved whatsoever, as my different bodily fluids were spat, shot, fired, sprayed, thrown, hurled and emptied the length and breadth of "Oxford Road." So, was it just the canvas to a lurid episode, in a time corridor that closed a long, long time ago? Eh!!!!!???

Tequila bottles looked so harmless. Do you remember they had a red plastic sombrero as the cap of the bottle? Fucking ludicrous! I held my head in my hands in the taxi, desperately trying not to hurl, as we sped down "Oxford Road", out of the City. All I could think of was that red plastic hat on top of the bottle, and "Speedy Gonzales." For some reason, Christine hadn't come out to look after us, so it was just me and Robbie, faced with the mountainous task of getting both of us into the taxi, while looking like a bad "Laurel & Hardy" sketch. It was autumn so it was a bit nippy once the sun went down, and it had been down for fucking hours. Don't ask me what year, but seeing as you asked, it was around 1990. We both nodded off in the warm cab, as it sped along the empty streets through Manchester. Rob woke me up, shaking my leg, and dry heaving.

Me; "What is it mate?"

Rob; "Toe, I'm fucked. I'm going to be sick. Stop the taxi."

Now I could have left him, and laughed like a cunt as he spray painted the taxi, but that would have meant us both walking to Stockport from Parrs Wood, so I acted concerned.

Me; "Hey driver, can you stop the cab for a minute, my mate's fucked?"

The cab screeched to a halt, and I helped my buddy out of the cab, just like any benefactor in a "will" would. Rob was in trouble, and as he doubled over, I noticed his hair touching the floor. If I'd have been in the same position, there would have been more of my hair on the floor, but I don't want to bore you with how long my hair was right now. Anyway, as he started to heave, I jumped in and grabbed his hair, and lifted it up in to a ponytail, high above his head, so he wasn't sick in it. He repaid my act of kindness by throwing his fucking gutful all over my jeans and my cowboy boots. It was even in my socks. He climbed back into the taxi, and fell asleep. As his sick cooled down, the warm bile cooled, and made my legs feel cold and damp. To make matters worse, the rancid stench was making me heave, so I finished the journey with my head stuck out of the window, in the cold night air, as "Sleeping Beauty" gurned in the moonlight.

Rob had a pair of faded "501's" which were his pride and joy. He customised them by adding black and white tassels down the outside of each leg. They were his middle finger to the world. Gigging, drinking, and probably, wanking, he never took the fucking things off. 50% leather "Joyboy", and 50% leather "Joyboy", but he assured me they were "Rock n' Roll." One night, we were walking down "Oxford Road" in search of a taxi, when two lads took umbrage to his "Rock n' Roll" pants. When Rob wore these pants, he would also try and shoe horn his feet into a pair of black cowboy boots, which he bought in Hollywood, that had a metal plate around each heel, and a metal plate around the toes of each boot. They looked like "Robocop's" going out shoes. Now then, if that wasn't enough, they were a size too small for him. You could see the knuckles on his toes, pressing tightly against the leather, like one of "Alvin Stardust's" old fucking leather gloves. As he hobbled down "Oxford Road" we saw the two lads looking at his pants and laughing. As we passed them, Rob swung his leg, and hoofed one of them, right up his arse, with his gleaming, tight fitting boot. The lads fucked off, and Rob stopped dead in his tracks.

Me; "What is it mate?"

Rob; I think I've broken my fucking big toe."

The boots were painful enough, but to know he now had a "fucked" foot inside one of them, set me off laughing. It was fantastic.

Rob; "Fuck off."

Me; "Come on, this is fucking great. Your feet are fucked. We've got to walk for fucking ages to find a taxi, and you are wincing like a cunt already. And to top it all, I heard your tassels go "Whoosh" as you swung your "Diver's" boot at that twat."

Rob; "My bastard feet. These fuckers are going straight in the bin when I get home. This is all your fucking fault."

They never did, and I would occasionally talk him into wearing them, so I could feed my own perverse sense of humour. He seemed to forget the pain he had previously experienced, and he would put them on at the last minute, before we left his house. Once we were in the taxi, it was too late. I was in for a fucking laugh that night. By the time we got to "Rockworld", he was in so much pain that he would have to take them off. So, he sat drinking beer in his white towelling socks that had four different coloured hoops around the top.

"Oxford Road" also boasted a few curry houses, which we frequented after the clubs had closed. Our favourite was the "Star of India" which unfortunately burnt down. We relocated to the "Koh I Noor" which was above "Rockworld." Luckily, if we went for a curry after "Rockworld", there was always a big crowd of us, because it was like a fucking "Wild West" saloon, once the clubs had closed. Opposite the "Koh I Noor" was "Rotters" nightclub. There was a huge glass window at the front of the restaurant, where we sat and watched the brawling punters from "Rotters" being slung into Police vans. "Rotters" was eventually knocked down, and the area was fenced off and turned into a car park.

One Summer Saturday night, I was standing outside "Rockworld" with Rob, waiting for a taxi. There was no urgency to the night like there was in winter, because it was still stifling, and the girls were dressed in what they had been wearing in the clubs. No fur coats, no jackets, no knickers. One of the girls from "Rockworld" came over to talk to us. She made it clear, early in the evening, that she liked me.

"Do you want to go for a walk?"

A poor opening line I admit, but it was late, and it worked. Besides, there was no fannying around, either it was "on", or I was in the next taxi.

"Yes", she said softly.

"Right then Robbie, you get a taxi, and get the fucking kettle on. I won't be long."

"Fucking hell, it's gonna cost me a fortune on my own, you cunt."

Rob set off walking down "Oxford Road", and his moaning faded into the distance. I grabbed hold of the girl, and we crossed the road into the car park, where "Rotters" had once stood. She wasn't shy, and as soon as we entered the car park, she was worshipping at the "Temple of Bell." I could tell that she was in pain, because the car park had a gravel floor, and her knees were beginning to take a hammering. Anyway, like a fucking modern day "Walter Raleigh", I picked up a huge board showing the daily rates, and laid it flat on the floor. I stood on the board, and she got back to work. I looked up and saw around a dozen people watching me from the huge window of the "Koh I Noor." I smiled and waved at them, as they enthusiastically replied. The girl then got on her hands and knees, and I parked for free.

The crowd in the restaurant started hammering on the window, while pointing at me and my "date", cheering, and condoning my ridiculous behaviour. Anyway, from out of nowhere, a guy drove into the car park, in a burgundy Jag, and parked next to me. Next thing, he rolled his fucking window down, and started having a chat, while I was gaining momentum, and building up a sweat. Unnerving to say the least. He introduced himself as "Steve", and from what I could gather, he was loosening his pants as we spoke. To give the girl her dues, she didn't flinch. I don't think she even noticed him drive into the car park. I couldn't see, but I knew from his body movements that he was wanking like a fucking madman. I finished before he did, and we left him, pulling his head off, in front of the restaurant crowd. Rob will tell you that I got back to his house before he did. I'm good, but not that fucking good.

# CHAPTER THIRTY

*"Let's Get The "World" In Motion"*

"Rockworld" Manchester, opened in the Autumn of 1990. Probably late September, or early October. I can remember, because I'd just been fucked off by that girl. You remember Rob's impression in the caravan? Course you do. The opening night was a fantastic night, as we stretched our legs in our new home, and found our bearings. Eye contact with the barmaids was first on our list, with the old, "And one for yourself love", thrown in liberally throughout the night. This would hopefully stand us in good stead during the years to come. There was always the question in my head, of whether I should try and date one of the barmaids because that would have been ideal wouldn't it? No more queuing at the bar, even when there was a dozen of us. The odd free drink now and again and you knew that whenever you fancied sex, she would be there at the end of the night. Hold on, fucking rewind that bit, yeah, you know, the bit about her being there at the end of the night. That also means she would have been there at the start of the night, so there would have been no chance of those fatalist encounters, while there was a pair of eyes burning into the back of my head all night from behind the bar.

I'm a fatalist. You know, you meet a girl who tells you that she was on her way to Sheffield, when her mate's car broke down. It was towed back home, where she had to wait for her dad, who was working the late shift, to get home, before she could borrow his car. He finally got home at 10pm, and because it was so late, she decided to drive to "Rockworld", or whichever club I was in. You have a great night, get laid, and arrange to meet again. You don't meet again, even though you both had a great time. It's just that the next week there is somewhere else for her to go. The next week, you meet a girl that went to Sheffield last week, because her mate's car broke down, and they couldn't get to "Rockworld." This week however, she's very much in "Rockworld", and it would appear that

I'm on a roll. Ring a bell? Hey, you're a fatalist too.

Like I said, before "Rockworld", there was the "Banshee" and "Jilly's." The "Banshee" was about fifty yards up "Oxford Road" from "Rockworld", and "Jilly's" was in the basement of "Fagins" the disco, which had just changed to "Rockworld." I'm not sure if he owned "Jilly's", but a guy called Danny used to stand on the door each night. Big fucker, who smoked a pipe, and just watched and weighed up everybody who came in the club. There was an illuminated sign as you entered "Jilly's", which showed a picture of a guy wearing jeans. Next to this picture there was a tick. The next picture on the sign was a guy wearing a pair of normal trousers. Next to this picture was a cross. Plain, simple, and easy to understand, it told you exactly what was expected, nay, demanded of you in our club. It was kinda "goofy" and cute in a certain way. Unless you tried to get into the fucking place in trousers that is. I saw Danny, on several occasions, grab numerous "trouser" wearing lads by the throat, or the scruff of the neck, and launch them down "Oxford Road." His reasoning was simple. We couldn't waltz into their clubs in our jeans, so they in turn could fuck right off.

One Saturday, there was a lad in "Jilly's", who was intent on making trouble. I didn't recognise him, and he'd punched a couple of the regulars. Danny must have heard about the trouble, and he came down the stairs, into the club. As he puffed on his pipe, he watched the guy squaring up to another regular. Danny leaned into the cloakroom, and picked up one of the "bikers" full faced helmets. He walked over to the guy and fucking whacked him across the head with the helmet. The lad fell to the floor, he was out cold. Danny put the helmet back, and dragged the lad up the stairs, out of the club, and on to the street. Not once during this episode, did he take his pipe out of his mouth, or utter one word. Fucking cool or what? I expected him to shout;

"The drinks are on the house" but that was too much to ask for, that would have been "blockbuster" film material. There were always loads of stories being "whispered" around our hallowed club about Danny, and he rightly or wrongly, became a legend. Somebody told me that he used to be a mercenary, and they had seen a picture of him, taken in the middle of a jungle, with some poor fucker's head on a stick. You know what Chinese whispers are like though, don't you. It probably started out as a picture of him taken at a fairground, holding a "gonk." However, I wasn't prepared

206

to try and validate any of the stories I had been told. Every time I went to "Jilly's" or "Rockworld" with Rob, Danny looked us up and down as we approached the club. From thirty yards away, we saw him staring down Oxford Road at us. Our strut was reduced to a fucking stagger, and we deflated our chests as we approached the door. He casually took his pipe out of his mouth. We both knew what was coming.

"Evening ladies."

"Alright Danny", we squeaked.

Did that mean our heads were safe from the "stick" for another week? I fucking hoped so.

"Rock" could also be found in abundance in Manchester, at U.M.I.S.T. This was the University of Manchester, Institute of Science and Technology, which was just off "Princess St." Sounds a right stuffy place doesn't it? Well on a Saturday night, it was a rocker's paradise. Pool tables downstairs with a shit hot jukebox, and loads of comfy chairs. There was a bar downstairs, and a separate room, where they had bands on from time to time. Rob saw Def Leppard and Iron Maiden in this room, way before they hit the stadiums, the old fucking gipper. Upstairs on the top floor was the examination hall, which was the main room, and they had a deafening rock disco every Saturday. Condensation dripped from the ceiling, as it mingled with the sweat that had been headbanged out of every fucker in the room. Wet, lank, matted hair stuck to everybody's heads, as we swung them to "Jane", "Carry on my wayward Son", "Crazy Train", "Ace of Spades", "Barracuda", "Elected", "Touch too Much" "Doctor Doctor", "Queen of Spades", "Stargazer", "Back on the road Again", "Rescue Me..." I'd better stop, because my thumbs are firmly in my belt loops on my jeans, and I'm ready to go.

When I first started going to U.M.I.S.T, I had no idea "Jilly's" existed, until a crowd of lads asked me if I fancied going. U.M.I.S.T. was all over by midnight, so they walked over to "Jilly's." I walked in and fell in love with the place immediately. So this is where all the girls had been hiding. Then there was the smell of greasy burgers and onions, sizzling away all night. Fantastic. The music was far more up to date than U.M.I.S.T. Plenty of Van Halen to sink my teeth into, plus a glut of high spirited Yankee bands, that all the girls danced to. I could tell that the experience of growing up was going to be just fine, and it was.

We were all in the "Banshee" one night, before "Rockworld" had opened. Malc came over with a load of bottles of "Rolling Rock" beer, which had just started being sold in the U.K. He handed us a couple of bottles each, and said, "Get those fuckers down your necks, and let me know what you think."

Well, the first thing I thought, was, "These bastards are free, are there any more?"

There was, but they weren't free. It didn't matter; Malc's marketing plan had worked. Between us, we supped every fucking bottle he had. He knew we would. The same happened when he started selling "Warsteiner" beer. One Wednesday night, he gave me, Rob, and Glyn a couple of pints to try. This was fucking "headache" material, but it was really tasty beer. The following Saturday, we all went out, and emptied his barrel of "Warsteiner" just as he had planned. It was that night that Malc revealed his plan, and said he had been negotiating for "Fagins", and it was all done and dusted, "Rockworld" would be opening in a month.

"Fucking hell… shit hot Malc. I hope you will still afford me the same privileges that I enjoy here."

"You're a cheeky cunt Tony. Here you are."

Malc reached into his jacket, and pulled out a red laminate card, and handed it to me. It was a VIP admission pass, which meant I wouldn't have to pay to get into the club. I pushed my luck.

"What about Rob?"

"Fucking hell, it's not a charity."

He laughed as he handed over another pass.

"I want to see the pair of you in there all the time. This is a fucking investment."

"Well, your going to make a tidy profit aren't you, because you'll have trouble keeping us out of the fucking place my friend."

The contents of Pete Dutton's boot at Heaton Park later confirmed that his gestures were a great move, and were rewarded favourably. This was all down to the way that Malc ran the "Banshee." He mingled and chilled with the punters all night. He knew everybody in the place, and made everybody feel welcome. It is still the best club I have ever been to, including the "Rainbow Bar & Grill." Malc helped move the magic of the "Banshee" into "Rockworld", and I didn't spill a fucking drop in the process. The "Banshee" didn't even have a closing down party, which is unbelievable, considering how special it was to everybody that went there. I suppose everybody was looking to the future, and the japes that were yet to happen. Besides, it wasn't like it was shutting, and there was nowhere left for us to go. We had a brand new hangout, all ready for legends to stamp tales of excess, daring, comedy, fun, skullduggery, double crossing, double dealing, double donging, romance and heroism, across the blank canvass of our virgin "Rockworld." "Jilly's" remained downstairs in the basement, and it turned into a self contained land based "Pirate" ship. "Jolly Roger?" Weren't they all?

During the last few weeks of the "Banshee" we all reflected on what a fucking blast it had been, and how the last six years had passed by unnoticed. Fuck all to worry about, and fuck all to do except play music, listen to music, or get laid to music. Lifelong friendships were forged over incoherent, drunken ramblings, drowned out by our music. Bands were formed and then broken up on the same night. Young hearts fluttered at a chance encounter, while the person stood next to them nursed their broken heart, vowing never to "fall" again. Girls turned up on time, and made your night. Others turned up late, launching their drinks over the girl that was giving you their number. Girls you had never spoken to before, pushed you into a dark corner and snogged your face off, when they'd had that one beer or wine too many. It was too late; I was up their skirt in an instant. That's where my time went, and that's why it whizzed by. Nothing else mattered, how could it? My world started and ended with black vinyl discs, with labels I can still describe down to a fucking tee, all etched into my memory like they've been there forever. Wars, disasters, great human endeavours, global famine, corruptness, racial and religious intolerance and bigotry, all passed me by, as I turned my hair dryer up to full blast, to drown out the news. Well, I was running late, and she wouldn't wait all fucking night.

One quiet Friday in the "Banshee", I was minding my own business, while failing miserably on the "Trivia" machine. A couple of weeks before closing forever, the place seemed to be winding down on its own. It seemed to know that the end was in sight. I struggled with a piss easy question and swigged at my beer. I felt a tap on my shoulder.

"Alright Tony."

"Alright Malc."

"What are you up to?"

"Filling your fucking pockets with cash again, by the looks of it."

"Well, tonight Tony, I'm going to do something for you."

"Oh here we fucking go. Let me guess, you'll swap me one of your crisp brand new fivers, for one of my old crumply tenners."

"No, not even close."

"Well, what is it?"

"See that girl over there?"

He pointed to a blonde, standing at the other end of the bar.

"Yeah."

"Well, she's a very good friend of mine, and she has just told me that she likes you."

I stared at her, trying to get a good look, in the dim lighting of the club.

"Well, what do you want me to do?"

"Come and talk to her."

"Nah, I'm not bothered Malc. I've blown all my fucking cash on this thing, so I'm off home after this beer."

"Look, if you stay and speak to her, you can have free beer all night."

"Do I have to fuck her?"

"Well, that's up to you."

"Right then, you'd better get me two Bud's, and give me a large wine to take over to the lady."

Me, free beer, and a blonde shouldn't appear in the same book, never mind the same fucking sentence. I'm piss poor at opening lines, but the beer helped me limp into some nonsense about different kinds of hairspray. It was clear that she would listen to any old bollocks, and I was indeed, "in." The beer kept flowing, and consequently, I got increasingly funnier. Well in my mind at least. You've gotta work with me here. She laughed like I was Tommy fucking Cooper or something, so I could tell that she was desperate to get laid. Not by me necessarily, but laid nonetheless. Now I'm no fucking oil painting, but as I squinted in the darkness, I could see that she looked like Peter Sellers, when he was trying to pull out Dreyfuss's tooth in one of the "Pink Panther" films. Remember the laughing gas, the blonde wig, and that fucking plastic melted nose? Well put a pair of knockers on him and move him from that castle on the side of that mountain, and into the "Banshee", and you have my date. I couldn't let Malc down, so I shouted up a couple more beers and headed for the toilet.

The toilets were downstairs, and were accessed by a set of stairs that had a landing halfway down. Desperate for a piss, I jumped down the stairs, three at a time, leaping like Rudolph Nureyev at his peak. As I approached the landing, I launched myself into the air, and cracked my head on a wooden beam that some fucker had put there when they built the place. I fell to the ground in a crumpled heap, bouncing off the walls, and cracking my shins on the stairs as I slid to a halt. There was nobody around, so I staggered to my feet and stumbled into the toilets. I looked into the mirror, and saw two of me. Alarming I know, but both fuckers looked shit hot, so I smiled, and drunkenly pissed on my foot. As I lowered my head, blood gushed down my face, across my jacket, and into the toilet. Up to that point, there was no pain, but introduce a bit of "claret", and your brain expects pain, so pain there was, and plenty of it.

Bearing in mind, it had taken me over an hour to construct my masterpiece earlier on, I was reluctant to wet my hair to see where the damage was, but I could tell by the blood that it was serious. I dabbed my head with a damp paper towel, and the bleeding finally stopped. I went back upstairs and changed my order to vodkas, to try and numb the pain. I sat nursing my head and several vodkas, and paid no attention to the girl, so she went and stood with a crowd at the end of the bar. Mike Harris turned up, and pissed himself laughing at my misfortune. He offered to take me to the hospital, but the bleeding had stopped and the club was still open, so it was free beers until closing. When we did leave, a girl I hadn't seen for a while rubbed my head as she said hello. The fucking thing opened up again, and the blood started streaming down my face, so Mike drove me to the hospital. To give him his dues, Mike had a date that night, but he fucked her off, so that he could witness my humiliation at the hands of the nursing staff. Half best-mate, and half Marquis de Sade, he roared down to Withington hospital like something out of the "Dukes of Hazard", eager to see me wince like a bastard.

As he opened the door, I expected a bevy of blonde nurses in white tunics, with breasts spilling out of the top like some kind of porn movie. You must be getting used to my success rate by now, so it's no surprise that an overweight "Hattie Jacques" snarled at me across the reception desk. She wasn't interested in how I had cut my head. To her I was just another drunken twat that was making her

"Ovaltine" go cold. With a fiercely cold expression, she reached for a set of hair clippers and told me that she would need to shave my head, in order to stitch the wound. She clenched her teeth, fighting the smile back into her mouth. She was fucking loving it, as I turned white at the thought of Peter Gabriel's "Foxtrot" hairdo. That was enough to stir me into action.

No way, you're not shaving my head. I'll let it heal on its own. No, I'm not bothered, come on Mike."

The nurse called me a vain old sod, and pushed me back into the chair. My face was covered in blood, so she soaked my head with a wet sponge and wiped my face. She combed my hair into a centre parting, so that my wound was exposed. She was having great difficulty getting a comb through my hair, due to the fucking gallon of hairspray stuck to it, so my poor head was subjected to further pain as she dragged a sharp toothed comb through my sticky hair.

"Have you been drinking?"

"Yeah, I'm leathered."

"Well, you can't have any anaesthetic then."

"What... will it hurt?"

"Probably."

She took great delight in slowly threading the needle so that I could see. My body went rigid. She held the gash together with her fingers, as she pushed the needle through my skin. I could hear my skin popping as the needle burst through, and a bolt of pain ricocheted around my body. It was fucking agony, and I'm sure she put a few extra stitches in just to piss me off. All of this just for a few free beers. Would I ever learn?

To me, this wasn't failure. There was another story to be had from this particular episode, along with many others over the years. My role in the band had been defined early on. The rest of the lads had girlfriends, partners and wives, so I was their sexual outlet. I put in the same amount of work when writing songs or rehearsing, and nobody could question my commitment or the pride I felt, but it was down to me to spread the word horizontally. When things didn't go as planned, I never got pissed off. Usually, there was a comical outcome to my failed attempts, and I would relish the challenge of recounting my tale, the funniest way I could. It was far better than just saying, "Yeah, I got laid."

Humility is something I have yet to experience. Throw

anything at me and I will turn it around, into something funny. I'm not afraid to laugh at myself, never have been. Some people can do it, but most people can't. I look for laughter when there is none there. I try and create it from nothing. There is nothing better than laughing until your sides hurt, gasping for breath you might wish you had saved, when your time finally comes, and your "birth certificate" is about to expire. I'll laugh at anybody and anything, so I give everybody the right to stand before me and throw the lowest punch, if it creates an unforgettable moment, because believe me, if I make it my decision to tear into you in the name of laughter, then your bones will smell of me.

Now this is where I don't get it, because the lads were exactly the same as me. With seven of us, you would have expected a couple of us to be tuned to a different station. One of us at least. I would enter a room, and find Steve and Andy doubled up with laughter, and I would immediately feel left out. I needed to know, because I knew that I would end up in exactly the same state as them, if only I could unlock the fucking box. I didn't know if it was me, I didn't care if it was me, just please let me in.

Looking back, it was weird. From the day this planet was created, be it from a scientific or religious viewpoint, our course was set. Our genes survived in whatever outlived the Dinosaurs, until they emerged as Homosapiens, millions of years later. Somebody related to me has fought with a Sabre toothed Tiger. My genes were around at the time of the Bible. I've been carried through Stone Age man, and I was doing fine when the Romans ruled Europe. I survived plagues and the Saxons. Two world wars couldn't prevent me from arriving, although it is evident that my genes didn't take the path that Mozart's and Beethoven's took. Bearing this in mind, we all ended up, sat farting in the same fucking van, at the exact same time. We could have missed each other by centuries, but we didn't. Drunken fuckwits, or cosmic Musketeers on astral horseback? I guess we'll never know. Now where did I put my fucking beer?

The following Wednesday I was back in the "Banshee", only this time I crept downstairs when I needed to take a leak. Malc spotted me and came over. I could see what was coming, I was going to have to shell out a fucking fortune for the beer I supped the previous week, and then get some "earache", for not honouring my word. Like a "Gent" he just checked that I was ok, and bought me a beer. I met a girl later in the evening, and I offered to give her a lift home, just in case. I parked at the end of her street, and without a word she unzipped my jeans, and set about me like I was a fucking strawberry Cornetto. I was close to boiling point, and my cowboy boots resembled something from the "Curly toed slipper Emporium of Old Baghdad." As I grunted and twitched, she sat upright;

"This is where I finish."

"What… you don't sw…"

"No, I don't."

I had to take desperate measures, so I kicked off my boots and yanked at my socks. I got them off just in time, and avoided making a mess of my car. She looked at me in silence, as I rolled my socks into a ball. I couldn't say,

"Here, hold these."

So, I wound the window down, and fucking launched them into the night air. I pity the old tramp that thought his luck was in when he found them, as a sockless toe pointed through his worn out old boot. The girl gave me a kiss on the cheek, said goodbye, and I roared off into the night, like Don Johnson in "Miami Vice."

"Pssst. Hold on. What about the tattoos?"

"What?"

"The tattoos. Tell them about the fucking tattoos."

"Fuck off."

"Come on, it's Rock n' Roll."

"Are you sure? Are they fuck."

"Yeah, you'll be fine."

Well that's that then. I've just talked myself in to telling you about tattoos. I didn't want to, because they are stereotypical of rockers, and for years were the biggest expression of a need to feel tough, by insecure blokes. However, tattooing turned into the art form it always has been, given a huge boost when girls entered the periphery of a male dominated world, as the appeal of ancient rituals and tribal markings sat next to hair and nail appointments. Rob had a pale green star on the top of his "tossing" arm, while I sported Paul Stanley's rose that looked like some fucker had tattooed it with their foot. We spent a couple of years just laughing and taking the piss out of each others pathetic attempt to make a statement. We wound each other up, over our dire attempts to establish ourselves amongst the tattooed elite of the hard rock industry. It soon became blatantly clear that this just wouldn't do.

Not only would it not do, it was a fucking embarrassment. The continual pummelling, of insults and ridicule took its toll and I soon began to resent my tattoo, and pretty soon came to hate the fucking thing. We were soon avoiding getting undressed in front of each other. Fuck off, I mean getting changed for a gig, alright? Things were going to have to change, and the choices were to have laser surgery, and effectively pay out cash, in addition to the original cost of the tattoo, and end up with fuck all. Either that, or shell out more cash, for more ink, for more credibility, for more coolness, for more great photos, for more girls.

Big noises were being shouted around the A.O.K. rehearsal room, and the threat of putting our money where our big fucking mouths were, was gaining momentum. One Saturday afternoon, we met up at the room to run through the set, tightening up for an imminent gig. As soon as we got in the place, Rob was into me about the fucking flower on my arm.

"Well it's better than your fucking star my friend."

"What star?"

"That fucking green thing on your arm."

"What green thing?"

He took his jacket off to reveal a brand new tattoo, covering his old green star. It was the American pin up, Betty Page, amidst a swirl of colours, with a twisting musical stave wrapped around her, and notes scattered all about it. Bastard. He swaggered right up to my face.

"Right then. What have you got to say about that fucker, you soft "rose armed" twat?"

"Well you've nailed my hat on good and proper there, haven't you, you sly fucker."

Fugsy opened a can of beer, lit a fag, and took his jacket off. He was also sporting a new tattoo that consisted of an exploding keyboard with notes and colours shooting out everywhere. My jaw dropped. Rob kicked more fucking dust in my face, by telling me that the musical notes on his arm were the vocal melody of "Gunpowder, gelatine, dynamite with a laser beam."

Enter Louis Molloy, tattooist to the stars, pervert of the parish, and spectacle wearer of the year 1993. If you're interested, Janet Street-Porter came second, and Christopher Biggins came third. Louis is a modern day Michelangelo. He's Van Gogh with perfect hearing, and a straight hat. He's Salvador Dali without the moustache. He's Albert Einstein without those daft fucking glasses....hold on a minute, fucking scrub that one. What I mean is, he's a clever cunt. Louis is one of the busiest most celebrated tattooists on the planet, never mind in England, and despite his demanding schedule, we managed to forge a friendship with him. He tested the term "friendship" regularly, by threatening to lean on the needle, if we gave him any lip, or to double the fucking price, if we didn't stop taking the piss.

We soon learned when to take the piss and when not to take the piss. For me, the best time to piss Louis off was when Rob was in the chair. This meant that Rob suffered for every bit of shit that was thrown Louis' way. There was an eerie reverence to Louis' shop, as people gulped and sweated in silence, waiting to be stabbed, hurt, and then fucking well charged for the pain they endured. One day, a lad poked his head around the door, and the bell clanged away. The place was packed, but silent, and everybody turned their heads towards the door. A guy reluctantly entered the studio and shouted to Louis.

"Excuse me. Do you tattoo knobs?"

Louis was deadpan in his delivery.

"Yeah, what do you want?"

Classic. Louis' reputation was, and still is, legendary, and that's why we waited three weeks for an appointment. Sure, I could get the fucking thing done tomorrow anywhere else, but we did a lot of research when finding a tattooist, and it was blatantly obvious to us where our choices lay. Louis is the best, so there's not even a fucking argument there. It's simple, if you want the best, you'd better pay the man, because if you don't, you are gonna be stuck with a tattoo you hate, for the rest of your life. Rob embraced the world of tattooing totally, and ended up with a full back piece. However, his back is that fucking humped, it looks like it has been tattooed on an open parachute.

We wound up at a couple of tattoo conventions with Louis, just to give him somebody to moan at really, while me and Rob got leathered, whilst shouting "Louis Molloy" at the top of our voices for two days. Now then, as you might expect, a tattoo convention is a fucking eye opener of an experience, even for the most travelled man on this clump of planet floating in the middle of nowhere. The event was held in Dunstable in Bedfordshire, and it was brilliant.

When we opened the door to go into the place we were greeted

216

with the sight of the meanest, dirtiest, hardest looking set of fuckers you have ever laid eyes on. I gulped as the door closed behind me, and I was thrust into a world that had existed for years without my intervention, so why did I need to be there now? If it had been a pub, I'd have slammed the door, and run as far away as my little legs would have taken me. However, once inside, a crowd of "Hells Angels" approached me and said in unison, "Hey, shit hot tattoos." There was no punch, or bike chain around the back of my head, and I suddenly felt at home. I even managed to smile at them, as I tried to control my heartbeat. It turned out to be the friendliest weekend I have ever spent, as strangers tapped beer bottles with us, in respect of the time and effort Mr. Molloy had put in on our arms and backs.

While Louis' brow furrowed in concentration at the big tattoo he was desperate to finish, me and Rob stood at the bar, sharing a beer with the biggest fucking "Grizzly" bear of a guy you have ever seen, as he cried at our jokes. When he left, we chatted to an old Sailor, who was covered in ink, before we shared a litre of vodka with an Axe murderer who had yet to be caught. Slowly, we were getting accustomed to our new environment, as nipples, cocks, and labia were flashed freely for any fucker that possessed a camera, film in the fucker or not. What eventually made me question everything, was a guy I met in the foyer. He must have been eighty-five years old, and he was pushing a metal supermarket trolley. He had fuck-all on, except his white Y-Fronts, and his slip on shoes. Inside the trolley were the rest of his clothes, neatly stacked. What I couldn't deal with, was the fact that he didn't have one fucking tattoo on his body. And that fucker was somebody's grandfather. All of a sudden, it was time to go.

They say that you should never scrimp on the cost of your bed or your shoes, because if you are not in one, you are usually in the other. Well, my advice for your life is that if you ever decide to get a tattoo, get the best, no matter what it costs. Oh, and shag as many absolutely filthy young ladies as you possibly can, whenever you can. I hope you are paying attention, because I don't want you blowing the dust off this fucking thing twenty years down the line, saying to yourself, "Now how come I don't remember reading that bit before?", as you are sat there married to the only girl you ever fucked.

# CHAPTER THIRTY ONE

## *"Just A City Boy"*

I'm not a mind-reader, but I know exactly what you are thinking. I was just thinking the same.

"What the fuck's happened to his band, did they get off their arses and play any gigs? Is this a different book?" Well forgive me for a moment, because I don't always know where this fucking thing is going to take me, and I think that is a great quality to add to something that I'm trying to make as honest as possible. As I write this, the spellchecker is going fucking wild, with vast swathes of red and green shooting across the screen, but after reading everything again, I'm happy with it, so what am I supposed to do? By saying that it's great to go off at tangents, I'm obviously doing the whole fucking thing arse uppards, and any writer looking at this will think I'm a complete twat, but it's the way I need to tell it. I could write it like none of us swore, to make it a little easier on the eye but we are all working class, and swearing goes with the territory, along with honesty, humour and irony. I loved the guys because of their rough edges, and the way we bared our souls to each other, not because of what we held back. We couldn't be from anywhere else, other than the city, no matter how hard we tried. Not that we wanted to be from anywhere else.

You don't get that with the middle or upper classes, you can't. They are too preoccupied with keeping a bloodline going to have any fucking fun at all. Big old crumbling houses that they can no longer afford to keep, with a coat of arms over the door, and some dodgy sherry in a decanter. Well, times have changed, and these twats are reliant upon us. These fuckers are unscrupulous vagabonds with a few acres to their name, and not a pot to piss in, so do you know what they do? They designate a couple of rooms in their house that they will open up to the public. Then they apply for a "Lottery" grant to bring the place up to scratch. Once they get the grant; and some of these fuckers have their fingers in the "Camelot" pie, so they decide who gets the grants; they have a complete new roof, and any building work that needs doing. Then they shoe-horn you into a couple of rooms, while you pay for the privilege, as the value of their estate doubles, thanks to our very kind donation. Yes you've worked it out; you don't need me to tell you. Cunts.

I would love to be a fly on the wall, when these young "dotcom" multi-millionaires turn up at their mansions, with their arses hanging out of their jeans, ready to buy the place for cash. They are the only people who can afford to alleviate the tweed wearing twats of their crippling debt, and then turn the fucking place into "Manumission", complete with the foam cannons and naked girls. Don't be surprised, "The meek shall inherit the Earth", apparently.

Glyn had been slogging away, and lined up more gigs. Cannock, Ashton, Newbury, Stoke on Trent, Stockport, Birmingham, and Workington, again. I didn't need to worry about finding my passport. I had a fucking perm on the picture anyway, so it was a bit of a blessing. Glyn received a telephone call from one of the researchers from Radio One. To be precise it was a researcher from Tommy Vance's "Friday Rock Show." Glyn hadn't sent a tape, but somehow they came into possession of a copy of the tape we made in Cardiff. The woman asked Glyn if she could use our tape in the "Battle of the Bands" competition, in particular, the track "Two Souls." Glyn agreed, and we took off on the road again. If you've been in a band, you know that getting your songs played on the local radio rock show is a fucking big deal, so when Radio 1 come knocking, you can forgive yourselves for getting legless on the back of it.

Anticipation, I fucking love it. It can lead to everything, or fuck all. Of course, it can also lead to some point in between, but to get the full effect, it has to be one extreme or the other. A ship without a rudder that you think you can steer. You don't have to try and steer it, nobody asked you to, but once you have made that decision to try, then the success or failure that befalls you is entirely in your hands, because you grabbed the fucking wheel. Well, I steered me and Rob into the hairdressers for starters, to get more blonde in our hair, just in case there were any surprise photo calls to negotiate. Then we were off down to "Affleck's Palace" in "downtown" Manchester, for a shopping trip, looking for waistcoats, washed out jeans, and bangles. We've never been ones

219

for sleeping in our own piss, or smelling like sweaty tramps, so we took care of it. We had several changes of clothing, all designed to turn pretty young female heads. On occasions, things got out of hand in town. Me and Rob wound each other up all the time about who had the longest hair.

After one afternoon in "Affleck's", we wandered around Market Street, asking young ladies if they had a few minutes to spare, just like these canvassing, double-glazing flogging, 0% credit card promising, save the seal whingeing, join my sect sodomising, freedom for Palestine/we hate Marks & Spencer faced twats, are doing nowadays.

Rob; "Excuse me love, can you spare us a minute?"

Girl; "Yes."

Rob; "Right my lovely, I'm probably wasting my fucking breath here, as it is clearly obvious to me; but would you take a good look, and tell me which one of us Rock gods has the longest hair. By the way, that is a fucking lovely skirt."

Girl; "Yours looks the longest."

Rob; "Eyes off my cock love, and concentrate on my hair if you will. It's flattering, but this is fucking serious."

Girl; "Well, your mate's hair is very long as well."

Me; "You've got to take into account, that this fucker has been staring at the sky while he's been speaking to you, so his hair looks longer because he's played his fucking trump card straight away. Anyway, I take it you are a lap dancer with those legs?"

Rob; "Watch out, he's a fucking snake. Don't listen to him, or the next thing you know, you will be in a fucking cubicle in Debenhams changing room, holding on to the coat pegs for dear life. So, mine is definitely the longest is it?"

Girl; "Well it's hard to tell. Does it really matter?"

Rob; "It certainly does my dear. Are you half Italian?"

Me; "While you are looking at my friend, may I point out his boots? If you take a closer look, it is obvious that either boot will fit either foot. Fucking remarkable isn't it?"

Rob; "Yes, and if you take a look at my friend's tan cowboy boots, it appears that he has no fucking boots on whatsoever, the ginger cunt."

The girl looked at her watch and said her bus was due, and wandered off, as we traded insults like two hookers arguing over their patch. Motorhead would have laughed their unwashed bollocks off at us, and then supped all our beer, before beating the shit out of us.

It didn't matter, Glyn had secured us a date on the Friday Rock Show, and we were confident things were about to change. I never studied Glyn at work, but I can see now that there was a work ethic he followed every time we had a gig. First and foremost, he knew that a gig was a chance to get away for a while and have a laugh, and nobody loves a laugh more than "Jonesy." Nobody. Secondly, he knew that once we were together, we would let our guards slip, and he could infiltrate us like a fucking Stealth Bomber, while planting seeds in our minds which would ultimately lead to our self-destruction, as the "Y-Front" wearing, smiling assassin revelled in his finely honed alcoholic battle plan. In layman's terms, we supped what he poured and paid for it dearly. He had no pretension that he was an "industry" mogul on his way up, or some maverick Svengali that was bent on getting us to the top. He knew that A.O.K. was a release from the shit that we all dealt with on a daily basis, but, just like us, he believed that there was a chance. None of us realised how slim that chance was, but we were all convinced that there was one. He is a rock fan, who loves his music with a passion. He loves drinking, he loves laughing, and he loves taking the piss out of those he loves. He can spot a twat ten bus stops away, and he lets them know by the ninth.

Glyn likes "people watching", and forming gangs within his own band. Innocent enough. Everybody passes the time of day with their noses in every other fuckers business; it's the way of the World. Gangs? Great, kind of schoolboyish, but this time with hand picked mates, and no outsiders. The trouble starts, when "Jonesy" has been watching you and you are not in his gang. Woe betide, if you have a nasty zit, or a badly cut fringe, or, God forbid, a fucking girlfriend that he has taken a dislike to. Well, you guessed it; I suffered all three in the same fucking week. It wasn't a big spot, but that's like saying my fringe wasn't that bad, or the girl wasn't that much of a fucking nutter. I can protest all day long, but "Jonesy" dismissed me completely, as a "Singing Detective" faced "Hog Humper" with a "Spinal Tap" fringe. I tried to stand my corner, but there were six in his gang, and I was on my own.

Thirdly, and most importantly, Glyn is not a shirker. Well, if you're talking about lugging amplifiers up and down stairs, of course he was. Honestly, there was only me that ever put my back into anything. They were a lazy set of twats, I can tell you. No, Glyn dug deep in the name of the band, and spent more than all of us, topping up the coffers when we needed it. If anything needed to be paid for, it was always split seven ways, and if we were still short, he bunged the rest in.

I've spent some fucking money in my time. I had an Ibanez guitar, a Kramer pointy headstock thingy, my candy apple red Charvel, and a custom built white explorer, just like Stanley's on the "Destroyer" tour. And that's not including the Epiphone, and a couple of battered old acoustics. Oh, and a fucking "Hondo II" Les Paul copy, which I had to play upside down. No, the fucking guitar was upside down, not me, you daft get. It just goes to show what a daft twat I was. "Strats" looked cool upside down, copy or not, and were the obvious choice for anyone with a couple of brain cells. Oh no, I talked myself out of the aesthetics and logistics of a symmetrical guitar, and fucked up good and proper as I struggled with an upside down Les Paul. Now just stop for a second and try and picture an upside down Les Paul. Fucking ridiculous isn't it? Now then, slowly introduce the "ginger" hair into the picture, and the guitar doesn't look so bad does it? Then there were several amps and combo's along the way, before ending up with a Marshall stack that was bigger than me.

I couldn't move for effects pedals, which were replaced with a state of the art Digitech GSP5 processor. The week after I bought the GSP5, they brought out the GSP10, which did everything the GSP5 did, with fucking knobs on, and was valve driven. It was a fucking beast of a unit that made me want to sling my transistor powered piece of junk as far as I could. The upshot of all this, is that the cost of the GSP5 was slashed by half, and I could have saved myself a few hundred quid, had I been in a coma for a week. Me and that fucking "Green cross code" eh. I knew it would come to no good. I also had a Nady 201 wireless system, just so that I could hang over the edge of the stage and give you that little bit more of me. How thoughtful. Throw in the cost of rehearsal rooms, accommodation, recording, petrol, van-hire, photos, beer, condoms, the fucking list goes on, and you have one skint sex god.

Taking all of this into account, Glyn matched me pound for pound, and then some. That's what I love about "Jonesy." He didn't need to put anything in the pot, he only had to book the gigs, and split the cost of everything between us, but he wanted to be a part of what was going on, and that meant feeling every high, and every low. So, besides his unquestionable commitment, you can see that the basis of his work ethic was to make sure we were drunk, and preferably in a vulnerable position so that he could lay waste to anyone he chose, with his hand-picked posse, illegal Polish vodka, and the odd bag of gold.

The gigs were great, but we were kinda stuck at the same level. Some of the places were packed, mainly because they were "rock" clubs, so people were there anyway, but we always went down great. Some places were less busy, but we always won people over. Glyn had bags of letters from people all over the place that had seen us and enjoyed it so much, that they kept in touch. The press never got behind us, and we naively believed that the public would make the difference, and force the press to accept us. The closest we ever got was on Alan "Fluff" Freeman's rock show on Radio 1, one Saturday night. Somebody sent a letter to him, asking if he'd play something by A.O.K. His reply went like this;

"A.O.K? Never heard of them. Here's some Iron Maiden instead."

It was clear, that gigging alone wouldn't take us to the next level which we craved, which we fucking deserved. When Glyn finally got the call from the "Friday Rock Show", confirming the date we would be on, we decided to celebrate a bit. Rob invited everybody round to his house for a few beers, while listening to us wipe the floor with the competition. We didn't know who the other bands were, we didn't care. They were up against "Two Souls", and they should be afraid, very afraid. Vodka, beer and pizzas were divvied up between us, and as long as you turned up with at least one of them, you were guaranteed a piece of floor to sleep on, and a fucking headache the next morning. On the Thursday, the day before, I phoned Glyn.

Me; "Glyn, I'm not going to Rob's tomorrow night."

Glyn; "Why, what's wrong, you soft cunt?"

Me: "I'm going out."

Glyn; "Fucking hell, it's not some tart, is it?"

Me; "No, I'm going to see Vixen at the "International II.""

Glyn; "For fuck's sake, they're shite. Come on lad, let's go and get drunk."

Me; "No, I've sussed it out. There will be nobody there, so I'm gonna stand right at the front and get noticed by them. I'll get invited backstage, and I'm gonna fuck that dirty singer, or the guitar player."

Glyn; "You're fucking dreaming. You'll be lucky if you can pull the drummer."

Me; "Fuck off, you'll see."

Friday night was a big hair night, even by my standards. Chewing gum, mouth wash, condoms, and an arsehole you could have eaten your fucking supper off. I squeaked into the "International II" and handed over my ticket. As I climbed the steps, I came to a halt. The cause of the grimace painted on my face, was split 50/50, between the size of the crowd, and the stinging arsehole rammed inside my jeans. The place was sold out. Every pox-riddled fucker with long hair and a knob had turned up with exactly the same plan as myself. Balding, short-arsed, big-toothed, no-toothed, one-toothed, dandruffed, cross-eyed, lug-eared, sex gods, blocked my way to the stage in their hundreds. These fuckers had been wanking over their Vixen album covers earlier the very same night, and they were full of themselves because the album covers hadn't resisted them earlier. Phantom of the Operas in frilly shirts, the fucking lot of them.

The singer and the guitar player looked like porn stars, but I couldn't get close. I considered feigning fainting, but I would have just been dumped on the street rather than being taken backstage, so I nuzzled into a space at the bar and drank like a bastard. I met a few lads that I knew, and I accused them all of being sad old wankers, who were only there because of some preposterous idea that they could actually get to fuck the girls out of the band. By accusing them of this ridiculous charade, they immediately knew the reason I was there. I supped up and fucked off, knowing that I couldn't hang around after the show, because these fuckers now had me sussed completely. Any failure on my part would have been round "Rockworld" like wildfire. The next morning, Glyn phoned me.

"Hey Tony, we came last."

"Fucking tell me about it."

It didn't have to be this way. There was an alternative ending, where I woke up in between the singer and the guitar player, in a "Vixen" sandwich, with Glyn on the phone telling me that Phonogram were so impressed with what they heard on the radio, that they were flying up to try and sign us. That's not too much to ask for, is it? There are bands the World over that have all experienced that. Different girls and different record labels I will admit, but it's all the same when the legends are written. "Saying" and "doing" are so far apart, they're not on the same scale. While I'm writing this, some lucky twat is lying on a yacht somewhere on the planet, with the sun on his back, and half a dozen beauties parading naked in front of him, believe me. I'm just stopping for a second, while I go get another ice cold beer from the fridge and reflect on the last sentence, then take a good fucking slurp while I salute that man.

If destiny is a predetermined course of events, then I wish it had a fucking mouth as well. Then at least, we would have known that on our particular board, the snakes outnumbered the ladders, ten to one. More importantly, we would have been armed with the foresight, that the Def Leppard/Captain Scarlet headsets we used at the Wheatsheaf" in Stoke on Trent, were a rock and roll faux pas, for which we should have been kicked senseless. It played havoc with my hair, and lasted two songs before I slung the fucking thing as far as my "Charles Hawtrey" arms would allow. We were all handed a headset each, convinced it was the future of a world of rock, zooming towards the 21st Century. There are loads of pictures knocking about from this gig, but not one of us have got the fucking things on. You can only take so many lads laughing into their pints, can't you? Somebody probably got six headsets for a right fucking bargain the next morning, on a cold Stoke market.

You may be thinking that radio had the last laugh at my expense after that fucking performance on the "Friday Rock Show", but I don't lie down that easily. It happened many years later when time was no longer an issue, and in fact, happened twice, within a very short period. The first time was during 1998, as England prepared to go to France for the "World Cup." After a dismal tour of America, they returned home after losing to the U.S.A. Ray Cokes had some competition on "Virgin" radio, to find a song which would apply to any of the teams entering the competition. I opened a bottle of vodka that Sunday evening, and listened to the rubbish being offered up. It was fucking nonsense, the lot of it, and the best they could choose, was some twat saying that if France won the "World Cup", and sang "We are the Champions" at the end, then they would really be singing "We are the mushrooms." Yes I know, I was supping the fucking vodka from the neck of the bottle by this time, as I fumbled for an out of focus phone.

"Hello, you're through to Virgin."

"What's all this fucking nonsense about mushrooms?"

"Well, it's the best we've had tonight."

"It's fucking rubbish."

"Well have you got anything better?"

"Of course I have, put me on air."

"It's not that simple. Although there is a time delay, I need an assurance from you that you won't swear on air."

"Will I fuck."

"Are you drunk?"

"What do you fucking think?"

"Well what have you got?"

"Do you know Supercalafragalistic?"

"Yeah."

"Well, my song goes,

> Super Gazza, Beckham chipped it, Shearer was ferocious
> Even though the warm up games were something quite atrocious.
> Hoddle's with the psychic, and they're talking hocus pocus.
> Super Gazza, Beckham chipped it, Shearer was ferocious."

Obviously, I was declared the winner outright, and they wanted the whole fucking rhyme printed on T-Shirts in time for the World Cup. Consequently, I could choose any CD's I wanted from their extensive back catalogue. Neither materialised, so I decided to retire from the world of radio.

That is, until I tuned in one night, to hear Uri fucking Geller conning the whole country, thirty years after he started this fucking charade. Of course it was to do with your old watches that hadn't worked for years. Spoons and fucking watches. His routine had never changed, and he was still making cash out of this sideshow. Only in England eh? I bet he's been kicked the length and breadth of every other country he's ever tried this heist in. Anyway, apparently, if you stared at your radio this particular evening, then your fucked watch would be as good as new. People phoned in, until they were told that "Uri" had now left the building. I phoned "Virgin" and told them my watch was ticking again. They passed me through to the D.J. straight away.

"So Tony, I believe your watch has just started ticking again, after "Uri" weaved his magic."

"No."

"Oh, well what happened?"

"Nothing."

"Sorry?"

"Nothing."

"Well why have you phoned?"

"Well, when you said "Uri" has now left the building, I hope it was by the fucking scruff of his neck, with a security guard behind him, the fucking time waster. We could have had some Van Halen on instead of him, the fucking loon."

The line went dead, but I had spoken for the nation.

Anyway, back to the story. By now, Glyn had somehow managed to wangle his way on to the books of a company called Trinifold Travel. Apparently, they were something to do with the "Who", and were set up to provide decent accommodation for bands travelling around the country. He was given a reference number, and he could book us into decent hotels like the "Holiday Inn" for a fraction of the price. Now we were unsigned in style. Swimming pools, Jacuzzis, and hot tubs. We let huge, gassy, kebab tinged farts rattle around all of them, as bubbles of iniquity popped at the surface, leaving you gasping for air like you had just run a fucking marathon. Not only had our gigs turned into luxury nights out, but our social calendar also felt the benefit, as we booked into fantastic hotels for nights on the piss. We couldn't believe it. It was cheaper for us to stay at the "Holiday Inn" than it was for us to stay in a filthy shit hole in some city centre back street.

The first time we took advantage of the offer socially, we all went to Birmingham, for a night at "XL's", which was a fantastic place. Once the news broke out about Glyn's super deal, every fucker we knew was on the phone, trying to make sure they had a place in a car. It didn't matter, as long as there was enough cars, Glyn could book as many rooms as he wanted, at the giveaway price. It was like the "Wacky Races" as we roared down the M6, with all manner of long haired reprobate, drinking beer and showing their arses for the benefit of any car that contained a woman under 60. You're probably ready to flick the page, dreading the thought of reading a few paragraphs about people you don't know, getting pissed, and talking bollocks, but I'm with you on this, so I'll spare you, this time.

The highlight of the jaunt was on the Sunday morning, when the human wreckage was silent, apart from the snoring, and the odd fart. I was sharing a room with Rob, and we were woken by voices shouting outside. I opened one eye, and the clock said 8 O'clock. Rob stirred, and tried to ignore the noise. Now before you fucking start, we were in different beds. Anyway, the room was dark because of the blackout curtains, so we drifted off again. The voices got louder, and Rob jumped out of his bed. He slid the glass door open and I joined him for a nosey. There was a Canadian Ice Hockey team staying at the hotel, and they were standing on the street below, shouting up at a window. They were obviously trying to rouse one of their team from his slumber, and get the lazy bastard on the coach, which was waiting outside the hotel. After a while, a guy appeared on the balcony of the room directly below us, and he started shouting back at the crowd as loud as he could. Rob ran into the bathroom, and reappeared with the waste bin, which he had filled with cold water. The guy was still shouting to his team mates when Rob leaned over the balcony and shouted; "Oi."

The lad looked up, and Rob slung the bucket of ice cold water all over the fucker, as he gasped, spluttered, and then reeled backwards with the shock of the rude awakening.

"Now fuck off, I'm trying to sleep."

Rob shut the window, climbed into his bed, and went back to sleep.

"Rockworld" had only been open a few weeks, and I was leaving there one Saturday night, with a girl I had just started seeing. Tall, long blonde hair, fucking amazing hairstyle, great legs, cute ass, hard toned body, a fucking great figure, eyes that undressed you to the point of violation, and a pair of lips you could have snogged all night long. No wonder she fucking liked me. Alright, alright. Fucking hell, you can't have a laugh around here, can you? Anyway, I swaggered out of the place on to "Oxford Rd" in search of a taxi, with a pretty girl who was wearing tiny black lace see-through panties under her dress. There were a few lads hanging around outside, who were taking the piss out of the "rockers" leaving their shrine. One of these wankers came over to me and said, "Hey, which one of you is the girl?"

"Fuck off" was my unoriginal reply.

228

The lad stepped up to me, and something hit him full on in the face. He fell to the floor like a sack of shit, and he was out cold. Was I Bruce Lee? Did I move that fast, that even I couldn't see the speed of my lightning fists? I checked to see if I'd manifested myself into a gleaming suit of armour, and rushed gallantly to the aid of the young lady with the raging horn. Nope, I was still wearing a shirt; open to the waist, with one of my nipples on view to the world. Hey, hold on a minute, I had black leather fingerless gloves on. I checked the top of my head, to see if somebody had plopped "Rocky Balboa's" black leather pork pie hat on my head as well, which would account for the "Apollo Creed" type dusting I had just handed out. Nope, the answer wasn't there either. Mike Harris stepped from behind me, rubbing his fist.

"That's shut him up" he laughed.

Mike Harris is a gentleman, and is one of the fairest people you will ever meet. He has impeccable manners, hates injustice, and is very intelligent. He dresses in the smartest clobber, and drinks Budweiser until he falls over. I've never seen him start any trouble, but I've seen him come to the aid of the underdog, the outnumbered, the persecuted, the mocked, the bullied, and the unable, loads of times. When we started getting some decent gigs, Mike turned up at my house with a Marshall 4 x 12, as a present for me, to assist in my quest for stardom. Yes you read it right, a Merharshall ferhour berhy twerhelve. That was beyond friendship that fucking gesture, wouldn't you say?

Along with his brother Chris, he followed a regime of fitness and boxing training, which can ultimately be used for personal gain outside the gym, if you are ruthless, low in morals, and lazy. See? Criminals are basically lazy. They want what other people have got, but without having to lift a fucking finger in the process of obtaining whatever it is they want. They don't want to work for what they think they can take with a bit of force. Mike and Chris never chose this path, even though I suspect they could have, and this is because of honour. Having grown up with them, I know exactly where this comes from. It comes from their Mum and Dad. If you are loved, then compassion becomes a component of your make up, and once this is instilled inside you for as long as you can remember, then I don't believe that you can ever be a vindictive person. Having said that, Mike used to give me a big fucking knuckle duster to hide in my sock until we were inside

"Rockworld", because I never got searched on the way in. The reason he carried it was because he never knew what the idiots of today were carrying with them. Yeah, that was a concept I could deal with. What I didn't like, was the thought of getting my toes stuck in one of the fucking finger holes, while it was rattling around my cowboy boot. How would I have explained that one to Malc and the Fire Brigade?

The following Saturday, we were back in "Rockworld", and I was talking to a girl that I vaguely knew. Unbeknownst to me, she had been seeing a lad who was also in the club, and he stood behind me trying to attract her attention. Mike was at the bar, and he was handing cans of Bud back to the lads. Each time Mike passed a can through the crowd, this lad banged into Mike, forcing his arm crashing into a complete stranger. Mike asked the lad if he would move to one side, while he passed the drinks through the gap. Mike smiled, and was totally civil with him.

"Fuck off" was the reply he received.

Mike hit the lad with a can of Bud, and it exploded in his face. The lad wobbled, and Mike belted him again. He went down, and that was where his Saturday night ended. Never mind, there was always next week. Mike turned to me.

"What is it with you?"

"Don't fucking blame me. I'm just an innocent sex god, minding my own business. Anyway, was that my fucking drink?"

That wasn't violence; that was self-defence. Violence is instigated by the perpetrator, not by the innocent bystander. What Mike handed out was pre-emptive self-defence, but it was action that had to be taken. If Mike had capitulated, then it became bullying, and no fucker was going to bully him or any of us come to think of it. It's far better to get battered than to be bullied. It might hurt a bit more, but in the long run it won't, because you have made your stand, and the wanker's fifteen minutes of fame become their fifteen seconds of fame, and you are back to fucking the girls they kicked up the dust about, in the first place. Like I said, nobody bothered with us, but we're all aware that bullying comes from jealousy and feelings of inferiority, so, move it into the world of "rock", and "girls" is the obvious place it will manifest itself.

The following night, Mike phoned me and said he would pick me up for our Sunday night at the "Phoenix." I'd not been up long, so I jumped in the shower and washed last night's lipstick off various places. When he picked me up, Chris was in the car with him. Chris loved rock music, but he wasn't interested in going to rock clubs, so I was surprised when I saw him.

Me. "Fucking hell we are privileged."

Chris. "Shut it rocker, and get in."

Me. "Should I nip back in the house and get you some bangles?"

Chris. "Fuck off."

Me. "What about a bandana?"

Chris. "What about a slap?"

Me. "This fine evening Christopher, I want to see you shaking your head to some Van Halen, or "Whoah oah Black Betty bam ba lam."

Chris. "I believe you had some trouble last night."

Me. "No, not me. The lad that woke up with fag ash all over his hair, and a fuck off black eye; he had trouble, not me. Anyway, don't you know, "The damn thing gone wild, bam ba lam.""

Chris. "Well, he's gonna get some more tonight. And fucking shut it with the "bam ba lams", or you'll get a "dig" as well."

Chris opened his jacket and showed me a hammer. Now Chris is a lovely fella, but he's fucking mad. A lad that can display every fucking emotion on the planet in 60 seconds, and finish by planting a kiss on your cheek. He loves Van Halen, Guns 'n' Roses, and the Who, and he can dance the bollocks off Michael Jackson. For a while I thought he was going to join the fold, grow his hair, and get some snakeskin boots. He didn't, well, not publicly, but I'm sure he's got those snakeskin cowboy boots hidden away somewhere. Anyway, with me and Mike the way we were during the Seventies and Eighties, he couldn't fucking hide from "rock" if he tried, and he grew to love a lot of it. He fell for the "Who" big style, and in turn, introduced me to some great music. Late '78 early 79, we queued up at his turntable to get "Live at Leeds" played after "Love Gun", which to be honest, was a pretty shitty album, which had followed "Who are You?" However, tonight, he was going to hit somebody with a fucking hammer. He questioned me all the way to the "Phoenix."

"What did he look like?"

"Well, if I told you he was tall, slim, with long blonde hair; I'll probably get twatted with the hammer. So, I'll throw "ugly" into the description as well, just to fucking save myself."

Once inside, Chris questioned me about every lad that passed by, but he never showed. Luckily, the lad couldn't find his sunglasses that night.

# CHAPTER THIRTY TWO

*"In The Summertime, When The Weather Is Fine"*

I love women, I always have done. The stories recalled in this book show that. I didn't always wind up with the prize, but it didn't matter. Women are very intelligent, and it scares most lads shitless. Me? I wanted to learn, and I would always dig deep, trying to find out what they wanted. Women are a totally different entity to lads. If it's "hard", lads are happy, but women need more. It doesn't take much to make them feel special, but most lads are too fucking lazy to spend the time making any kind of effort. I knew from the start that women were in control, completely. Now I didn't know it at the time, but by knowing that simple fact, life was going to be a damn sight easier, where the opposite sex was concerned. I put it all down to propaganda. No, not propaganda, I mean a "proper gander" you fool. You know, a right fucking proper gander, either up a short skirt, or down a tight fitting top, my man.

Eyes. I was always attracted by a lovely pair of eyes. They let you into secrets about what the girls were thinking. If they could apply their eye make up correctly, girls could look as dirty or as innocent as they fucking well wanted. Each and every one of them. They say that your eyes are the windows of your soul. If that is correct, then it also stands, that your arse is the window of your hole. Your eyes may indeed tell a lot about you, but I think your hands give a deeper insight into the person that you are. For instance, if the knuckle of your middle finger stinks of shite, you are probably bored, and sat on your own. If the knuckle of your middle finger smells of "lady", then you have probably blown all your cash, and you are in a taxi with the said "lady", speeding back to her place. If the knuckle of your thumb smells of "lady", and your middle finger stinks of shite, you have probably gone that bit too far on your first date, and I suspect you are a "chancer." If all five of your knuckles on one hand smell of "lady", you are probably in the fucking taxi on your own, on your way home, after dropping her off, and declining the fucking "coffee", the dirty mare. Either that or you've been married to her for ten years.

It didn't matter how good you looked, or how funny you were, at the end of the day, it was the girls who said "Yes" or "No." They revelled in the power of being able to fuck your night up completely, by deciding whether or not, to let their "drawbridge" down. Some lads can't broach the subject for fear of embarrassment, but I've always been inquisitive where girls are concerned. Let me know, and I'll see what I can do. Women are funny, unpredictable, dotty, sexy, friendly, strong, vulnerable, and lovely. I have only ever used one chat up line, and it got me nowhere. It wasn't really a chat up line, but either way it fucking failed. I met a raven-haired young stunner in the "Banshee", and I had my sleeves rolled up, wallowing in the decadence that was the 80's. She had a thick mane of black hair, skin tight jeans, and a black leather jacket. Obviously I said "hello." She smiled, told me her name, I told her mine, and she asked what I did for a living.

"Me… I'm a lab technician."

"What, they let you work in a laboratory looking like that?"

"No, I mean labia. You know?"

I nodded at her jeans. She laughed, and although she liked me, she said she wouldn't fuck me for being so cheeky. I didn't get it. If you made them laugh, I thought it was guaranteed, with toast in the morning.

One night, I was at a party. I met a wistful, pretty young thing that took a liking to me. She led me out into the garden, and gazed at the stars. She was completely into the night and its secrets. The moon, the stars, the zodiac signs, the Universe. She loved it all. In fact, she couldn't contain her excitement, as she invited herself to tear at my jeans. I whispered in her ear as I lifted her dress.

"Have you ever seen a meteor?"

"Oh, yes, loads of them."

"Hold on, let me fucking finish love. Have you ever seen a meatier cock than this?"

Her answer was exactly the same as before, so I zipped up, and fucked off.

Another night, I was kinda set up with a girl, who maybe I should have stood my ground with and walked away, but she was tall, blonde, with a great figure, and I was drunk. A crowd of us went for a curry after "Rockworld", and I arranged to meet her the next night. This was during my "dry" period, and I was climbing the fucking walls. This was all self-inflicted, as I had made the decision to steer clear of anything permanent, either sexual or otherwise for a while, but on this particular occasion, I had let my guard down. I drove to her house the following night, and my guts were popping and fizzing, due to the spicy load rumbling around my stomach. I drove slowly down her street, searching for her house number. My car crawled to a halt, and I stopped under a street light. As I turned the tape off, I let go with the biggest, dirtiest fart my body has ever produced. It was the sweetest, hottest, longest abomination I have ever given birth to. You know the one, it fucking stank of lungs. I was wafting like fuck, when she opened her front door. She got the wrong end of the stick completely, and waved back with a beaming smile. She slammed her front door and ran to my car, acknowledging my over enthusiastic interest in her. She jumped in the car and said "hello". She didn't speak again, and I could see that she was holding her breath. Her face turned purple and she threw the door open, gasping for air. I broke the silence.

"Fucking hell, is that you? You fucking stink."

She laughed her head off, and then fucked my brains out. Slippier than the deck of a "Boston Whaler."

I don't know if you felt this way too, but it was fucking electrifying trying to contain the anticipation, which was the driving force behind a single lad's night out. It must be the same, no matter which clubs you go to, or the music you are in to. I wasn't shallow, well maybe I was, but I was only as shallow as the punk, rasta, rockabilly, or whoever, who went out to enjoy the music they loved, while hoping to get laid in the process. Now you tell me, if you can, what is wrong with that, and what is finer than that? Fuck all, that's what. Sometimes, you had to work at it. A stolen glance at the bar that turned into a game, seeing who could keep their cool the longest, before you admitted defeat and steamed in, threatening all sorts. Other times, you couldn't wait that long, as the animal inside the pair of you took over. There was no need for words; it was all in the eyes, as both sets of breathing got deeper. A great night in a great club could be made ten times better if there was a chance of casual sex thrown in. As you both edged towards the toilet, you knew how it was gonna turn out, but it was worth the wait, as the anticipation threatened to burst the very skull that contained your innermost, filthiest fantasies.

She didn't speak. She didn't introduce herself, or ask my name, nothing. She was pretty. "Mighty fine" they'd say in Texas. I looked over my shoulder, just to make sure she was looking at me. I shouldn't have bothered. I could tell by her eyes that it was me she wanted. This is the time when your mates can't help you, nobody can. Either you can deal with the situation less than five minutes away, or you can shatter your mate's illusion of you, and make excuses and a sharp exit, as they shake their heads in a huddle, expecting more, after you had "bigged" yourself up for months and fucking months.

Anyway, I handed my drink to the nearest guy, and followed the girl into the toilet. I don't know why, but it was always more comfortable taking a girl into the lad's toilets. The girl's toilets were totally alien, and made me feel like some kind of fucking pervy weirdo. Don't get me wrong, I'd be in there in a fucking flash if that was the only option, but "home territory" was always the battleground of choice. A bit of mutual appreciation for ten minutes, that's all we wanted, and then back into the club to a few "back slaps", or giggling looks of disbelief for the girl, from her girlfriends, and then a few more hours of rock. From what I can remember it was fucking fantastic. A dirty expert hand job mixed in with a porno style blowjob, followed by a good fucking fingering that lasted until each eye was looking at the other. Funny, but I can't remember what I did in return!

The chase was always exciting, but once I was ensconced in a relationship, I was yearning for the thrill of it all. I went to clubs with girlfriends, and felt resentful as I noticed a new gorgeous face standing on her own, or with her friends. However, I would have felt exactly the same if I had been with that particular girl, and a new beau appeared. I was confused, I couldn't figure out what I wanted. Then it came to me. I wanted it all. I put this down solely to my fascination with girls. There are few things better than making a girl howl with laughter. To see a girl laugh is a magical moment, especially if you have had some part in it. It showed me that I had crossed the divide, and I could feel just as comfortable as when I was talking to the lads. I fucking loved leaning into a girl's ear to speak, and being totally engulfed in their perfume, while being close enough to lick the soft skin on their sexy necks. To watch them pull away laughing, was a moment to savour indeed.

A lot of lads were far too serious when they met a girl. I know you have to make some kind of impression, but lads, and especially lads in bands, just talked about what they had done, or what they were doing. It was all "Me, me, me". I gauged my success by a girl's reaction to my tomfoolery. Laugh at them, laugh at me, laugh at anybody, but laugh at something. That was the key. There are ships at the North Pole that can't break ice like I did. Lads are basically insecure, and a lot of them use the terms "slag" and "easy" when referring to our heavenly opposite sex, especially the ones they don't stand a chance with. This shows their ignorance, misunderstanding, and fear of females. Everybody knows, lads are by far the "easier" of the species. Girls are very intelligent, and know that if they so wish, they can beat us hands down, if they choose to live a life of sexual excess. They know that they can go out every night, and do the same as the night before, because we are such gullible, tunnel-visioned fools. Lads became scared, because they knew that if they turned out to be a let down, after all of their preening and chest puffing, they would be crucified over a few white wine and sodas, while the girls watched a male stripper. We have nobody but ourselves to blame for this. We can't have it both ways. "Girl Power" has been around since Eve's fig leaf blew off in the wind, don't let the Spice Girls kid you.

Girls grow up far quicker than lads, so while we carry on like teenagers in our mid twenties, they advance to another level, while still being able to deal with our immaturity. I don't know if this is built-in to a woman's body, but I think they are equipped to deal with childish antics from an early age, to prepare them for motherhood. Lads take far longer to understand what is going on. As I write this, I am in my early forties, and I am only just advancing to the next level, after the teenage delinquent stage. Britney Spears? I'd rather go on Brittany Ferries. Now Anastacia… she's a different ball game entirely. Girls in the Eighties were glamorous, and I wanted my very own "videobabe." Sometimes I was lucky, but most of the time, well, you know me by now. All of a sudden, "politically correct" became the latest soundbyte, and girls in tight dresses and high heels were no longer relevant. Well in who's fucking book exactly? Because I know six other lads for starters, who loved them just as much as me.

Not counting Daisy Duke, the "Bionic Woman", and Chris Evert, I have fallen in love three times. All of them strong individuals, who had a staggering effect on me, and I can see a common link that drew me to each one of them. I know I could have fallen in love many more times given the chance, but it's all history now, and it was draining, especially as I had some kind of parallel musical agenda running most of the time. I always wondered, how many girls there were in the world that I would fall in love with, if time wasn't an issue, and geography wasn't a problem. There must be thousands and thousands. It's the same for everybody, including you, it must be. Anyway, the first time was during my late teens, and lasted almost four years. At the time, music was equally as important to me, and I experienced two fascinating journeys at the same time. The second time was when music was my total existence, and through no fault but my own, it was doomed. I shouldn't have started what I knew I couldn't finish. By the third time, I had grown up, slightly, and it is still going strong after thirteen years.

I met Mandy through the rock clubs, and we were married in 1997. Our paths crossed continually over the years, until one day, the stars were aligned, and for a split second in time, we could either deal with what was in front of us, or we could let it slip away forever. Luckily, she had the mind and the heart that gave her the strength to change our history. She is a lovely woman, who is beautiful from her very soul. She is the rock upon which my life is built, and she loves me far more than I deserve. I'm not really sure what I bring to the "table" that makes her stay there, and I know that "worlds" can turn upside down in split seconds, so I take nothing for granted. I don't own the girl, and we are together purely through choice, which is a fucking great thing. I can't see round corners, and I can't look into the future, but at this point I would be more than happy to die in her arms when I'm ninety-five years old. However, I am totally aware that "tomorrow" is another day, and she could quite easily be married to somebody she hasn't even met yet, for the last forty or fifty years of her life. The lucky man. Three times is more than enough for any man, and I feel blessed for the good fortune that befell me. Before this however, there was plenty of, as my dad puts it, "birding" to be done.

Although I was in a great band, had some great, great times, and met some lovely girls, I had a nagging obsession gnawing away at me all of my fucking waking hours. My thoughts were hijacked time and time again, by the vision of me, and two girls in a threesome. After all, history dictated that lads in bands got more than their fair share where girls were concerned. The hedonistic lifestyle totally appealed to me, and I knew that I was missing out on the one thing every straight guy dreams of, without considering for one fucking moment, whether I could actually manage it or not, if ever I was in that right place at that right time.

So, lets hear it for Tony Bell, who left "Rockworld" and climbed in the taxi, with two young ladies, who had called my bluff, when the conversation got around to sex. The taxi ride was like a game of "Twister" without the fucking mat, and my best mate was thrashing around, trying to get out and join in the fun. I ushered the girls up my stairs as quick as you like, and I went into the bathroom. I could hear the girl's voices getting louder and louder, as I scrubbed like fuck. They were arguing about who was going to go first, so I made my way out of the bathroom to calm them down. Me, trying to calm somebody down right at this moment in time? That's a fucking laugh. As I stepped out of the bathroom, my mum came out of her room, to see what the noise was. I shut my eyes and pretended I was sleep walking. She was having none of it. Mum and dad were cool with girls staying, but it was the bad language being shouted around the house that she didn't want to listen to. God help me when she reads this then. Anyway, she asked them to leave, so I strangled my best mate.

About two weeks later I met two girls who were rather posh, but were also rather dirty. They asked if I wanted to go for a ride after "Rockworld", and I was soon heading south out of Manchester towards Styal Woods. As long as my mum wasn't there, I reckoned I was sorted. The full moon shone on the big pair of breasts, as they were handed over to me in the back of the car, as we sped along Kingsway. By the time we got to Styal Woods I was threatening all sorts, and I very nearly phoned the fucking police to report myself. Like before, it had started well, but the decision on my part, to strip off and chase the girls in just my cowboy boots, bangles and waistcoat was my undoing. Not because the girls weren't up for it, oh no, this one was my fault. Being a clumsy twat, I slipped as I chased them and fell in a puddle, rolling around in the mud for far longer than planned. It was right up my back, in my hair, and all over my little shivering peach of an arse. It took them about fifteen minutes to stop laughing, as I pulled my skin tight jeans back over my cold, soaking wet, filthy legs. They dropped me off at home, still finding it hard to conceal their fucking schoolgirl sniggers. As I walked down the empty street with my shoulders shrugged, I noticed a can in the gutter, so I gave it a good fucking boot.

The first time I ever saw a girl's "cool" bits, I was about twelve years old. I was playing football in Didsbury Park, with a couple of lads from school. We stopped for a rest, and sat on the grass talking. One of the girls from our class came over to talk to us. As cool as you fucking like, Kevin Bissett asked her if we could have look down below. She said "yes", and we followed her into the bushes, where she pulled her jeans down. We stood there in silence, staring at the soft, downy, triangular mound. She said that we could touch it, and one by one, we cleared our dry throats, and rubbed, with no particular skill, or direction. I reeled back, like the fucking thing was going to bite me. I had no idea that there were any other parts to it. In total, we spent about ten seconds between us, touching it. Totally contented with our encounter, we strode out of the bushes as men, and carried on playing football.

"Was it 3 – 3?"

"No, 3 – 2, you cheating fucker."

I'm getting good at this, because I know what you are thinking, again. If there was sex and rock and roll, then there must have been drugs, mustn't there? Well, you're not wrong. I've had a few spliffs in my time, we all have. My problem is that I don't smoke, so it wasn't the easiest thing to adapt to, so I didn't. I've read about bands, whose sole existence was to get as fucked up as possible, on all manner of illegal cocktails, but I'm not the one to sit and pass judgement. Temptation is everywhere, be it a pussy or a needle, and it's down to the individual, where he lets himself get caught. To me it's simple. I'd rather have the blonde in the big shoes and short kilt every time, than a night of paranoia, shivering, and hallucinations. Having said that, cannabis is a mellowing experience, which I think everybody should try, at least once. Only then, can you make any kind of valid point about the argument for, or against. I've never once considered taking Ecstasy or Heroin, I can't think of anything worse. So, you can take your theory about cannabis leading to harder drugs, and shove it right up your tightly-clenched, half-wiped sphincter. I've lost count of the times I've sat in a pub with people who were smoking and drinking, slowly killing themselves, and polluting every other fucker in the process, while they pontificated about how cannabis would damage the social fabric of society, if it were legalised, the fucking hypocrites. They don't understand that it might as well be legalised. I don't know of anybody that wants cannabis, who can't get hold of it. The people that smoke cannabis are laughing at you, because they are smoking the biggest fucking spliff they can roll, whilst watching the latest "Newsnight", with some wanker telling the country that it's under control. You can appoint a drugs "Tsar", you can fill newspapers with "crackdowns", you can interview a "smackhead", and parade him around as some "media misfit", who probably had a shitty upbringing, but it won't go away. Some people will sit at home, smoking the fucking biggest spliff you have ever seen, listening to Steely Dan, with an ice cold beer or a nice glass of "red", while the rest will be out getting drunk, smashing glasses into each others faces. Hey, don't worry, this is legal. My mum is teetotal. Don't you get it?

The biggest hurdle has got to be taxation. The government receives huge revenues from fags and booze, but how would they create a department to collect tax on cannabis? It would cost millions and millions, just to set up. I have an "off the wall" idea, which I think would make a good film. If cannabis was legalised, then there would be designated outlets, and regulated prices. If the government could undercut the dealers, which they could, then millions of pounds would be diverted from the dealers, straight into the government coffers. Now, the dealers would be slightly pissed off with the "New Boy" invading their patch, as there was nothing they could do. Or is there? My idea revolved around a story, where the dealers got together, and decided that something should be done, to save their livelihood. A threat is made to the government, that if the legalisation goes ahead, then the Prime Minister will be assassinated. No, even worse, the Queen. The government can't back down, as the changes in the laws have been given Royal assent. What can they do? I'll tell you what they do. Tommy Lee Jones is hired from the "States", and he wipes every fucker out, before taking the bullet, like the hero he is. You can always count on Tommy!

# CHAPTER THIRTY THREE

*"All The Leaves Are Brown"*

My dog "Kerry" was a super little guy. I often wondered what he made of me, as he watched me change from a small kid, into a tall, long haired fella. Did he have any recollections going back that far? I don't know. You see, to me, he didn't change physically, not from him reaching the age of about two anyway, but me and Steve were shooting up, and changing daily. He must have been bored, because he turned into a thief. One day I looked out of the window, to see him shaking a small animal in his mouth. I was shocked, because he never had a nasty temperament, and also because he was so fucking lazy. Sometimes, when I took him for a walk in the park, he just lay down when he'd had enough, and wouldn't walk any further. Numerous times, I had to pick him up and carry him back home, like a tired toddler, who'd had enough for the day. Anyway, I dashed into the garden to rescue the poor creature, but when I got close it turned out to be a full roast chicken. I don't know where he got it from, but he was fucking loving it, so I left him to it. It made a change from the chewed up plectrums I used to find on the grass, on the morning of a gig.

My Nan lost her false teeth once, and she couldn't remember where she had left them. She tried retracing her steps, but she still couldn't find them, so we searched everywhere. "Kerry" was dozing in front of the fire, and we sat down to think of any places we might have forgotten. I was looking at the dog while talking to my Nan. His face looked strange, so I crouched next to him to take another look. As he turned towards me, I could see my Nan's teeth perfectly positioned over his own top row of teeth. I sat down next to the miniature Ken Dodd, and slowly prized the teeth from his jaws. When he stood up, I found the bottom set of teeth where he had been lying. When the laughing finally stopped, my Nan phoned the Dentist.

For once, I was early in plenty of time to catch the train to the

"Salisbury", so I sat and had a beer to pass the time. It was autumn, and "Kerry" had been rolling around in the soggy leaves. He nudged my bedroom door open, and came in to see me. While I was stroking him, I picked the leaves out of his fur, and dropped them in the bin. As I pulled the large leaf from his tail, I discovered that it was a flat piece of dog shit. I almost dropped my fucking beer.

"Aaaah fuck."

Kerry dropped his head, and pulled his tail between his legs. He knew exactly what it was, and left the room quietly. Heaving, I ran to the bathroom and washed off my "chocolate" glove. I went downstairs, and found him fast asleep in front of the fire. I gave him a pat on the head, and left him in his world of cats.

# CHAPTER THIRTY FOUR

*"Ring Of Fire"*

The band logo, which adorned our magnificent backdrop, was designed by our very own, "Sir" Steven of Kenny. Steve was the most "Bohemian" of the gang, and was always willing to lend his artistic bent to whatever it was, that was required to further our cause. Two hundred years ago, he would have been the dapper gent in the tall hat, with the long lacy shirt, gracefully nudging out of the sleeves on his elegant coat, as he stood scratching his bollocks in his tight britches. Steady ladies. He is the smiling gent, on those Christmas cards in the picturesque village, in a time before electricity was invented, when candle was king. That's right, the man with the scarf, and arms loaded up with presents. Simple wooden toys in the toy shop window painted in bright colours thrill the expectant children. Steve joins them at the window and they all smile as the glow of the candles adds a cherub like quality to every happy face. It's a pity that the Christmas card wasn't made later in the evening, showing Steve stumbling around "Ye Olde Inn" talking bollocks, while necking that fucking spirit with bits of gold floating around in it, showing his arse and knackers to all and sundry, while burping the alphabet. That's more like it. That's my Steve.

We decided that we needed some T-Shirts to sell to the punters, so after we all threw our two pennerth in, we walked away, leaving Steve to sort it all out. Steve was already a graphic designer, so he knew how to draw the fucking thing for a start. Also, he knew how to arrange the colours, he knew the suppliers, he knew the printers, and he knew if we were being ripped off. He was by far the most qualified man for the job, plus, it didn't help that everybody else was a lazy twat, and consequently, not really interested. Before we knew it, we had boxes of the fucking things, and not many gigs. We all had a few T-Shirts each, and so did everybody's girlfriend. Then we sat and stared at this big fucking pile of T-Shirts. We had gigs lined up, and we were confident we could shift the T-Shirts, especially as Steve got us a great deal, which meant we could sell them for three quid, and make a profit. Who could resist a top quality T-Shirt, for a fucking giveaway? Nobody, surely. We started gigging, and immediately found an inherent problem. I developed a nasty habit of walking around clubs when I was pissed up, telling punters that if they wrote to Glyn and bought a demo tape, then they could have a free T-Shirt. I thought nothing of it and stumbled happily around the clubs. I was sat at home one night, when Glyn rang me.

Glyn: "Alright?"

Me; "Yeah. What do you know?"

Glyn; "Well, I know that I received half a dozen letters today, all asking for demo tapes."

Me; "Shit hot."

Glyn; "No, it's not shit hot, because every fucking letter is also claiming the free T-Shirt that you fucking promised them."

Me; "Fucking hell Glyn, it's only a T-Shirt. It's a gesture, people will remember our name."

Glyn; "OK then, why are there no letters from any lads then? They're all from girls, you fucking snake."

Me; "I can't help it if girls talk to me. I can't make lads talk to me."

Glyn; "I wouldn't mind, the fucking things only cost three quid each."

He agreed to send out the T-Shirts with the tapes. The following night he phoned me again.

Glyn; "I've got another five fucking letters here, all implicating you in the great fucking T-Shirt giveaway. And guess what? Not a fucking fella in sight. I hope you got laid for this."

Me; "No Glyn, nothing."

The next evening, the phone rang again.

Glyn; "Are you having a fucking laugh?"

Me; "What's wrong now?"

Glyn; "Another five fucking letters, that's what's wrong."

This carried on for a while, and Glyn sent out the "soon to be" dusters, free of charge.

London beckoned. Glyn got us another gig at the "Marquee" so I went down a couple of weeks before, handing out flyers with him. The tiny area of Soho was the centre of the music and film industry, with offices stacked on top of each other, in alleyways you could barely get your fucking shoulders through. Ghosts of British rock darted through the shadows behind us, sneering and ridiculing our pathetic attempt to convince the people in the know, that we were the next big thing. The date on the calendar in the Greek café on Wardour Street may have changed, but the present was only there because of the past. People eeked out a living from entertainment, which supported whole families, even though they were nothing to do with music or films. Be it the Greek, who fed the secretaries of the conglomerates, or the sandwich shop assistant who sold a sarnie and a can of cola to the runners and motorcycle couriers. Or the street cleaner who picked up the fag packet, slung out of the window of the Jag, of the president of "so and so" records, or the traffic warden who stuck a ticket on that fucking Jag, right down to the drug dealer who crept upstairs and made the deal without uttering a word.

Everybody was there because Hendrix had been there, because the Kinks had been there, because "The Yardbirds" had been there, because "Clapton" had been there, because "The Who" had been there, because the "Stones" had been there, because "Floyd", "Purple", "Lizzy", "Free", "Queen", "Slade", and "Bowie" had all been there. Oh, and me and the boys. Midweek "fillers" maybe, but if there was a book containing every single person who had played at the "Marquee", and it was in alphabetical order, then you would see my name before you saw "Gilmour", "Mercury", "Hendrix", "Daltrey", "Lynott" "Jagger", "Naylor", and "Kenny." And no matter how insignificant I am, how much you hate this book, or how wank you thought my band was if you know me, there is fuck all you or anybody else can do to change that fact. Fuck all.

A few companies said they would come to the gig, but the general consensus was, that "Ozzy" was playing in London the same night, so there was somewhere else for people to be. We knew people would have their priorities, and quite fucking right too. I nearly went along to see him myself. A couple of A&R men turned up, but nobody was waving cheque books, well, apart from us lot waving them at Glyn, to pay for our merry fucking jaunt. I wasn't ready for going home afterwards, so Rob joined me in a crawl around a few bars before heading for the "St Moritz" club. Glyn was a bit pissed at us, because we had a gig at "Derby Hall" in Bury the next night, but mainly because he had to work the next day, so he couldn't spend the night in London on the lash. We told him we would be on the dinnertime train back to Manchester, so he agreed to pick us up at "Piccadilly" station. Glyn was stony-faced, as we waved him off, laughing with two fucking over priced bottles of beer in our hands.

We met up with a girl from Manchester who was living in London, and who had turned up at the "Marquee." We went for a few beers with her and a few of her mates, who turned out to be strippers, who had been working earlier in the day, at the same peep show where we had been ogling away, while fiddling with our small change. It's a small fucking world isn't it? I didn't recognise any of them, because I couldn't see any of their faces earlier in the day, as we had to stoop to peek through tiny letterboxes, in a makeshift wooden wall. The baby oil had long since been wiped from their curvy bodies, and they were no longer "dildo" dartboards.

Of course, it was "Jonesy" who diverted us into this den of iniquity, after a few pints and a sound check. We mingled in between grimy, smelly, dirty old men in macs, with wispy grey hairstyles, which up to that point, I thought was a stereotype for the unloved, sexless, middle-aged, socially defunct loner. These fuckers had no dignity at all, as they elbowed past the young upstarts for the prime wanking, drooling, letching positions. To my surprise, the place didn't smell of old man's "wrist chowder" like I had anticipated. No, it stank of shite, like these bastards hadn't washed their arses for months on end. Fucking disgusting the lot of them. "Old Holborn", beer, and shit, not the obvious bouquet to choose when meeting a young lady dressed in her finest sexy lingerie. Then again, there was a screen between the girls and the punters, so the rancid stench may not have been so pungent for them. It couldn't have been, or else they would have fucked off and slung the cash back at the smelly twats. No, that fucking smell was reserved for the fools on the wrong side of the screen.

Back in the "St Moritz" club, we sat and had a few beers with the guitar player from Love/Hate, while listening to his booming narcissistic drawl. Not that he was interested in me and Rob in the slightest; it was purely for the simple reason that he wanted to fuck one of the strippers who was sat with us. My plan for the night only involved the girl from Manchester, as we needed somewhere to sleep. Sure enough, she invited us back to kip at her place, so we jumped in a taxi and headed out to New Cross. We turned up at Euston the next day and slumped into our seats, on our way home.

Hold on, what happened between getting back to her flat, and getting on the train at Euston? It's not like me to skirt around great sexual marathons, fuelled by alcohol, hold-up stockings and perfume, is it? Well, there you go then. I got fuck all. Don't get me wrong, I tried, and very nearly succeeded, but she played that little bit too hard to get, and I was drunk. Not the best fucking combination, but it didn't matter. My arse was resting against a radiator keeping me nice and snug, and it was costing me and my mate fuck all. Yes, fuck all let me tell you, in one of the most expensive cities in the world. Now that was a result.

Glyn met us at "Piccadilly", and we set off to Bury. Glyn was wincing, and appeared to be in terrible pain. He was waving a prescription in his hand, and was desperate to find a Chemist's. Now I don't know if it was down to the lifestyle, but occasionally Rob, Glyn and myself suffered from haemorrhoids. This particular time it was Glyn's turn, and he was in fucking agony.

Me; "What's wrong?"

Glyn; "My fucking arse is on fire. I need some cream, and fucking quickly."

He drove along, talking through clenched teeth like some fucking "Brooklyn" racketeer, while trying to avoid the bumps in the road. His stance reminded me of a championship winning jockey, as he "rode" the van, with his arse cheeks barely touching the seat. We both knew what he was going through, but he got no sympathy. This particular day it wasn't us, so he got what we got, when it was our arses that were playing up.

Rob; "I bet your arse looks like a turkey's face, with those fucking horrible red bits hanging down."

Glyn; "Fuck off, I've had a doctor's finger up there this afternoon."

Rob; "Glyn, these perverts will tell you anything. Doctor my arse. Anyway, some people would pay good money for that, including you."

Me; "Jonesy, your arse is like the neck of a ketchup bottle at the best of times."

We stopped at a Chemist shop, and he picked up his cream. He disappeared into a pub a few doors down, and all was silent for a few minutes. He reappeared a new man, walking tall and smiling. He jumped into the van and roared off.

"Glyn." "Now fuck off, the pair of you."

Derby Hall was running smoothly. The PA and the gear were set up on time, and the punters were turning up early. The only problem arose when Rob couldn't find his bag, which he thought he had left at the "Marquee." His bag contained his hairspray, his shampoo, his hair dryer, his bangles, his combs, his bracelets, his boot straps, and his hair straighteners, so, as you can see, it was fucking serious. The bag finally surfaced, and I avoided sharing my hairspray with him. Although we were close, it fucking grated on me when I had to share my hairspray with anybody. I'd pretend to carry on getting ready as normal, but my beady eyes were locked on to the fucking liberties being taken with my VO5 gel spray. It always ended in an argument, as their fingers went bright red because of the amount of time they had my fucking nozzle pressed to the max. I don't mind admitting that I snapped a couple of times, only momentarily, but for a split second nonetheless. I mean, who in their right minds would forget their hairspray if they were serious about all of this? Not me, that's for sure. I forgot my Digitech effects unit once, and had to drive an hour back to Manchester, but never my hairspray.

The obsession with our looks and particularly our hair seems effeminate now, but we never thought of it that way. Nobody did, whether they were in a band or not. That was the 80's for you, and for a time, the early '90's, God bless 'em. Under the stage lights I would cringe as the bitter taste of hairspray ran into my mouth, mixed with the sweat, but it made a great photo. During the '80's, it was kind of expected, the unwritten rule. It didn't matter what type of rock you liked either, if it flourished in the '80's then it had big hair. Needless to say, the bands I liked all had big hair, and were crucified for it, but every fucker else had it as well. Thrash bands sang about death, destruction, and global politics, all with big hair. Funky dudes like Dan Reed and the Electric Boys, plied their trade with the first Van Halen album in one hand, and "Sly" in the other hand, all with big hair. The Black Crowes injected a needle full of "blues" into their arms, while teasing their locks. Avant Garde metal was supplied by the innovative Queensryche, and their hair products. Pomp parped its way back into the '80's consciousness, courtesy of the gloriously groomed, "Simmons" owned, "House of Lords." The balladeers, like Michael Bolton, Richard Marx, Heart, and Foreigner, all crooned away for us, while the silhouettes from the lighters made them look like fucking dandelions. Even Ozzy wore hairspray in the '80's.

The clubs were full of lads and girls that had taken a hell of a lot of time getting ready. Lads wore tighter jeans than girls, they wore more bangles than girls, and they wore more hairspray than girls. When you walked into a club, you could gauge how good you looked, not by the amount of women that looked at you, but by the amount of lads that looked at you. "Isn't that homosexual?" I hear you gasp. Well maybe, but not this particular time, not this particular decade. Everybody had been through the same ritual earlier in the evening, and it was only manners to "doff" your cap when somebody had got it oh so right. Hair was "cool" with me, but there were certain things lads should avoid at all costs:

## Umbrellas

Come on, if you used an umbrella you looked a cunt. You deserved every fucking derisory comment you ever got if you carried one of these fuckers about. The problem was that it took a conscious effort to obtain one. If it was a black gent's umbrella, then this showed that you had thought about it, and you had come to the conclusion that this was how to look "cool" with an umbrella. Believe me, there is no "cool" way. Alternatively, you had a tartan, or flowered, or pink, or paisley umbrella, which had been nicked from your mother/sister/girlfriend, at the last minute. Forget about it, just get wet. You'll soon fucking dry out.

## Nicknames

Nicknames are OK, unless you made up your own, and then spent time telling other people what it was. Nicknames are a term of endearment, created by your closest friends, and contain elements of the rare qualities that make you special to that close group of friends. People who made up their own nicknames didn't have a fucking clue, because they tried to make them sound cool. They missed the point completely. Nicknames dwell on your idiosyncrasies and quirky traits, which have been observed by your mates over years and years. I spent far too much time talking to the people that make up the first sentence of this paragraph, to have any fucking kind of respect for anybody with a nickname, and if you had an umbrella as well...

## The "Hump"

A lot of lads got the "hump" if you made any kind of comment about their girlfriend. This was like an ice pick ripping into their frost bitten hand of insecurity, and they didn't fucking like it. If you wore your heart on your sleeve, and spoke the truth, then they knew where they stood, they could keep you at arms length, and they appreciated the girl they were with ten times more than before. This was obviously the point where the problems arose. You see, and I've been guilty of this myself in the past, if you are with a girl for a long time, you get lazy. If you are with a great girl, then there will be a fucking long line of filchers and furtlers desperate to bang her, and they would all give 100%, because they have silently worshipped her from afar for months.

Meanwhile, you have slipped into what has, quite honestly, become a shoddy performance, in terms of being a boyfriend and a lover. Apart from not wanting to lose the girl, you have got to step up a gear again, and make the effort to make your lass feel every bit the fucking princess you told her she was all those years ago. So, in these situations, everybody is a winner, all except "honest" Tony. What they didn't realise was, that it was the weasely fuckers who said nothing, that they should be wary of. If you are dating a babe, everybody will be thinking the same. Only, my honesty may shock you, and take your eyes off the real issue of the silent snake creeping around the back of you, while you are far too busy puffing your fucking chest out at me, for being a lad. Chill out, you're taking her home.

## Sunglasses

Sunglasses are great... providing that you wear the fucking things in the sunshine, preferably on holiday abroad, and only if you look like a fashion model. I'll let you into a secret. Sunglasses don't work on every head shape. Sunglasses disguise ugliness to a certain extent, but its better not to start that carry-on, because there comes a time when you've got to take the fucking things off in front of some girl you have conned for the last month, and now it's the start of the rainy season. Either that, or you make the wrong decision to wear them in a rock club, where everybody will just fucking hate you for it.

251

Too many ropy '80's rock bands made the wrong decision of every band member wearing sunglasses on their album covers, despite them being shot indoors, in the rain, in the snow, in fact anywhere where it wasn't sunny. Heavy Metal, as a genre, had a tacit understanding that sunglasses were one of the coolest items to be seen in, if you had long hair. Consequently, most bands between 1978 and 1991 looked like the "Banana Splits." The worst sight I ever saw was some idiot with a pair of sunglasses perched on his head, while he wore a pair at the same time. If that wasn't bad enough, he had a pair hanging around his chest, on a dayglo pink string, the twat. I can't remember why I did it, but I still cringe to this very fucking day. So let that be a warning.

# CHAPTER THIRTY FIVE

*"Out In The Fields"*

The 80's were a boom time for rock music, even though Dave had split from Van Halen, and Kiss were on their knees. I didn't care about the different guitarists, or that Gene had gone "Hollywood." As long as I could go and watch Stanley belting out "Strutter", then everything was fine. Aerosmith had been and gone, but they had also come back again. Journey, my other band, were still creating melodic monsters of songs, but if you weren't a fan you wouldn't know they existed. Also being listened to, shagged to, and wanked to in the Bell bedroom, were, Balance, Reckless, Rick Springfield, Saraya, Aldo Nova, Honeymoon Suite, Little Caesar, Stan Bush, Ratt, Skid Row, Santers, Triumph, Coney Hatch, Survivor, Streets, Nightranger, Craaft, Black n Blue, Sabu, Van Zant, Stryper, Danger Danger, Fate, Warrant, Tesla, Joshua, Dan Reed, White Lion, Jagwire, Teeze, Pretty Maids, Virginia Wolf, Winger, Jimmy Barnes, Giant, Aviator, Icon, Kim Mitchell, Dokken, Touch, Strangeways, TNT, Antix, FM, XYZ, Heavens Edge, Bad English, Vinnie Vincent, White Sister, Hughes/Thrall, King Kobra, Living Colour, Signal. And that's just for fucking starters.

Now then, did you finish the list and smile, or did you slam this fucking thing shut, and walk off in disgust at my pathetic choice of music? Yeah, well according to everybody you talk to, we all like shit. Which particular shit do you listen to smart arse? On top of this, I still had all the mainstream rock bands to go at as well. Wasn't I the lucky one? Whitesnake simmered nicely from their inception, with some fucking outrageous songs. Then, in 1987, they blew the fucking roof off the world. It was fantastic watching the planet surrender. AC/DC, Scorpions, Rainbow, Lizzy, Bad Company, Ozzy, they all kept going during the '80's, and supplemented my foray into the life force coming from the "States."

Donington festivals were a great occasion, and gave us a fantastic excuse to go missing for a few days, doing nothing but drink, shout and wank. My first one was 1984; er that's Donington, not wank. It was a blistering hot day, and I got scorched to a fucking cinder while watching Gary Moore, Accept, Y&T, Ozzy, and Van Halen, who were all excellent. Oh yeah, Motley Crue were on as well. The sun went down, AC/DC came on, tore the fucking place up, and then fired their cannons. I was speechless. In 1988, 110,000 people turned up, and two unfortunate souls lost their lives. The highlights were Guns 'n' Roses, Dave Lee Roth, and Kiss. Paul Stanley screamed "110,000 people can't be wrong", and they were off, into "Deuce." I fucking loved it, the band that wouldn't die, not for you, not for anybody. My band.

Donington took a good couple of weeks preparation, as we gathered tents and firewood ready for the event. Glyn had a checklist as long as his arm. The most important commodity I took with me was a rake of Diocalm tablets. They rattled around inside me, and bunged me up, so I didn't need to take a shit until I got home. Stone-Age man wouldn't have used the toilets at Donington, they were fucking disgraceful. The problem was that when I finally did get to take the mother of all shits several days later, it came out like fucking Oxo cubes. That was bad enough, but it felt like they were in a fucking box of twelve. 1994 was the only year that I became a casualty. Too much vodka and high jinks meant I was helped out of the arena two songs into Aerosmith's set. I was slung into my tent, relieved of the rest of my alcohol, and left in the recovery position, while I lay motionless in the increasingly chilling summer dusk, listening to Tyler belting out the rest of the show in that cool hat.

By 1996 it had gone a bit daft, with two stages, and a load of fucking bands I had never heard of. Come to think of it, there were two stages in 1994, unless it was my fucking eyes. Yeah, I'll put that fucker down to my eyes at the minute, because I was fucked. Let me get back to you on that one. Anyway, 1996. I was only there to see Kiss and Ozzy anyway. After a day on the beer, I was finding it hard to cling on to reality. Just when I thought I'd gotten the hang of it, Kiss came on and prized my fucking fingers off. Rob's back gave way during Ozzy's set, and a St John's ambulance was radioed into the site, to assist with the crooked man who had walked that crooked fucker of a mile. He lay gasping for air, as me and Glyn flicked him with our toes, to check if there was any life left in him.

Glyn; "You'd better grab his beer."

Me; "Good idea. It's fucking full, and he's spilling it."

Glyn: "Pass it here."

Me; "Fuck off."

I started to swig Rob's beer as Jonesy tried to grab it out of my hand. Rob lay eerily still as we squabbled over the liquid "booty." The ambulance was with us in minutes, and two guys jumped out trying to help. We explained what had happened, and they spoke to Rob to see if he could move.

Me; "Look, I've seen this before. You grab his arms, and I'll grab his legs. If we both pull, his back will click back into place, and he'll be fine."

Rob was trying to protest, but he couldn't get the fucking words out. Fortunately, the guy from the ambulance saved him.

"No, you can't do that, just leave it to us. Let's get him in the ambulance and we'll take him to the Medical Centre."

Me; "Aaah fuck it then, just leave him there. I'll stand on him for a better view."

Glyn was choking with laughter, as Rob was loaded on to a stretcher, and into the ambulance. We waved goodbye, as he lifted his head ever so slightly, and mouthed the word "cunts." We gulped his fucking drink so fast, that it splashed out of the glass and into our eyes, as we laughed at the white metal doors of the ambulance being shut, taking away our "fucked" mate. Honestly, he wouldn't walk anywhere, the lazy twat.

As the darkness enveloped the warm summer night, Kiss hit the stage, and me and Glyn nodded in approval, as Stanley took control.

Glyn. (Swigs his beer and shouts) "DO YOU KNOW WHAT I'D FUCKING LOVE NOW?"

Me. "What?"

Glyn. "A fucking big spliff to get us in the groove."

Me. "Yeah, cool."

Glyn. "Well my friend, I managed to get these fuckers out of Rob's pocket as he was being loaded on board the ambulance."

Glyn opened a packet of fags that has about twelve joints inside. He threw a spliff into his mouth and lit it, as the glowing embers "bobbed" in time to "King of the night time World."

Glyn. "I'll smoke all of these fucking things rather than hand them back to that soft cunt."

Me. "Well pass the fucking thing on. Don't forget, you've got a long fucking night ahead of you with the barbecue, when you get back to the tent. Please tell me you've gone one step further this time, and booked some fucking strippers for when we get back."

Glyn. "Do you think I would be stood here watching these old fuckers if there was a crowd of strippers waiting to show me their pussies, you fucking idiot?"

Me. "Just fucking burgers then is it?"

Glyn. "What do you think? You know I would never serve up just burgers. That's a fucking insult, that is."

I think Glyn lit a new joint for every song they played. Either he was having the fucking time of his life, or it was the only way he could deal with the complete fucking lunacy of it all.

After the gig, I walked with Glyn to the Medical Centre, only to find that Rob had been discharged with a handful of painkillers. We walked back to the tents, and found Rob fast asleep, with a belly full of hot chicken. Oh yes, he'd managed to cook himself a fucking magnificent supper, but he was just that bit too poorly to stick some extra fucking chicken on the griddle for the rest of us. Glyn fired the barbecue up from its dying embers, handed out the beers, and we were off, talking bollocks, munching some fantastic marinated chicken, under the stars. Steve was sat nursing his thumb, which had been slammed in the van door the previous day, and it was pissing him off. Glyn asked Steve to pass him one of the gas lights, so he grabbed it by the glass top. Steve was so drunk, that he forgot that the glass was red hot. He screamed and dropped the light as the searing pain rushed through his already fucked thumb. The poor lad was almost in tears, as the laughter drowned out his screaming.

In total, between the vans and the cars, set up in the "Wagon Train" circle, there must have been twenty of us having the fucking time of our lives that summer. Glyn had arranged everything, as usual. He booked the sites, ordered the tickets, packed the inflatable mattresses, bought the firewood, and loaded the barbecue and charcoal. Again, he took charge, and providing we gave him twenty quid, we could eat and drink as much as our fucking bodies would allow. This was a fucking bargain, because I knew that Glyn would be up a couple of nights before we set off, creating some magnificent marinades, for us to drizzle across the succulent chicken he was going to prepare. He knew that we expected it from him, and he rose to the occasion every fucking time, no matter how drunk or stoned he was. If there was a light under the barbecue, an ice cold beer in his hand, a spliff in his other hand, and his beloved "Journey" on the ghetto blaster, then "Jonesy" would stay up all night, and I mean all fucking night.

The only problem we encountered was some chap that cadged a lift down to Donington, in a car that was with us. As he had cadged the lift, he didn't think he had to contribute to the cost of the trip, even though he was given a shit hot bed to sleep in. Also, he "lifted" one of the litres of vodka, which again, he hadn't contributed to. Without spending a fucking penny, he had slept like a log, and he was now asleep in the sunshine, lay on the grass during "Ozzy's" set, drunk on our alcohol. Rob and Glyn were fuming, so they eased the litre of vodka and coke from under his arm. They took the lid off, and took it in turn to dangle their sweaty bell ends over the neck of the bottle, as they topped it up with piss. Of course, the lad was parched when he woke up, and took a big fucking swig of his freebie. He was a cheeky cunt, because once Glyn had the barbecue smoking away after the gig, he joined the crowd of diners, who had paid their money, and tried to freeload a fucking gutful of Glyn's culinary masterpiece. I like Glyn, because he will always say what everybody else is thinking, even though it makes you cringe when you hear it, and that is why you never said it in the first place. The sparking embers and "spitting" chicken had this lad salivating like a fucking idiot.

Glyn; "Right, pass this chicken down. If anybody hands a piece to that cunt, they will get this red hot fork on the back of their fucking head, and there will be no more food for them. So, it's up to you. I'll feed the cunt when I'm good and ready."

Nobody passed the chicken down, and Glyn tossed a few gnarled bones down to him, once he had shredded every last fucking piece of meat from the bones. All the lad had to do was offer a few quid towards the trip, but for some reason he was hell bent on getting a fucking freebie. Well, he didn't reckon for Glyn Jones that warm, drunken, stuffed, comfortable, stoned, happy, summer's evening.

The 80's belonged to Bon Jovi, but they never really interested me. Sure, we all sat up when their debut album came out, but when album number two and three were the same, you kinda wished they would have failed after their first album, which in "rock" terms, would have given it a "classic" status. Fans of the band will argue that what they provided was a signature sound, like all the great bands before them. Fair enough, but girls don't pay that much attention to music, besides knowing when their asses look cute, while shaking them to a particular record. So, their critique of something I hold as dearly as music was fallible. I saw Bon Jovi loads of times, supporting Kiss, and a couple of times on their own, and I was impressed by the amount of good looking girls that turned up to watch them. Anybody would have thought that us lot were playing. It didn't matter; they did just fine without me anyway.

The music that I loved flourished during the 80's, and a week never went by without me discovering a new band, or a new band being thrust in my face from one of my trusty magazines, but you would be hard pressed to find an article about us. We did o.k. in the fanzines, but "Kerrang", "Raw" and "Metal Hammer", the national magazines, were frugal with their support. They didn't blank us completely, but we expected more. Maybe they did too.

The '80's were drawing to a close, and I had milked them for all they were fucking worth. I had been in clubs and bands for the majority of the decade, and I had made some great friends during this time. Low morals pushed me into some sticky situations, but I must stress that I love women. So, it was down to weaknesses on my part, and not some misogynistic streak in me, that led me to chew more than I could bite off.

I was walking down "Oxford Road" one day, when I heard somebody call my name. I turned around to find a pretty young girl hurrying to catch up with me. I didn't recognise her, but she knew me.

"Hello" she said.

"I'm sorry, I'm not being rude, but I don't know you."

"I've just started going to "Rockworld" with my sister, and I noticed you in there last week. I heard somebody say your name, so that's how I know who you are."

"Well come and have a chat next time you are in there."

"I will. Look, this may sound funny, but I'm a photographer, and I wanted to ask if I could take some photos of you?"

"Are you taking the piss?"

"No, I'm serious."

"Why me?"

"Well, I think you are a good looking lad, I love your hair, and you seem o.k."

"What kind of pictures?"

"Oh, just some black and whites, different poses, nudes."

I could see that she was serious, and the "weirdo" alarm went off in my head.

"No thanks, I'm not really into that. I know that it's art and what have you, but I wouldn't feel comfortable. Anyway, the pictures could end up anywhere, and I'd never hear the fucking last of it from my mates. Sorry."

"I'll fuck you."

"Right, better give me your number then."

She gave me her number, and carried on her journey. I watched her, just to see if she stopped any other strangers with her bizarre requests. Well, how fucking easy was that then? Minding my own fucking business in the middle of Manchester, and right out of the blue, offers of sex with a pretty stranger. Then it slowly dawned on me, this was a set up by Glyn and Rob. I kept checking over my shoulder to see if they were hiding down some side street with the girl, having a good old fucking laugh at my expense. I slung her number in the first bin I passed, determined not to be fooled by them again. Yeah, it all made sense, I would have noticed her in the club, I noticed everybody. Not only were the 80's making me older, they were making me wiser. Mr. Jones and Mr. Naylor would have to set their alarm clocks a damn sight earlier, if they wanted to catch me out any more. I saw her a couple of weeks later, and she wouldn't give me the fucking time of day. Turns out, it wasn't them, she was genuine. So, Glyn and Rob had fucked it up for me, even when they hadn't fucked it up for me!

As the barmaid shouted "time" on the 80's, I met a girl who, although she was blonde and pretty, would never ever get her fucking hand in her purse. It never bothered me before, I didn't really expect it. You know, I was grateful if a girl bought me a drink for every ten I bought her, that wasn't the issue, but to go out time after time and pay for absolutely everything, when to be honest, the single life was still very attractive, pissed me off no end. To top it all, she didn't like sex very much, well not with me anyway, and one of the few times we did it, we stumbled into bed after a night on the town. As she squatted over me, she started pissing, and didn't fucking stop. As she tried to stand up on my bed, it squirted in my mouth and in my eyes. Finally, I'd gotten a fucking drink out of her. She said nothing and went to sleep. My bed was soaked, so I crashed on the floor. Well, what do you say the next morning, as the tangy whiff of stale piss burns your nostrils? Do you make a joke of it? Do you say nothing? I opted for the latter, and it was all over. I didn't necessarily object, but it would have been nice to have been warned. It certainly bothered her more than it bothered me, so I couldn't work out why she did it. Anyway, second-hand gin and bitter lemon isn't the greatest fucking drink in the world!

# CHAPTER THIRTY SIX

*"Climbed On Board A Westbound 747"*

We gigged regularly from the start of the new decade, and even managed to get ourselves filmed by some Australian TV channel called Network 7. To be honest, none of us had ever heard of them, but it didn't cost us anything. I don't know what came of the film because I never saw the fucking thing, but I bet we looked cool.

Glyn turned up one night, with some good news and some bad news. We had the chance of a support slot on a small national tour. Hooray. It was supporting Dare. Boo. It was 1991, and they were about to release their second album. We had some serious reservations, because we hadn't gotten on that well with some of them the last time we played with them, so we were sure we would get stitched up, sound-wise. However, it turned out that our old friend Jon Hull would be mixing the sound on the tour, so we knew everything would be o.k. Before you can support a band, you have to stump up hundreds of pounds, sometimes thousands, just for the privilege of being looked down upon, fucked about, and generally treated like shite, which didn't lie well with us.

Now you can call Gene Simmons the greediest, most mercenary musician on the planet when it comes to money, but every band that ever supported them has had nothing but the utmost respect for the guy. Apparently, Simmons and Stanley will do anything they can, to help you enjoy the experience of, which for many, is a very limited lifetime. Paul and Gene don't need to prove anything to anybody, and you sure as hell ain't gonna blow them off the stage and steal their crowd. I'm sure this goes for Coverdale, Roth, Tyler, and the rest. The problem with bands being twats arises at the start of their career, when it could go either way. They maybe have one or two albums out, and are under pressure for a single to chart. The last thing they want is a band from the same country, never mind the same fucking city, looking ten times the rockers they will ever be, with attitude, and a set full of fucking stompers. Well this is the situation we found ourselves in with Dare.

I was standing at the bar in "Rockworld" with Mike, filling him in with the details of the Dare tour, just to check if he was o.k. to come away for the gigs. He helped lift the gear in and out, and then drank himself rotten, just like the rest of us. He was always up for a night out. I was moaning because I looked so fucking pasty, and was banging on about going away, to get some colour in me. Mike mentioned a quick holiday at short notice, and we were off.

Mike; "Where should we go?"

Me; "Somewhere hot, with loads of girls. I don't know…Spain maybe."

Mike; "What about the Greek islands?"

Me; "What about L.A.?"

Mike; "Yeah, great idea."

The next morning we booked two flights to L.A. We hired a car, and decided to sleep where we fell, so there was no accommodation included. After what seemed like three weeks on the fucking plane, we landed at LAX in the middle of the night, full of the free in-flight drink and peanuts. My next shit was going to look like Sun-Pat Peanut Butter alright. We picked up the car and turned on the radio. "Whole lotta Love" faded out and "Separate Ways" came marching in, the first two fucking songs we heard, without even changing the dial. It was just like being in my old Fiesta. We sped along, trying to find a hotel, desperate for some shut eye. I was starting to nod off, but something caught my eye. It was the Great West Forum, home of the "Lakers", but more importantly, it was where "Kiss Alive II" was recorded. We had been driving for less than twenty minutes, and I had just passed my spiritual home. I waved my fist in salute. The next sign told us we were entering Inglewood. Hey, now this was cool. This is where Brian Wilson came from. Inglewood turned into Watts district. This was the scene of the Civil Rights demonstrations in the '60's, which were done for all the right reasons, but was now a gang infested neighbourhood. We turned around, got on the 405 to Hollywood, and fucked off.

We found a right shit hole of a motel, and managed to sleep for about an hour, jet lag being the fucker it is. We were up before the sun, so we showered, had breakfast and headed for the beach. I was in the sea dead on 8.am, and I was out of the fucking thing before one minute past, it was bastard freezing. I put on every piece of clothing I had with me, and we fell asleep on the empty beach. I don't know how long we'd been asleep, but when we woke, the whole fucking place was buzzing. Skateboarders, rollerbladers, joggers, musclemen, musclewomen, street artists, babes, sand artists, back packers, tattooists, jewellery vendors, T-Shirt vendors, Ice-Cream men, musicians, mime artists, dogs in sunglasses, volleyball teams, gymnasts, guys on stilts, break-dancers, food vendors, gays, lesbians, straight, black, white, yellow, Asian, Hispanic. It was a fucking amazing cross section of America having fun, and I loved it. We stayed all day, and then headed back to "Hollywood."

We booked into a motel on "Sunset Strip" that made last night's digs look like Hefner's "Playboy" mansion. The pool had green slime covering the water, and the broken windows were taped together, holding them in the frames. Our room had a window missing, and the wardrobe door was propped up against the wall. This was a fucking dive alright. I had a shower and dried my hair, as Mike jumped in after me. No, not after me, like he was fucking "after me." Jeez, what is it with you weirdos? This was a big night, my first night on the "strip", so I tried to get my hair as big as possible. I was in the middle of an almost perfect construction of a rock and roll hairdo, this fucking planet hadn't seen the likes of before, when there was a knock on the door. I turned my hair dryer off, and a voice shouted;

"Police, open up."

I was confused, I was sure I had just heard somebody shout "Police." The voice shouted exactly the same again. In a split second, my brain sent loads of images racing around my mind. Was this a hoax? Was it in fact some piece of scum that had seen us enter the motel earlier, and was out to rob us? Probably. Why would the Police be banging on my door? Had there been a murder in the motel, and they were looking for witnesses? I approached the door, not knowing whether to open it or not. I looked down and saw my big black hair dryer in my hand, which, in a split second, could easily be mistaken for a gun, which could lead to the back of my head resting on the window twenty feet behind me. I didn't want to be the subject of a "sorry" letter from the L.A.P.D. to my mum. I physically gulped, I remember that, and I threw the fucking thing on my bed. I reached out my hand to open the door, and then I pulled it back, not knowing what to do. All of a sudden, the door flew off its

263

hinges, and a cop stood there, filling the gap where the door had been. He had his hand on his gun, but it wasn't drawn. My hair dryer was slightly bigger, but I wouldn't have stood a fucking chance. Let me tell you now, that I was fucking relieved. I sighed and my shoulders shrunk down low. I was safe. I didn't know what he wanted, but I hadn't done anything wrong, so whatever it was, it was a mistake. Then he spoke.

"Where's the kid?"

I was stunned. I couldn't speak. He repeated himself.

"Where's the kid?"

"What kid?"

My mind was that fucked up, I almost believed I had one with me. The cop walked up to me.

"The owner said he heard a child screaming on this floor, so he called us."

"There is no child. Not in this room."

The cop heard sounds coming from the bathroom.

"Who's in there?"

"Just my mate, he's having a shower."

He opened the door, and found Mike, ankle deep in shitty water in the bunged up bathtub. Mike looked at me.

"What's going on?"

"They think we've got a child in here?"

"What?"

The cop was satisfied.

"Sorry, there's been some mistake here."

The cop left and the hotel owner fixed our door. He seemed to be apologising as he fixed the hinges, but I think he was Russian, so we couldn't understand a fucking word he said.

Well, if anybody deserved a drink in Los Angeles on this particular night, it was me and Mike. Out on the "strip", it was party night, so we gate crashed the evening. As we passed the "Rainbow" I heard "Dance the night Away", which was followed by "Somebody get me a Doctor." Well that swung it for us; they were playing Van Halen II from start to finish. We grabbed a drink, wandered around and bumped into Adrian Vandenberg. For me, this dude had the best fucking hair in the universe, so we said hello, and sang "Wait, wait, wait, 'til the shit hits the fan." Isn't that awkward silence fucking horrible? Back at the bar, some guy told me that Dave Lee Roth was a regular here. Fucking hell, would Dave make an appearance? He didn't, but I could live with that. My first night in L.A, I spent pissed up in Dave Lee Roth's local. That's one for my Grandchildren to yawn at.

The next day we set off for San Diego, via La Jolla, just because it was mentioned in "Surfin' USA", and then on to Las Vegas, a couple of days later. The original draft of this book had reams of pages, documenting the whole fucking trip around the "States", and it was starting to read like something Bill Bryson had written, so I fucked it off. There's a time and a place for those road trip type of books, and the time is not now, and the place is somewhere else.

In between arriving in San Diego, and arriving in Las Vegas, we also spent some time in Tijuana, down old "Mehico" way. Fucking hell, this place was pure madness. Whole families grabbed you as you crossed the border, begging and crying for your cash. If you could get past them, you were literally thrown into a taxi, by a crowd of drivers that herded you towards the cars. We managed to get past these first two hurdles, but were stopped by the Police shortly after. Every spaghetti western Mexican I have ever seen, got out of the car, manifested in one fat, sweaty, toothpick chewing, greasy, mirrored sunglasses wearing, 70's porn film moustache sporting, cop. Again, we were questioned by the local constabulary, this time for apparently walking down the road in the sunshine. He took our passports, and I thought it was going to be the last we saw of them, as we sweated it out in a cell, all because we had long hair.

Something always happens to me in these situations. My eyes fix on the furthest thing on the horizon, and I just wish I was there. This time it happened to be some hills, which I knew were in California. You know, there's somewhere else that's in your field of vision, where you wouldn't have to deal with the shit you are currently having to deal with. I bet it's the same the split second before you have a real bad car crash, I've lived this one a thousand times. Out of your car, there is a safe place you can see not too far away, where you would be safe from the situation only milliseconds away. If only you could... BOOM!!!!!! They searched our bags, and I honestly expected a huge chunk of dope to be planted on one of us. Then we would have been somebody's "bitches" for the next ten years. Well, stranger fucking things have happened. Luckily, they let us go, so we carried on our journey.

We drove for five or six hours before we reached Las Vegas,

which turned out to be amazing. Not for the architecture or the ambience, but purely for the fact that every scrap of material, from the steel, the bricks, the cement, the carpets, the feather head-dresses, right down to the last light bulb and sequin thong, were taken along similar routes to those we had taken, for hours and hours on end. All to be assembled in the middle of nowhere. Then, Bugsy and his mates must have hoped and prayed that the regular American people would want to travel all the way to Vegas, just to hand over their cash by the billions. Well, they got it right. Like I said, this isn't a fucking travel book, so don't sit there moaning that I could have told you a bit more about the American experience. If you're that interested, get off your arse and go see. Alternatively, buy my next book, "The American Experience."

We stayed in Vegas for three days, and then headed back to L.A. We left around lunchtime, so there was time for me to have a few beers before we set off. We stopped for gas on the outskirts of the town, and I jumped out of the car to take a leak. As I walked across the forecourt, an old lady slipped and fell over. I ran over to help her, but because of the beer, and the fact that there was no fucking grip on the shiny soles of my cowboy boots, I fell over as well. I stretched out an arm to try and balance myself, but I crashed down on top of her, in a perfect "Stone Cold Steve Austin" body slam manoeuvre. She was groaning, as I helped her to her feet. I apologised, and helped her into the shop. I turned to our car, but Mike was missing. Where had he gone? He wasn't there. I returned to the car and found him lying across the two front seats crying with laughter. We went back to L.A., set up a base in a motel on "Sunset", and partied the rest of the holiday away.

Now I do like writing, and I don't know if I'll ever get the chance to do something like this again, so should I include every encounter that involves a girl? Well, that's not what this book is all about, and it is predictable if it's just sex without any dynamics, or peaks and troughs to the story. I'm all for sex, but I'm trying to put myself in the position of reading this as if it had been written by a complete stranger, because that's what I am to you. I wouldn't want to read a list of the people you have fucked, with a description of what happened with each one, no matter how tasty they were, because that is of no interest to me at all, as I appreciate mine wouldn't be to you. I am also aware, that parts of my story may not sit that easily with you. Well, firstly, I wouldn't be too sure about the bad language used. Is it necessary? Who gives a fuck? It's in, and it's staying in. This book has made me take a good look at myself. I've stripped myself down, and built me up from scratch again. All the same components as the original model, but I think I've assembled a few things differently this time.

# CHAPTER THIRTY SEVEN

### *"Got Brass, In Pocket"*

The lads knew I was home, but they gave me a couple of days to get over the jet lag, before they started harassing me. I should have gone to Ladbrokes, because I'd have put the fucking lot on "Jonesy" being the first one rattling my cage. True to form, he rang early on purpose, just to piss me off; my 3-1 shot first over the line.

Glyn; "Fucking hell, you've missed it while you've been away."

Me; "Why, what happened?"

Glyn; "We've been offered the support on the "Magnum" tour. It's a full U.K. tour, including the Manchester Apollo, Hammersmith Odeon, and the N.E.C.."

Me; "Fucking hell Glyn, that's fantastic."

Glyn; "There's a problem though. It's gonna cost ten grand. I've got the fucking brass, and it's in my pocket as we speak, but it'll need to be split between the lot of us, so we're all gonna have to pay just under two grand each."

Me; "Do you know what my problem is with this?"

Glyn: "What?"

Me; "This country is full of cunts just like me and you, who pay no attention to support bands, and see their time on stage as drinking time, or time for japery. Plus, I'm fucking skint at the minute, which means I'd be indebted to you for the next few years."

Glyn: "I know, everybody has said the same. The lads even mentioned the tossers who would be stood at the bar calling you wankers."

Me; "Hold on, I've seen you do that at our gigs before."

Glyn; "Well, at least I know you're a bunch of tossers. That's not so bad is it?"

Me; "No, I suppose not."

Glyn; "Anyway lad, I've saved us some money on the "Dare" tour. I've split it with Dan's band, so they are sharing the costs."

Me; "What?"

Glyn; "Don't worry, we've got all the best dates, I've seen to that."

The tour started, and me Glyn and Rob went to the "Tivoli" in Buckley, North Wales, to get a feel of what to expect. Dan came on stage in a pair of jeans, black cowboy boots, and a pair of polka dot braces, hanging round his knees, with no shirt on, sweating like a bastard, with his "Slash" locks entertaining the first few rows. Yeah, this was what it was all about. This was cool. We were fucking itching to get on. Dan's band was great, and so too, must I add, were "Dare." We dived backstage with Dan, and had a few beers. As the gear was being loaded into the vans, a crowd of girls approached us. One of them started talking to me, nuzzling her head into my shoulder. Rob handed me a beer, in addition to the one I was holding, while the girl whispered in my ear. Without any warning, she dropped to her knees, and opened my jeans. She blew like a fucking veteran of the wind section of the "Halle" orchestra, as my eyes rolled around my head. I finished my beer, and then started my new drink, as my mates watched without fucking blinking. I tried desperately, not to make a sound, because I didn't want my mates to know the fucking noise I made, when my kettle boiled.

We joined the tour in Norwich, and played at the "Waterfront." We still had the crack with Vinnie, but the rest of them avoided us if they could. We got bollocked for selling our T-Shirts for three pounds apiece, when "Dare" were charging ten pounds each. Although it was a free market economy, unless we put the price up to eight pounds, we couldn't sell them in the theatre. Now then, that is a prime example of "slapped arse girly pants" if ever you've fucking heard one.

They had a tour manager, called "Drac", who thought he was looking after "Elvis", or "Led Zeppelin." He looked like somebody had nicked him from outside a club, and burnt him out on a piece of waste ground. He spoke to us in a demeaning cantor, and I wish with all my heart, that I would have belted the fucker around the head with my Charvel, I really do.

We bought a pair of comedy rubber tits in Great Yarmouth, which you had to place around your neck like an apron, before parading around with them on. After the laughter died down, and we had all tried them on, the sad reality dawned on us that at least four of us didn't look any different with the fucking things on.

269

One night, after we had played, I grabbed hold of Vinnie, before he went on stage.

Me; "Vinnie, Vinnie. Quick."

Vinnie; "What is it?"

Me; "Come on. We've got this girl in our dressing room, and she's up for anything, and she's been asking about you."

Vinnie; "What's she like?"

Me; "Well what do you fucking think? She's fucking ugly, but she's got fuck all on, and she'll fuck anything."

Vinnie; "Can I come and have a look?"

Me; "Of course you can. That's why I came looking for you."

His eyes lit up, as he gulped at his beer. He entered the dressing room behind me, and stared at the girl, totally bewildered and puzzled. His face gave this immediate look of disapproval, as he leaned forward and peered closer at her, to try and take it all in. Christ she was rough. It took Vinnie a good ten seconds to realise he was actually looking at Rob. Rob was wearing the big flabby tits... or was he? No, no, he had the fucking things on, yeah, he did. Sorry mate. He had a red bandana around his neck, to hide the string holding the tits on. He had eyeliner on, and his knob was pushed through his legs, so that you could only see a pubic triangle, as he lay across an old couch. Totally fucked. Lumpy, and bursting out in some places, and saggy and smelly in others. The couch on the other hand, looked o.k. for its age. Rob tried to entice Vinnie in a high pitched voice.

"Hi Vinnie. Want some fun?"

Vinnie cracked up, as we took pictures of this cross between a "Reuben" and a "Picasso." It was the worst "reader's wives" picture you have ever seen.

"Wulfren Hall" in Wolverhampton was a great place, and was packed. Earlier in the day, we were sat around after we had unloaded the gear. We were having a beer and a laugh, when "Dare's" second guitar player strutted over to join us. He nuzzled in between us and said;

"Alright boys?"

Rob looked at me, I looked at Steve. Steve looked at Glyn, Glyn looked at Andy. Andy looked at Noel, and Noel looked at Fugsy. Each one of us raised our eyebrows at each other, but nobody said a word. The raised eyebrows said the same thing to every individual;

"Which one of us should tell him to fuck off?"

He started up again.

"Right then. How's my support band?"

Rob; "Look, if you don't fuck off, I'm going to support your chin with my fist, you cunt."

Allllllllllllllright Robbie. Way to go. I've heard him come out with some one liners, but that was top three, definitely. The lad carried on.

"Hey, let me buy you a drink out of my Per Deims."

Rob; "Fuck off you cunt. Just keep walking until your fucking hat floats... fucking Per Deims."

He wasn't wearing a hat, but the message was loud and clear... and funny.

During our slot, Darren Wharton told Jon Hull to fuck the sound up, because it was too good for a support band. Jon threatened to knock him out if he didn't move away from the mixing desk. He's a nice lad Jon.

After the gig, I walked back to our dressing room, with two girls who were desperate to put on a show for me. Alright, I was on my own, with a bottle of free beer, for fucks sake. Anyway, I walked around the back of the stage, quite lonely, in search of a few mates who I could tell about my freebie. As I got closer to the dressing room, I heard Rob's voice. He was arguing with Glyn.

"No Glyn, it's a fucking farce."

"No mate, it's not. Trust me, you are wrong this time."

Booming voices spilled out into the corridor. I could understand. Rob was pissed off with being on tour with "Dare" because it had cost us, and they weren't our favourite band. However, I could also understand "Jonesy." It was a step up the ladder; it was advertising we seriously needed. I stuck my head around the door, and they both looked at me. Rob was first on my case.

"Come on Tony, it's a fucking farce. You know that don't you?"

Me; "What is?"

Jonesy started.

"Is it fuck. You're wrong, the pair of you."

I hadn't said anything, because I didn't know why they were so pissed off with "Dare" in the first place.

Me; "Hold on, what's a farce, what's wrong?"

Rob; "That fucking bit of skin, between a woman's fanny and

her arse; it's a "farce" isn't it?"

Glyn; "Is it bollocks."

Me; "Glyn's right."

Rob; "What?"

Glyn; "Told you, it's called "Biffins Bridge" you wanker."

Me; "Hold on, I call it the "Chin rest", so you two fuckers are wrong."

Three men who were normally totally inseparable, unable to agree on the name of a tiny piece of coveted land, because they all doggedly believed they had been there first. And not a fucking Arab or Jew between us.

Bristol Bierkeller, a couple of days later. We ate "Dare's" food and drank their rider, while they were playing. Fucking sad I know, but that was about as "rock and roll" as we got. We played a few more gigs, but they cancelled the gig at the "Astoria" in London, which didn't half fuck us off, especially when we found out the reason, but I won't go into that here.

Vinny told me the reason, but I'm sure he wouldn't remember telling me, all these years later. So, I'd probably end up with a fucking lawsuit against me, or end up brawling at the next "Thin Lizzy" reunion sideshow. To which, my answer is…you're either fucking "rock and roll" or you're not. Don't make excuses for situations you had control over, when they got out of hand. There is nothing to hide behind, it happens to us all. Just fucking enjoy your life for the chances you took, when you took them, because no fucker is gonna remember you, one hundred years down the line. You should be fucking pleased if you are remembered for anything at all, outrageous or not. The more outrageous the better, obviously. If it bothers you in the slightest, what you got up to, then do me a favour, and fuck off.

As we were contracted as the support, and had paid for the privilege, they owed us this one, which was rearranged for a later date, along with an additional gig at the "Tivoli." "Dare" carried on into Europe, while we went back to "Rockworld." A few weeks later, Darren Wharton appeared in "Rockworld", with a small entourage. Rob nudged me, and said nothing. As he passed us, he stopped to speak.

"Hey guys, what have you been up to?"

Rob beat me again.

"Growing our fucking hair. What have you been doing?"

We knew he had been in Europe, but we weren't interested. He said nothing, and moved on. So, it was down to Rob "Loudhailer" Naylor, that they did all they could, to try and fuck us about for the last two gigs. We fucking loved it. We didn't have to pussyfoot around any more, or mind what we said, not that we ever did. All we had to do was try and antagonise anybody we could. The icing on the cake was having a good fucking laugh watching the singer rub baby oil on himself, and then spray water on top of the oil, just before he went on stage, so he looked all sweaty. Nice.

We gigged sporadically for the rest of the year, and drank throughout, when it should have been the other way around. It was December 1991, and Glyn phoned me one evening.

Glyn; "It's only me. Have you seen "Kerrang?""

Me; "Yeah, I've been trying to ring you all fucking day."

Glyn was referring to an article confirming that "Danger Danger" were playing one U.K. show at the "Astoria." I liked them; they had a laid back party attitude, just like Kiss. Bon Jovi must have been so pissed off with them, because by 1988, Bon Jovi had spent four albums trying to write "Bang Bang", a song on the first "Danger Danger" album. Glyn asked if I fancied going to London to watch them.

"Yeah, you can count me in. Have you asked the rest of the lads?"

"Yeah, yeah. Look I've got to go, I'll see you later."

"OK."

I was just about to put the phone down, when Glyn shouted;

"Tony."

"What?"

"I forgot to mention, if you're coming along, bring your fucking guitar, because we're supporting the cunts."

"Fucking brilliant."

That's why I couldn't get through to him all day, because he'd been sorting the gig out. It was part of an idea by "Shades" records, just off Wardour Street, and was billed as "American Dreams." They sorted out gigs for American bands who wouldn't normally come over to the U.K. even though they were popular. They weren't massive, well not here anyway. It was an underground kind of thing, which immediately meant it was cool. I don't know how it worked, but there must have been some kind of enticement involved. We got to London early, and watched the band run through their sound check. Great musicians, tight as fuck, with the backing vocals sampled straight from the albums. The sound was immense. Not only would I be up on stage playing in front of a packed "Astoria", I could then go and watch "Danger Danger", and all for fucking free.

The manager of the "Astoria" gave Glyn a stack of tickets for the gig, and told him that if we sold them outside, we could keep the money. He divided up the tickets, and pushed us outside into the cold January air. All of a sudden, we were hustling the crowd, to see if they wanted any tickets at face value. Most of them thought it was some kind of fucking hoax, and the tickets were forgeries. Meanwhile, they handed over exorbitant amounts to the touts, who they recognised from previous gigs. In the end, people took us up on the once in a lifetime offer, and we cleaned up. This would have been a straightforward "result" had it not been for the touts. They circled us like a pack of fucking hyenas, demanding to know who we were working for. Glyn was as pissed off with them, just as much as they were with us. He matched them word for word, screaming "Fuck You" into stranger's faces. We got rid of every ticket, and dived back into the warmth of the club.

Backstage, we pranced around like "Priscilla, Queen of the Desert" fixing our hair and bangles in anticipation. When it was time, we fought to get on that fucking stage; all dressed as savvy as we possibly could be. We were wearing that much silver, in the form of necklaces, boot straps, earrings and bangles; you could have made a replica F.A. Cup out of them. Throw in our fillings, and you could have made a Dakota DC3 plane. We took our positions on the stage, and exploded into "Why can't love Survive?" The heaving crowd backed us all the way, and we were off. "Loving the Danger." "Time is a Luxury." "Talk is Cheap." "The Bible Song." "Blessed", and a fucking stonking cover of Kiki Dee's "I got the music in Me" completed the shortened set. Not a fucking "filler" in sight, not one. Honestly, you don't know what you missed, you really don't.

Glyn taped the gig on video, and if you didn't know otherwise, you would have sworn that it was our show. Of course, when "Danger Danger" came on, the fucking roof came off, but give me some credit. "Danger Danger" were brilliant, and even threw in "Shout it out Loud" as an encore, with the singer on drums. Before he was a singer, Ted Poley was the drummer in an 80's US band called "Prophet." I've still got the album "Cycle of the Moon", which was a cross between "Pomp" and "AOR." It was one of those albums that you were supposed to own, if you were remotely "in", whatever the fuck "in" was where a record was concerned, but it was only ever a four or five out of ten at best.

After the gig, there was a party in the upstairs bar, which included as much fucking free beer as your body could hold. I sprinted upstairs, as fast as my legs would carry me, only to slow down to a crawl, when I realised it was my turn to drive the fucking van back home. I tried every fucking bribe I could think of, to get one of the beer guzzling fuckers to swap with me, and drive home on this particular night. The night I wouldn't have gone home. The night I would have tagged along with the "L.A. Centrefolds", a bunch of strippers who had turned up at the show, and in turn had latched on to "Danger Danger." They certainly didn't recognise the band, so I could have easily walked a few steps behind, and pretended I was the shy quiet one. My mates laughed in my face, and opened beer after beer, and guzzled the fucking lot in front of me, while burping beer soaked insults right in my face. There was nothing I could do, except wait for my mates to fill their fucking boots with freebies. I couldn't argue, I'd been there countless times, and they always took me home safely. The worst bit was when they opened their beers directly in front of my face, so the spray would hit my face and my lips. I licked my lips and tasted the most fucking minute drop of beer, but that was enough to let me know what a great night I was missing.

In Great Yarmouth, in addition to the big rubber tits, we bought a plastic skull, which was on a stick that was around a foot long. We spent ages passing it between each other, and we basically all did the same rubbish impression of a bad ventriloquist, turning the head from side to side while talking to each other. We all laughed at each other's pathetic attempt to entertain the rest of us, with a plastic head on a stick. Now that's sad enough, but we actually gave the fucking thing a name. "Tommy", if you are interested. I can't point the finger, because I don't know who decided to give the fucking thing a real name. However, if it was me, then I deserved to have been beaten senseless with the fucking thing. In fact, if it was me, somebody should have ripped my leg off at the hip, and kicked the shit out of me with it. Anyway, "Tommy" made an appearance in the bar at the "Astoria." I walked into the bar, and noticed Glyn talking to Jonathan King. Shit hot, were we being lined up to appear on some revamped version of "No Limits?" I couldn't hear what they were saying, so I walked up to them, to try and "earwig" the seeds of our future. As I crept behind Glyn, his booming voice stopped me in my tracks.

"Well why don't you go fuck yourself then?"

Turned out Glyn was a fine judge of character. I diverted my attention immediately, and joined the lads. Steve Kenny had his leather jacket zipped up, and pulled up over his head, so you couldn't see his face. Rob slid "Tommy" into the top of Steve's leather, and Steve grabbed him with an arm that had been zipped inside his jacket. Hey fucking presto, we had a singing dancing skeleton in our presence. To make him one of us, we bought a long wig, and he joined the gang as a fully fledged rocker. A hole had been made in "Tommy's" mouth, so a fag was placed inside. Steve sucked on the hollow plastic tube, and Tommy came alive, puffing away like Eddie Van Halen. Steve wandered around the room, trying to join in conversations, while twisting the head this way and that. Most people ignored him completely, and he finally came to rest in the middle of a crowd of A & R men. With his spare hand, he rubbed "Tommy's" chin, which made him look like he was totally engulfed in the "showbiz" conversations taking place. Steve leaned forward to listen to the wise words being spoken, and in doing so, he burnt one of the A & R guys heads with the fag he had completely forgotten about. Fucking classic, it was probably long overdue anyway. He returned to the crowd and unzipped his jacket. Tears were rolling down his cheeks.

"Sorry lads, we're not gonna get signed tonight."

"Fuck 'em. Fuck them all."

Jonesy was back.

I finally coerced the drunken fools into the van in the early hours, and set off back home, proud with myself that I hadn't touched a fucking drop all night. Around an hour into the journey, I fell asleep in the outside lane. Luckily, the motorway was empty, and it was only the raised ridges of the hard shoulder that woke me up, just like they are supposed to. I sprang to life and stopped the van. Whoever, or whatever, had decided that it wasn't my time, so along with a van full of precious cargo, I stopped at the services for a couple of hours and caught up on some sleep. I drove through the rest of that icy cold January night, with the windows open. It makes me shiver just thinking about it. Well it would, wouldn't it?

# CHAPTER THIRTY EIGHT

*"Child In Time"*

The "Danger Danger" gig took place in January 1992, around the time that the whole "Seattle" scene exploded. Nobody could touch "our" rock music. It was on the radio, it occupied the top positions on the "Billboard" chart, and if that wasn't enough, it was heavy rotation on MTV. We had every base covered, thank you very much, and we were here to stay. Girls, fast cars, sweaty lean torsos, mounds of teased highlighted hair, gleaming teeth, lighting rigs that could be seen from space, songs that made girls cry, slow motion videos, we had it all. I was made for MTV, if only I could get near the fucking thing, or so I thought. Let me tell you how it happened.

One Saturday night I went out, and had a fucking fantastic night. Nothing different really; just a great night out with the lads from the band and our girls. I woke up the next morning, and rock was dead, or to put it another way, the rock I loved, was dead. The police had a suspect, and he had confessed to everything, but it didn't matter, "rock" was dead. To be honest, I saw it coming, but if you ignore these things you think they might go away. No fucking chance here matey. The prime suspect had a cardigan, unkempt collar length hair, and one of those fucking horrible Fender guitars that Buddy Holly played. Are you sure? I thought he wore eyeliner, didn't he? Yeah, that's right. Hey buddy, didn't Motley Crue wear eyeliner? Yeah, once upon a time.

This new music was totally alien to me. I didn't like it at all, even though I knew it had come at the right time. It was a new era, just like it was when I started out in rock music. The lyrics were different for a start. They expressed the angst twisted up inside the younger generation. It was a "Doc Marten" to the "nuts" of the music I loved, which was mainly based around love lost, and love found. A black hood was slipped over the phrase "ooh baby", and it was passed to the Hangman. Even I could see that it was a breath of fresh air, but don't you dare ask me to like it. Every generation of music lovers need something to worship, something to call their own, safe in the knowledge that their peers wouldn't understand it. We all went through it, and every youngster thinks they are the only one it has ever happened to, and quite right too. We're all searching for our own "Beatles", "Stones", "Elvis", "Zeppelin", or "Sex Pistols." Something to piss other people off with. Where did I fit into all of this? Yesterday I was somebody who pissed people off. Today I was somebody who was pissed off. Was it just a gentle nudge to help me on my way, when I had been loitering in the queue marked "adolescence" for far too long? If it was, why didn't anybody tell me about it? Was I just supposed to experience it for myself? Is that the plan, are we all supposed to experience it for ourselves? Does it make us better people? Is that just the way life goes? No warnings, nothing.

All of a sudden, the last link to my childhood, my growing up, was severed. Every piece of music I ever loved was linked to the next piece, consistently throughout my life, in a complex rich tapestry, which imploded in 1991. It wasn't just rock that died that day. Slade, Marvin, Abba, Tavares, Luther, Queen, Aretha, Bowie, The Stylistics, Chic, Earth Wind and Fire, 10CC, The Who, Stiff Little Fingers, Love Affair, Tom Jones, The Beach Boys, Barry White, The Eagles, Hall & Oates, The Mamas & the Papas, Frank Sinatra, The Jacksons, Diana Ross, Simon & Garfunkel, Squeeze. The whole fucking fabric of my identity came tumbling down. I honestly thought I would live forever. That day, I finally took it on board, that "Hey, shit, I'm gonna die some day."

I had a wardrobe full of skin tight faded jeans, paisley shirts, leather waistcoats, dayglo vests, fingerless gloves, and bandanas. One day I was David Geffen's undiscovered gem. The next day I was a cunt. What was I to do? Three quarter length shorts and a "Soungarden" hooded top would have made me look just as much of a twat. I kept my shirts and got some black 501's and some work boots, and tried to fade into the background, but I couldn't. I still had a fucking massive mane of hair, and I wasn't ready for letting go. Musically, the band was swimming against the tide, and we surfaced momentarily, gasping huge gulps of air, before going under again. We carried on in a world we barely recognised. The fun, the spectacle, the chance, the humour, the glamour, the fucking "Benny Hill" of it all, was removed from "rock" music overnight. The bands we liked were being dropped weekly, and before we knew it, the music we loved had become nostalgic.

The best club in town was now Rob's house on a Saturday night, before we went out. Rob was the D.J., serving up Mr. Big, Tyketto, No Sweat, Hardline, Extreme, Giant, plus the classics from not so long ago. You were guaranteed three things; a great laugh, great music, and great women. The crowd was hand picked, and it was strictly invitation only. Throw in as much beer as you could quaff, and it was hard to beat. Surely I could pull at Rob's house. Yeah I could, but it turned out to be myself that I fucking well pulled in the dead of the night, when everybody else was asleep. Wanker, that's me.

One night, Rob was taking requests. He wouldn't fuck off, so I asked him for "Ogre Battle", just like any reminiscent, dewy eyed sex god would. As that magnificent opening riff made every fucker sit up and listen, the phone rang. Rob killed the music, and picked up the phone, as we all listened.

"Hello. Yes I'm Rob."

He paused.

"What do you mean, I'm a cunt?"

We all fixed our eyes on Rob, and the room fell silent as he listened to the caller.

"What do you mean; you've got longer hair than me? Listen lad, I've got the best fucking hair you'll ever see, you cunt."

Silence.

"Very tough, you sad twat. My teeth? What about my teeth? Ken Dodd? Fuck you."

Rob turned to me.

"Hey Tony, this fucker says I look like Ken Dodd."

I spat my beer back into the bottle, struggling to keep the alcohol that was left, from spilling on the carpet. Rob has a couple of caps on his teeth, which to be honest look fine. However, as he is the king of comedy, he has always made an issue about them, and has continually taken the piss out of them himself. Thus, elevating his brand of comedy to a different level, and winning the sympathy of pretty girls at the same time. The wily old fox. He carried on listening.

"Yeah, Tony Bell, that's who I was talking to. What do you mean; he's a bigger cunt than me?"

"Tony, he says you're a right fucking wanker."

Me; "Who is it?"

"I don't know. Hold on, he's saying that you are probably still a virgin, and your fucking hair is like Joanna Lumley's, so he's got a fucking sense of humour at least."

Rob returned to the phone.

"Yeah, well if you've got my number, you probably know where I live. Come on over, I'll knock your fucking teeth out."

"What? No, I'm not collecting them you cheeky cunt. Now fuck off."

Rob slammed the phone down, and turned the music up.

Me; "Who was that mate?"

Rob; "Nobody."

Me; "What?"

Rob; "There was nobody there. When I picked the phone up, the line was dead, so I made the conversation up."

Me; "Joanna Lumley? You cheeky fucker."

Rob; "Never mind that, what about Ken fucking Dodd, twatty? You could have disagreed."

Me; "Yeah, I could have."

We were finally saving money on the amount of hairspray we bought, although it wasn't fucking easy for any of us to adapt totally, but we all looked fine and dandy either way. Gigs changed, as lads turned up to watch us in hooded tops and shorts. Most of them were just following the trend, and they didn't mind a good tune, despite the social comment, or lack of it. The biggest problem I encountered was having to move up at the bar, to accommodate the new pretenders to my throne.

Aerosmith were still massive. Nothing seemed to affect them, even though they mellowed to fit in with radio play lists, the housewives choice. Now don't expect me to sit here and tear a strip off of Aerosmith, after all they have done for me over the years. Everybody has a reason for doing what they do, so let's leave it at that. Kiss wouldn't lie down. They kept going, enduring the same shit they had to deal with in the Seventies and Eighties. Nothing probably changed for them, because they didn't fit in with Purple, Free, Queen, Zeppelin, Lizzy, Van Halen, Aerosmith, Bad Company, Styx, Speedwagon, Journey, Meat Loaf, or any other band from that era. Oh, I tell a lie. Kiss had one band who they walked hand in hand with, and that was Slade. For me, Kiss was a natural progression from Slade. Without Slade, I may not have gotten it at all, it may just have been that little bit too "left field" for me. I didn't know it at the time, but after Slade, I expected Kiss. Slade were Thursday night Top of the Pops, silk scarves, Radio One, Christmas party, scuffed platform shoes with the faintest whiff of dog shit on them, all with electric guitars, and a bunch of songs that you only had to hear once, to know the words.

Kiss were Las Vegas, Broadway, P.T Barnum, Empire State, Arena filling, vaudeville, million dollar showgirls. I'm not having a dig at Slade, just the contrary. It's obvious that Kiss saw Slade, and loved what they saw. Equipped with endless amounts of cash, a 24/7 way of life, and the American dream, they "did" Slade how they wanted to see Slade, songs and all. So, between the pair of them, they came up with enough quality material to keep me going if I live to be three hundred. Kiss put the world to rights at Tiger Stadium in Detroit, in 1996, when they donned the make up once more, and proceeded to show once again, that you can employ the most articulate, graduate, "right on", lefty, "Rolling Stone" hack, to destroy them, and Kiss will blow them into oblivion, with the loudest A Major chord you have ever heard, followed by a D and an E. "Rock and Roll all nite and party every day", you fuckers.

Van Halen lost Dave and gained Sam, and carried on without blinking an eye. I never saw them without Dave, it just wouldn't be right, would it? For me, I have that oh so precious memory of watching the "classic" Van Halen swashbuckling across the stage, stealing everything in sight, from young girl's tears and hearts, right down to my very fucking breath, and it is something I am so reluctant to forfeit. Anyway, they only became REO Speedwagon, with a great guitar player. AC/DC wouldn't budge. They led the way, barging through in strict 4/4, giving not a fuck. Eric Carr, Freddie, Phil Lynott, Randy Rhoads, Stevie Ray Vaughan, John Bonham, Bon Scott. People's heroes passed away, but not before leaving us with magical memories. Most of the bands I liked were driven underground, and became a minority. "Thunder" was the best new British band. They had a great singer, and dished it out like classic "Bad Company." Five years earlier they would have been bigger than Def Leppard.

To be honest, we weren't affected in the slightest by any of this, because we had no status to lose. We didn't have to cut back from arenas to theatres. We didn't have to sell our jet because of plummeting royalties. We weren't moved to a subsidiary of the label as a tax loss. We had no contract that could be ripped up, signalling the end of a bountiful career. My girlfriends didn't suddenly change, from turning heads to turning stomachs. Well, that depends on who you fucking talk to really, because to bring the subject of my birds into the open, suddenly lays me wide open to a barrage of insults, mixed in with some fucking horrible "looky likies", from a set of lads who made it their duty to belittle each other at every opportunity, providing there was a big crowd present.

In terms of our own success, we peaked right at the beginning, and stayed on the same club circuit for years, interspersed with the odd prestige gig here and there. We were writing some great songs, so ignoring the demographics, we went right into the studio and recorded the fucking things. We were going to do the impossible; we were going to "save" rock. Ideas were flowing, we were gelling better than ever before, and we were confident that "Time is a Luxury", "The Bible Song", and "A Little Excitement" were going to elevate us to the status of "Saviours." The fact that I've got to write this fucking thing to explain our intentions, shows that our quest quickly took on the strange fucking features of a pear. Glyn doggedly retraced the steps he had taken for the last five years, knocking on every door he could think of. Some were opened, only for us to be politely refused. The ones that weren't opened, he pissed up against, then wiped his knob on the handle.

We tried to work out what was going wrong. We were all sticklers for melody and arrangements, and we knew what we were doing wasn't shite. We wouldn't have wasted so much fucking time if it was. We weren't idiots; we knew we had something to offer. It's all down to perseverance and conviction. I can't remember who, but somebody once told me that "Video killed the radio Star." It wasn't just me either, all the lads remembered somebody going on about it. So, we sat down and decided that was what we needed.

Our mate Jimmy Heron lived in Cullercoats, on the coast near Newcastle, and he made videos. He used to sing in Sam Thunder for a while, and originally came from Bolton. Rob got in contact with him and told him our plan. Jimmy invited us up to his place for the weekend, to go over a few ideas. Glyn slung the cement mixers out of the back of his van, set up a few rows of deck chairs, and handed out the beers. We squeezed into the portable seaside scene and fucked off up the A1. We played Jimmy the demo, once, twice, probably many times, during the vodka frenzy that ensued. I woke up feeling dreadful, apparently we had been out. I couldn't remember a thing, nothing. After a few brews, I started to have flashbacks of the previous night. The bright lights of the club, a curry house, a taxi, yes I had been there. The lack of cash in my pockets confirmed everything. It suddenly dawned on me that Fugsy wasn't there.

"Where's Fugsy, did he pull?"

Jimmy beckoned me over to the window. A solitary figure struggled across the beach, dragging a canoe over the sands, into the icy North Sea. In his other hand was a tin of beer, and in his mouth was a fag. It was early, it was freezing, but Fugsy was on holiday. He set off in the calm waters, swigging his beer, as if he'd been doing this all his life. Rob distracted me.

"Hey Tony, did you know that Bobby and Jackie Charlton used to live in this house?"

Me; "What, two World Cup winning brothers lived here? That's fucking fantastic."

Rob; "Did they fuck, you daft get."

His phrasing was perfect. It implied I was a gullible idiot, and he changed the subject straight away. One nil to Rob. This was another ruse that started out of boredom, in an attempt to make one of us look a daft twat. All you had to do was casually enter a total fabrication into a conversation, but there had to be enough sense to the fact, so that you made a mental note of the fact, and questioned it later. If it was you that was laying the seed, you changed the subject immediately, so the others wouldn't smell a rat. See, I fell for the "Charlton" story because I knew they were from the North East somewhere. It didn't matter that I didn't know exactly where, that's what Rob relied on. As soon as you acknowledged the nonsense you had just been fed, you were done for. "Did it Fuck", "Do they Fuck", "Are they Fuck", "Is it Fuck", "Was I Fuck", "Can I Fuck", "Will I Fuck", "Do I Fuck", "Does she Fuck" "Are we Fuck", "Did they Fuck." Take your pick.

We were sat listening to "Seven seas of Rhye" one day. The song fades into "I do like to be beside the Seaside." Rob stopped guzzling his beer for a second.

"Did I ever tell you about my Gran's boarding house in Blackpool?"

Me; "Yeah loads of times, you boring twat."

Rob; "Well, in the early Seventies, she was sat on the pier one day, singing along to this song, as a brass band played. I'll never

283

forget that she told me that after the song finished, the conductor told everybody that it had been recorded, and it was going to be used by a band called Queen. So, my Gran is on that song somewhere."

Me; "Is she? That's fucking amazing."

Rob; "Is she fuck."

I was target practice, easy prey.

Jimmy kept to his word, and a couple of weeks later he came down to Manchester, to spend the weekend making a video. On the Saturday morning we all met at the mill in Ancoats where we rehearsed. Most of us had only had a couple of hours sleep, due to partying with Jimmy all night, and we looked fucked. Jimmy, despite the proverb, was confident he could polish the turd that was A.O.K., as he planned to film the video in black and white. Ancoats was silent, as we unloaded our guitars from Glyn's van. Strange, roll the clock back a hundred years, and these mills would have been fucking heaving with a vibrant workforce. The streets would have been crowded with bodies weaving their way to the mills, which were pumping away at full capacity.

The 80's saw these vast complexes decaying, as they had been for decades. Somebody had the foresight to whitewash the walls of these derelict buildings, and turn them into rehearsal rooms for bands, of which there were fucking hundreds in Manchester. Although it was only a further twenty minutes in the car, if you had to catch the train to Piccadilly, it was twenty minutes walk from the train station. The side streets behind Piccadilly station were littered with young kids lugging their guitars towards Ancoats, with a bag of leads in their other hand. Stray dogs roamed the streets, growling for fuck all, as they crossed the road, weighing up whether to attack you or not. Well, a fucking whack with a guitar case certainly made their mind up for them. The damp rooms we chased rats across, have now been converted into luxury apartments for the children of the Millenium, and the place seems to be thriving again.

We led Jimmy up to our floor in the lift, ready to show off our gaff to him. It's only when we brought in an outsider, that it dawned on us what a shit hole we had let the place become. For the first time ever, we reeled back just as Jimmy did, at the stale smell of rockers that had been locked in the room for days on end. It was a bit fucking sharp on the nostrils I can tell you. We waded through the coffee cups, dried out tea bags, McDonalds cartons and porn mags, and stood by our instruments, ready to rock. Jimmy looked around, and shook his head. Most of the walls were covered with centrefolds from our specialist magazines, and the rest of the walls were filthy. It was a right fucking state and would have taken hours to clean up, before we made the video. Fugsy disappeared into the rickety old elevator and set off, in search of what, I had not a fucking clue. He returned ten minutes later, like the cat who'd got the cream.

"You're not going to believe this. The top floor is one fucking huge room. It's not been split into units yet. It's like a fucking aircraft hangar."

Hooray for Fugsy. We clambered into the lift to inspect the new venue, which we were sure would become the answer to some "trivia" rock question, in years to come. It was perfect, so we moved the gear upstairs, and set up a stage. We quickly encountered the slight problem of there being no fucking electricity up there. We clucked around like agitated chickens, fretting wildly, as Fugsy lit a fag. Like Clint, Brando, De Niro, McQueen, Grant and Gable, all rolled into one, he swaggered past us, picking up a screwdriver on the way. He prized the cover off a huge electricity box attached to the wall. We fell silent as he started splitting wires, and joining them again. He plugged in the ghetto blaster, and we had sound. It had taken him all of about twenty minutes. Fugsy was king.

We filmed "A little Excitement" time after time, to give Jimmy enough footage to work from. Glyn went missing, and appeared again five minutes later, wheeling a shopping trolley out of the lift.

Glyn; "I saw this fucker outside, and I thought we could use it. Jimmy, you get in, and I'll race around with you in it, while you are filming. It'll be like one of those flashy film cameras that are set up on a rail, to follow the action without shaking."

Jimmy climbed in, and Glyn jetted him up and down the vast room. Glyn was fucked, his cheeks were bright red and he was out of breath. Jimmy said it had worked brilliantly, but I wondered if our gazes would be focused on the hungover buffoons charging around, when the video was finally made. We had filmed rehearsals and gigs before, but this was something new for us and we loved it.

At this point, I couldn't understand how bands complained about the rigours of touring, recording, photos and video shoots. What possibly drove them to join the circus then? On top of this, some of them reaped huge rewards, for getting drunk, stoned and laid. I didn't understand it, if you had your health, then this lark was a fucking doddle, and no mistake. My experience was limited, but I couldn't grasp how being with your mates, and making music, could make some people so pissed off with it all. The biggest bands in the world started out exactly the same as us, with a gilt edged dream, only for some of them to tell you that it is not the life they wished for. They jumped on to private jets, while we argued over whose turn it was to sit in the front of the van. The unlucky twats who were loaded in with the gear soon had their own drinking gang, and whoever was in the front would be begging for somebody to swap seats, just to get in the "green room." You were told, by a rabble of tone deaf drunks, to go "fuck yourself", as the party in the back got louder. Meanwhile, Glyn moaned like fuck if your knee rested on the gear stick as you drifted off to sleep, while lifting his arse cheek to share his kebab.

Our van, well, Glyn's van, was a white long wheel based Mercedes, and my heart rose every time I saw it. Like Pavlov's dog, I had become conditioned to expect a regimented routine based on a sensory experience. For the dog, it was ears, a bell and food. For me, it was eyes, a van and fun. Glyn had a way of packing it, that utilised every last square inch, and he always ended up with the speakers arranged as seats, so there was at least somewhere to sit, when your drunken carcass was slung in along with the bags. After one gig, he asked me to help him load up, as he couldn't find any of the lads to give him a hand. Nothing fucking new there then. I agreed, as I spotted familiar beer-holding shadows dart and hide in the dark recesses of the club, as their teeth glinted through expanding grins, the lazy twats. I had met a girl, so I went to tell her I was gonna help Glyn sort the van out. Things had got a bit heated in a quiet corner, and she said she would wait for me. As I walked away, a guy stopped me.

"Alright mate?"

"Yeah."

"I thought you were really good tonight."

"Thanks."

"Is that your girlfriend?"

"No, I've only just met her."

I could sense what was coming. He was her ex.

"She's really nice."

"Yeah."

He wasn't angry, so I ditched the "ex" idea. Was he a voyeur?

"I saw what you were doing."

Yes he was.

"What?"

He caught me right off guard, and before I could tell him to fuck off, he was in to me again.

"Look, if I can smell your fingers, I'll buy you a beer."

I started laughing, but his face was serious, so I pushed my luck.

"Two beers and it's a deal."

"OK, what are you drinking?"

"Bud, get me two Bud's."

He went to the bar, and I stood there wondering what the fuck was going on. As he pushed through the crowd, I had an idea. I shoved my right hand down the back of my jeans, and had a right good fucking scratch of my arsehole. My arsehole that had been confined to my sweaty skin tight jeans as I tore about the stage for an hour, under the burning lights. My arsehole that had not yet had the pleasure of a palm full of shower gel, or the slightest blast of fragrant aerosol. My arsehole that due to the furnace of the club I was in, was not dry. The lad returned with two beers, which I grabbed with my left hand. He stood there silent and raised his eyebrows, indicating that he had fulfilled his part of the bargain, and now it was my turn. I raised my right hand, and rubbed my fingers around his nostrils. He pulled back immediately, but I thrust the fucking things into his face, trying to get inside his nostrils. His lips curled, and his face creased as he started spluttering. He looked like somebody had emptied a full can of "Mace" into his face. For a split second I got angry. My arse wasn't that fucking bad. That was an insult. He gasped as he spoke.

"Fucking hell, that's horrible."

I thought he was going to be sick. He didn't take up the offer of a further sniff, and he left the club in a right fucking state. I went to the toilet, scrubbed my hands, supped my freebies and made my way back to Glyn, only to find the van fully packed.

Jimmy returned to Manchester a couple of weeks later, with the finished video. We gathered at Rob's for the screening, amidst a pile of pizza boxes, beer cans and vodka bottles. Jimmy did us proud as we "hammed" it up in slow motion, looking rather fucking dapper, even if I say so myself. You want a song? Well "A little

287

Excitement" was a groovy little fucker. You want a rock video? Well Jimmy caught us in our natural environment, of being together, and "rocking" like fuck. You want hair? You've come to the right place honey. We sat in silence, witnessing a fucking great moment in our history. The room got smaller, as seven chests swelled with pride. We turned to each other without saying a word, and then focused on the TV screen again. We handed out the beers, rewound the tape, and watched it until the sun came up. We now had another tool to bombard the companies with, but outside our own little world we wondered if there was any place for the music we made. Again, people were interested, but nobody bought into the idea. Not even the rock shows that had emerged on TV, playing video after video. When we should have been down, we were up. We didn't care; we were now available on video.

# CHAPTER THIRTY NINE

*"Boom Boom, Out Go The Lights"*

The summer of "92" turned into autumn, and we gigged as often as we could, culminating in a gig at "Rockworld" in November. We had a load of new songs in the set, all with a harder edge, but they still had that all important component that made a girl shake her ass and move her feet at the same time. "Well that's not fucking special" I hear you cry. "Thousands of bands have that effect on girls." That's exactly the point. We could do what Van Halen did. Could your band? We started with a new song called "On the Edge", and it was a big menacing fucker of a song. The hairs on the back of my neck stood up, and I knew the rest of the lads felt the same. For me, this was it. I didn't care about the latest fad. If I could still feel this way five years later, then we were doing something right, if only for each other. Gone were the epaulettes, gone were the tassels, and gone were the bright colours. It was strictly, black, leather, honest, hairy, heavy and melodic.

We didn't know who we would appeal to, but at least we appealed to us. Bands like us fell by the wayside because they weren't already established when "grunge" changed the world. All of the big mainstream bands like Aerosmith, Van Halen, Leppard, Bon Jovi, AC/DC, Ozzy, weren't affected at all. They laughed in the face of "grunge" and then turned their attention back to the sold out "arena" tour they were just about to embark on. Although we had been at it for over five years, to be thrust into the limelight at this point, would have been a fucking nightmare. People would have thought we were a new band, stuck in a "Spinal Tap" time dimension, where sad twats reigned supreme. Obviously, we would have had no fan base whatsoever, and I would have been begging for my job back, three months after I left the fucking place, after vowing never to return, as the record company told us they had made a bad decision. Anyway, everything came full fucking circle, as these innovative, happening, new bands turned up with their

"Kiss" lunchboxes, saying that the last great song they heard was "House of Pain" or "Girl gone Bad" from "1984." These were the very bands they rebelled against in the first place.

Being in a band puts you in the enviable position of being able to write songs you want to hear. No matter how much of a music fan you are, if you are not a musician, then you have got to wait, and pray that somebody writes songs that you will like. Then, depending on how popular each particular band is, you may not ever get to hear the song, which may be the one to change your whole fucking life. Think about it, you may never ever get to hear the song that would be your favourite song in the world, ever. Forget your top ten songs. Somewhere, hidden on this planet are hundreds of songs that would melt your head, but you're never gonna hear them. Just in case you are interested, and if you are not, then it's just to take up a bit of room, but in no particular order, I'll give you a list of songs that I love. It may give you an insight into who I am, or it may just make you think "Wanker." However, bearing in mind what I have just said, I am totally aware that there are songs I will never hear, which would make me wipe these fuckers off the board tomorrow.

| | |
|---|---|
| "Heaven must be missing an Angel." | Tavares. |
| "Dance the night Away." | Van Halen. |
| "I can't tell you Why." | The Eagles. |
| "The Rover." | Led Zeppelin. |
| "Rock Candy." | Montrose. |
| "Gentle on my Mind." | Dean Martin. |
| "Knocking at your back Door" | Deep Purple. |
| "New York Minute." | Don Henley. |
| "Hungry Heart." | Bruce Springsteen. |
| "Girl can't help It." | Journey. |
| "Mary's Prayer." | Danny Wilson. |
| "Dream On." | Aerosmith. |
| "Love Gun." | Kiss. |
| "Got to get you into my Life." | Earth Wind & Fire. |
| "Dreamtime." | Daryl Hall. |
| "Stargazer." | Rainbow. |
| "Wouldn't it be Nice?" | Beach Boys. |
| "Far far Away." | Slade. |
| "Silly love Songs." | Wings. |

| | |
|---|---|
| "Let it Go." | Dan Reed. |
| "Signed sealed Delivered." | Stevie Wonder. |
| "Thank you for the Music." | Abba. |
| "Highway to Hell." | AC/DC. |
| "Waitin' for the Heartache." | Jimmy Barnes. |
| "Laughter in the Rain." | Neil Sedaka. |
| "In the Summertime." | Mungo Jerry. |
| "Help Yourself." | Tom Jones. |
| "Promises." | White Sister. |
| "Slow n Easy." | Whitesnake. |
| "Abraham, Martin and John." | Marvin. |
| "The fairy fellers master Stroke." | Queen. |
| "Baba O'Reilly." | The Who. |
| "Still in love with You." | Thin Lizzy. |
| "Let's go round Again." | Average White Band. |
| "A Li'l ain't Enough." | Dave Lee Roth. |

Well, there's one 90 minute tape full already, but I could be here all bastard night reeling off songs you fucking hate, so shut your moaning for a second, and carry on reading, you whingeing twat.

Anyway, with "Rockworld" under our belts, we stretched our legs and went away for the weekend, courtesy of Glyn's cut price deals. Nottingham Friday and Birmingham Saturday. It wasn't for wimps this fucking picnic. Friday was total mayhem, and we made the decision to set off for Birmingham early, so we could all sleep off some big hangovers. It wasn't easy, as most of us looked like we should have had a nametag tied around our big fucking toes.

However, we made the right decision, because as soon as we got to the Holiday Inn, in Birmingham, we all drifted off into a fantastic slumber that lasted until well after it was dark. Glyn woke us in time for "Final Score", and we carried on drinking as soon as we woke up. Big, white, fluffy, hotel dressing gowns and pineapple towels on our heads showed that we meant fucking business this particular evening. There was some major scrubbing, buffing, polishing and soaping going on, as we danced around supping beer and vodka to the fucking excellent compilation tapes I had made. "So this is Love." "Still of the Night." "Baby now I." "Rock you like a Hurricane." "Naughty Naughty." "Love in an Elevator." "Tears are Falling." "Modern day Cowboy." If your fucking foot wasn't tapping, then you must have been an amputee. Between the seven of us, we all had different definitions of the word "cleanliness", even though we had all made an effort to look as dapper as possible. To me, cleanliness is scrubbing your arse until any shitty, claggy lumps are washed clean away from your hairy crease, until it smells like fucking daisies. To others it meant twisting their arse tags and pulling them until they snapped, leaving a smelly wick. To some, it just meant merely pushing them up out of sight, saving them for their delving fingers, back in the very same room, later that evening, when they thought the rest of us were asleep.

Anyway, I placed the porn mags on the radiator in the bathroom underneath the mirror, paying particular attention to the angle that the mags lay against the wall. Too upright, and the fucking pages buckled and folded, mid-stroke. Get it right, and providing you had remembered to lock the door, you were fucking flying. This particular evening, I was the "Red Baron." Loop the Loops, followed by gravity defying twists and turns reader, let me tell you. I got a bit carried away, and the fucking towel flew off my head a few times, but I couldn't care less, the door was still locked, and it was hours 'til "showtime." By the time I left the hotel I was sweating vodka, "Jonesy" had seen to that. "Personal bests" were put to the test, as we all fell one by one. I could tell I was in trouble, because I'd never had so many best mates in one fucking evening.

I woke on the Sunday morning, to find Glyn and Rob sat on the bed, laughing like bastards. I checked my hair, just to make sure the fucking thing was still there, and then I checked my knob. Well, with this pair pissed up, anything could happen when there was a hopeless drunken mate lying at their mercy. In these situations, what would be the worst possible situation to find yourself in? Go on think about it. What would fill you with the most horror? I know mine. Somewhere in the back of my mind, there is some dark recess that conjures up some fucking horrible images, especially when I am at my most content and happy. No matter how great things are going, there is a nagging in my mind that some fucking colossal catastrophe is waiting to make an appearance in my life. The happier I am, the more I expect something to come and tear my world apart. So, I can't even fucking appreciate the good times properly, because I'm waiting for the Grim Reaper with his hair clippers, Beelzebub with a "ginger" hit list, Jimmy Saville with that fucking "Jim'll fix It" letter that I sent in 1976, begging to meet ABBA. Oh, I suppose you were too fucking cool to consider anything so soft weren't you? Why don't you just admit to your past and enjoy it for what it was. We can't be cool for every fucking second of our lives, so drop the act, and smile about all of the times you've made a complete twat of yourself. Anyway, getting back to the point I'm trying to make. This uncomfortable feeling I get at the strangest times, is it all part of the human condition, to reaffirm the sanctity of the situation, and multiply my gratification for the good fortune bestowed upon me? I dunno.

Anyway, on the lighter side of the macabre, I have already dreamed up the ultimate jape to mess with the minds of your drunken best friends. I never played this trick on any of the lads, and this will be the first time they have ever heard about it. Rob and Glyn both came so fucking close, but I couldn't find my wicket keepers gloves. Firstly, after a big night on the piss, when your drunken mate wakes up, tell him how hammered he was. He will no doubt already be aware of the fact. Turn the conversation around to food, and bang on about what a fantastic piece of corn on the cob you had for lunch yesterday. Then go about your business as usual. Time will pass, and he will eventually go for a piss. As he lets go with last nights slops, he will notice the piece of sweetcorn you have strategically placed under his foreskin as he lay snoring and farting all night. As you can see, this is why I never went through with this. The look of horror would be priceless wouldn't it? Well, you do the fucking maths!

Getting back to the arsey, sweaty, porn laden, crusty tissued, Birmingham hotel room, Rob and Glyn were still laughing.

Me; "What is it?"

"Fugsy." They both said.

Me; "What's happened?"

Rob; "He's got no eyebrows."

Me; "Fucking hell, who's done that?"

Glyn; "All of us. Well, all except you, you drunken twat. He's not fucking happy."

Me; "You tight fuckers."

Glyn; "Aaah, we were pissed."

His defence was weak.

Rob; "It's alright for you Jonesy, I was there when he woke up. He looked at me, and I was horrified. He didn't have a fucking clue, so he jumped out of bed and made the coffee. Happy as fucking Larry he was. He was saying what a great fucking time he'd had, when he walked into the toilet. All of a sudden he fell silent and then stormed out."

Me; "What happened?"

Rob; "He was fucking angry. He came flying out of the toilet and demanded to know who had done it."

Me; "What did you say?"

Rob; "I told him that Dan had done it."

Me; "What, you blamed Dan?"

Rob; "Well, it was Dan… and me and Glyn, and Steve and Andy, and Noel."

I got dressed and tried to avoid Fugsy for as long as possible. I left the room and walked towards the lift. Fugsy was waiting for the lift, and he looked like a rubber doll. Although it was initially amusing, I knew how he felt. If it was me, I'd have been fucking livid. He said nothing, so I stood next to him in silence. This wasn't funny in the slightest. Inside the lift, he turned away from me, but the lift had mirrored walls, so I could see him wherever I looked. He then had to suffer the indignity of joining a queue to check out of the fucking place at the crowded reception, as the people stared and pointed in silence. He was a broken man.

I sat in the back of the van, opposite Fugsy, for what turned out to be the second most awkward journey of my life. He said nothing, nobody did. The van was our "inner sanctum", somewhere that was nothing to most people, but it was so fucking special to all of us. This particular day it was like a hearse, carrying the corpse of something that had previously been full of life. I was relieved to be out of the fucking thing after a long, long journey. I spoke to Glyn later in the day, and he was back to normal, eagerly organising our next night out.

A couple of days later, he picked me up on the way to the rehearsal room. When we got there, we opened the door, to find a space where Fugsy's keyboards had been. He had been there before us, and the sad thing about it, was that he had been there on his own, without us, in a silent room that had echoed with our laughter, sometimes on a nightly basis. It must have taken a lot for him to make that decision. He must have been so pissed with us, because he didn't tell anybody his intentions, he just upped and left. The chain had been broken, and it had been broken by the person who I had come to think of as one of the strongest links. He was the guy that never ever had to be asked if he fancied a night out. He was the guy that slept in the rehearsal room until he worked out how to programme the sequencers that were patched through his keyboards. He was the guy that threatened to twat the headlining bands if he thought they were fucking us about, just so we wouldn't get a sound check. He was the guy that was everybody's nomination for the "Dead Pool" if we ever got signed, because he didn't know when to stop when he was with his mates. He was the guy, who we could all start amazing yarns about, with the phrase, "I've got this mate called Fugsy..." from here you could go practically anywhere.

The lads turned up, and we went straight to the pub. Did we want another keyboard player? I didn't want another keyboard player, I wanted Fugsy back; we all did. He was our keyboard player. He was just one of the gang. We sat and waited, hoping he would just turn up again, but he didn't get in touch with any of us. The music we played wasn't even yesterday's news; it was the day before yesterday's news. We still loved it, but there was nowhere to go with it. We couldn't progress, because nobody was getting signed. Not with our fucking hair anyway, and I wasn't about to "bob" the fucker off for anybody. New bands flourished, like they always had done, but melodic rock, that "baby" of the late '70's and '80's, keeled over and hit the deck in the most ungracious fashion.

Britain always had a great "club" scene, but we had been on it for years, and this is where our heroes were banished to, so what fucking chance did we have? The prospect of progressing was now zero, it probably always had been, but my lifelong dream had now been given a wake up call. Not the gentle wake up call, when you are awake before the alarm in the summer, as the Sun gives you a gentle nudge to tell you that the larks are singing. Oh no, this was the wake up call that came from the Butchers shop in 1978, when the alarm alerted me in the pitch black, and the fucking wind and hail beckoned me through the icy sleet on a dark Saturday morning, to dupe me into climbing into a freezer full of ice, time and time again.

We met again, a few days later, and Steve and Andy said they didn't want to start the search for a keyboard player, which could take months and months. Circumstances and time had finally crossed paths in late 1992, creating the moment for us to end the band. A moment sooner and we wouldn't have considered anything so absurd. A moment later and we would have been that awkward last guest at the party, when all you want to do is go to bed. We had all come to terms with the fact that we weren't going to make a career out of the most exciting, coveted business on the planet. I could never envisage Rob or myself giving up on the band without a fight, but there was nothing to fight for any more. I wasn't angry, and I certainly didn't blame anybody for the decisions they had made. There was no way I was going to try and talk them round, because I knew that A.O.K. was a massive part of all of our lives. I respected them far too much to ask them if they had thought about it properly. Of course they had, I could see it on their faces. I hadn't seen this look on anybody's face in the last five years, and although it was a sad moment, it showed me that I was special to them because they shared their emotions with me. It's easy to be one dimensional with people you meet on an irregular basis, like band members, but we transgressed that blip early on, and forged some great friendships. We agreed to split the band up, and then organised our next piss up. We had run our natural course, and parted the best of friends. It makes me wonder if the "eyebrow" incident was subconsciously pre-planned, to give us a nudge in the right direction, so we could end it all with a bit of dignity.

We all went to "Rockworld" the following Saturday, and had a good fucking drink, to say goodbye. People had heard we had split up, but nobody could tell. Flaming cocktails, beer races, laughter, and a crowd of beautiful girls. It was like we had just landed the biggest fucking deal on the planet. We all talked earlier in the week, and everybody agreed we should go out "all guns blazing." We wound each other up all week until we were all fired up to fuck. Sometimes I scared myself with how cool we could all look, given the right amount of preparation time, and the right amount of alcohol, but this particular night we did ourselves proud and surpassed even our own expectations. Call me arrogant, call me biased, call me whatever the fuck you want, but we looked like rock stars. Everybody knew about mine and Rob's hair, and the shit we gave each other, and other people about the length of it, because most people didn't come fucking close. And we told them so. Everybody knew that Steve Kenny was the guy that should have been on a fucking poster on every Rock Chick's bedroom wall. Everybody knew that Andy Chemney made the art of shit hot drumming look effortless. Everybody knew that Noel Fraser had the looks and the "jaw" to make it on to prime time U.S. television, should he ever choose to do so.

Then there were the girls. We always had a crowd of great looking girls with us, whether we were fucking them or not. Mostly we were, but people liked us for our humour and honesty first, so the good looks and raging sexual appetites were a bonus. The gigs were gonna be so fucking hard to give up, but apart from not playing music, things didn't really change that much. I was always trying to drink as fast as I could, gig or not, just so that I could grab the two bottles of beer that were still waiting on the bar for me, while not breaking contact with the blonde's eyes.

The bands that had previously considered themselves our "competition" faded away, leaving us to get as pissed as we could. They didn't like it, because although we didn't have a band any more, you were aware the second we walked into a place, from the sudden increase in the crowd and the noise, or by the way that girls edged around us. That sounds fucking big-headed doesn't it? However, most girls were great fun, and just out for a laugh, because we were jokers. Some however, laughed along with the other girls, and then told me they were going to fuck my brains out later. Angels, the fucking lot of them. A girl asked me why we had split up. I pointed to Rob and Steve.

"Because I hate those fuckers."

She walked off as another girl spoke into Rob's ear. I couldn't hear what she said, but Rob looked over his shoulder, and pointed to me.

"Because I hate that cunt, that's why."

A few lads from other bands came and asked us about it. Rob dealt with them, as only he could.

"Look, you weren't fucking bothered before, so don't act interested now. Go on, fuck off you cunts."

You still couldn't get a fucking Rizla between us. We hadn't split up we had just stopped playing music together. We were just as strong. Most of us got married, most of us had children, and most of us had met the best set of friends anybody could wish for. Although I had failed to "make it", I didn't care. Along the way, purely by chance, my path crossed with those that made my life such a laugh. Anybody would be grateful just for that, but there was so much more.

297

# CHAPTER FORTY

*"That's Me In The Corner"*

Well, you've stuck with me all of the way so far, and I hope you've laughed at least once or twice, at some of the ridiculous situations we faced during our youth. Not one of them serious, but hey, they were serious enough at the time. Anyway, how do you wrap up a book that has never really gone anywhere? Can a book about failure be a success? It seems a big contradiction to me, but fairytale endings rarely happen. For every U2, there are a million A.O.K.'s. I'm not bitter in the slightest, because I know damned well, that "Bono" would be half the man Steve Kenny is. "George Michael", maybe a great man, but he is only a shadow of the colossus that is Glyn Jones. Throw the "classic" Van Halen into a melting pot with Kiss, and their combined "might" would only come up to Rob Naylor's knees. Shane McGowan likes a drink does he? Well give him Steve Ferguson's number. You think Charlie Watts is laid back, while "carrying" his band? Well step forward Andy Chemney. When you got bored of your Jon Bon Jovi posters, did you wonder where the next "film star" rock singer was coming from? I didn't. He was the singer in my band, Noel Fraser. I saw something in each of them that raised my spirits. Although we had finished the band, we never strayed far from each other. Something that turned out to be a blessing of sorts.

In 1996, the lads, without request, joined hands with Mandy and myself, along with our families and friends, and walked with us on a journey straight into the abyss, and out the other side. Not one person let go until the journey was over, and it was only because of the strength of everybody concerned, that we finally made it out. Our Daughter, Taylor Alice Bell was born on 25th October 1996, and she was five weeks premature. There were major problems with her delivery, and she was starved of oxygen for a dangerously long time. When she was born, she was lifeless, silent, grey, helpless, and looked like she needed her mum so badly. Doctors and nurses came rushing from nowhere, injecting her and fitting pipes and monitors into her, while talking in a frenzied conundrum of words I didn't understand. Then it hit me, I was convinced that she was dead, and I became hysterical, screaming and shouting, while Mandy sobbed uncontrollably. Taylor was taken out of the delivery room, and we were left on our own with a nurse trying to explain what was happening. I tried to listen to what she was saying, but it just didn't make any sense. It wasn't the reasons she was giving, it was the actual words I couldn't understand. It was plain English, but nothing was registering in my mind, and I couldn't identify the words, no matter how simple. I just couldn't make out what was being spoken to me. Mandy grabbed my hand, not to comfort me, well it was to comfort me, but also to let me know that she couldn't make any sense out of what was happening either. My head was ready to explode as we hugged and cried. I didn't even know where Taylor was. She was whisked away without any warning, and we feared the worst. After what seemed like the longest time, a nurse popped her head round the door and smiled.

"Do you want to see Taylor?"

In a split second, normality had been restored. Me and Mandy looked at each other, totally ravaged by the last twenty minutes of our lives. We both spoke.

"Is she alive?"

"Yes, but she's very poorly."

I couldn't believe it, my heart gushed like it was about to burst. I grabbed hold of the wheelchair, and I whizzed Mandy down to the Special Care Unit, where we noticed Taylor straight away. She was a lovely pink colour, just the way all babies should be. She had loads of dark brown hair, and was long, slim, elegant and beautiful. I held her tiny hand, and kissed her for the first time in my life. She was the nicest smell, the softest touch, and the most intense feeling I have ever experienced. The moment my lips touched my baby, our own creation, I crumbled. In a split second, Taylor opened a door inside of me that I never knew existed. It was a short cut to my heart that nobody had ever found before. As she tugged on the door, our initials were already carved, inside a big, big heart on the front of it. I thought I had experienced everything, but in she breezed like a breath of fresh air, and blew everything away that I had clung to so dearly. Effortlessly, she stole my heart, and showed me what I had been searching for.

She stared silently at her mum and dad without blinking. Her legs were outstretched, rather than in the foetal position that babies adopt, and she already looked weary of this world. Mandy clung on to her baby without saying a word. I knew that Mandy was feeling guilty, but it was nobody's fault, and certainly not hers. Your mum is the safest place in the world when you are small, and that was all Mandy wanted to be for her precious little girl. Being parents for the first time is hard enough, but the situation we were in had never even entered our thoughts, and so it shouldn't have. We were totally devastated. I always wondered if the sound of your newborn child crying relentlessly would drive you crazy, but at that moment, it was all I wanted to hear, just once.

We phoned our families and friends and explained the situation, and they all rushed to the hospital. Mike was on his way to a weight-lifting competition in London when I phoned him, and I heard his tyres screech as he made a handbrake turn, and headed for the hospital. It must have looked like we were fussing over nothing, because when they turned up, Taylor was a lovely colour, and was quite long, despite her early appearance. Smiles broke out as we laughed about the fate that lay ahead regarding her looks. Would she be a babe like her mum, or would she be unfortunate enough to favour my gene pool? A nurse took Mandy and myself to one side, and asked us if we would like to have Taylor christened. Our hearts sank, as a Doctor explained that her Adrenal glands had been destroyed. Apparently, they produce adrenaline, which keeps your heart beating. Taylor had been given injections of adrenaline, as her body could not produce it. Although I had no great desire to have Taylor christened, I stood by Mandy and agreed. Mandy has faith, not just in God, but in the goodness of mankind, and it was no time for me to put my cynical head on, when nothing could have resolved the situation. The vicar came to the hospital, said a prayer, blessed her, and gave us a certificate. I could barely speak as I kissed Taylor.

"I'm so sorry Taylor."

She blinked, as my tears fell on her face. Mandy was drained, and couldn't summon up any words. There were no words to say. She was ripped apart from her very core. Every last ounce of her love was pouring into her little girl.

We spent the night in the hospital, unable to sleep. Exhausted, we wandered up and down the corridor, checking on Taylor, and then drifted in and out of sleep that never lasted more than a couple of minutes. Morning came, and Taylor's first twenty-four hours passed quietly. One day old, and I felt like I had known her all of my life. Loads of people came to visit the second day, and we showed her off for every single one of them. I told Mandy that Taylor could recognise my voice, because she moved when I went near her. Of course, I was dreaming.

I was holding her hand when Rob and Christine turned up. Rob gave her a kiss and said.

"She looks ten times better today, doesn't she?"

"Yeah, maybe they can take her off these monitors soon."

I was in denial. The nurse looked at me, but she bore no expression whatsoever. No smile, no look of sadness, no raised eyebrows, nothing. The lack of anything told me that I was wrong. She couldn't have made it any clearer if she had shouted it in my face. In the evening, we sat on the bed in a daze; we hadn't slept for nearly three days. We were shattered. Mandy held my hand, and her grip softened as she fell asleep. There was a knock on the door and we jumped up. We had been asleep for ten minutes. A nurse came into the room.

"It's time to say goodbye."

Her gentle whisper was full of sadness. I dropped my head and reached for Mandy's hand. I couldn't offer one single word to comfort her. Me, big mouth, Mr. Wise Guy, with an answer for everything. Well not today. I tried to be strong, as I led Mandy down the corridor, but I have never been so scared in my life. I wanted to run as fast as I could, to make sure I didn't miss Taylor, but I also wanted to walk as slowly as I possibly could, praying that she would wait for her mum and dad, extending her miniscule life for a few precious moments longer. I was no more prepared than Mandy for any of this, and I wished that somebody would help me down the corridor. Maybe they did. When we entered the Special Care Unit, a nurse was removing the last tube from Taylor's nose. The nurse picked her up ever so delicately, and passed her to her mum. I was crying out loud at a scene I had taken for granted and expected to see for eight months, but one I would never see again. Mandy gave her a great big hug, and whispered in Taylor's ear with that reassuring warmth that dad's just don't have.

"Hello my baby. Now what's all this fuss about?"

Mandy was so strong. I was just the idiot that had been

involved eight months earlier. Mandy carried Taylor. She bought the clothes, she bought the magazines, she felt every kick, she threw up, she took the vitamins, she picked the curtains, she practised the nursery rhymes, she spent hours picking names, she had sleepless nights, she complained of swollen feet, she nagged me to decorate. She loved every single minute of being a mum, and now it was about to be taken away from her. I hugged Mandy as we cradled Taylor in between us. This was my first family hug. It wasn't meant to be this way. Taylor's eyes gradually closed, and her chest heaved as she searched for breath. Mandy kissed her and hugged her tightly.

"Sssh, go to sleep darling."

She stroked Taylor's hair and kissed her goodbye. I hugged my baby and told her that I loved her, and thanked her for two days that I would never ever forget. As we held her in between us, Taylor's breathing faded as we hugged and cried. The room fell silent and she was finally at peace.

Writing this has hurt me like nothing you will ever know, or I hope you will never know, and I have cried from start to finish of every single letter. Taylor would be ten now, and she would have wrapped me around her little finger. I was supposed to keep her safe. I was supposed to make her life wonderful; I was supposed to protect her. I was supposed to chase the lads down the garden path, for daring to fall in love with my angel. All I could do was watch in silence, as my baby weakened over the short thirty six hours she was with us.

> *"You'll never know that the cow jumped over the moon.*
> *They put him back together again.*
> *They fetched a pail of water.*
> *He had ten thousand men."*

We hit rock bottom with the mightiest crash, and lay there motionless, unable to function, while trying to come to terms with what had just happened to our family. It wasn't just us, our families and friends were in this with us, and a lot of fantastic people grappled for the torch between themselves, determined to lead me and Mandy into the light again. All of a sudden, the floor of "rock bottom" gave way, and we plummeted headlong into the darkest, scariest free fall of the Human consciousness possible. We were both scared to sleep, because of the nightmares that lay in wait for us every night. Our families and friends stood up when we needed them to, and their lives changed as they adapted their routines and work patterns to support us. I thought I was strong enough to deal with the situation that was threatening to drown us, but without the people that cared, we would have just been another sad statistic, I'm sure. My brother Steve turned into the hero I always knew he was, as he watched over us while not knowing what to do himself. They felt helpless, we all did, but every one of them was paramount throughout our grieving and healing process. I sat with Rob, and I would talk all night, just like the night before, and the night before that, and the night before that, asking just one question. "Why?" I can't remember when we first laughed again, but I'm sure we were with Rob and Christine.

Taylor was cremated at Rochdale Crematorium, and the place was full. People were spilling out of the church, and into the grounds. Although I'm sure they would have loved her, the majority of the people present had never seen Taylor, so their presence was purely as a mark of love and support for Mandy and myself, at a time when we were desperate for anything. The thought of burying your child should never have to enter into anybody's mind, but the day was forced upon me, when I had to carry my little girl's coffin past all of my family and friends, to a place where I had to offer her up to someone, something, maybe nothing, for safekeeping until Mandy and myself are ready. Ready for what, I don't have a clue.

Even in my lowest desperate moments, I couldn't say with any real faith, that we will meet her again someday. At best, it's a nice thought, which offers a temporary comfort to the surreal world you find yourself in, but the chances of it happening? Sadly, I very much doubt it. Naively, I thought Taylor would be a perfect little girl who would outlive her mum and dad, have a great life, and make us so proud. You couldn't blame us for thinking that, no, for expecting that. After all, that's what happened. You had children, you loved them to bits while watching them grow, suddenly realising you had grown old yourselves. Nothing comes close to the bond between you and your children, no matter how short and treasured your time together, but the day had come when I had to walk to the front of a massive silent crowd and carry Taylor to her final place of rest, and let her go.

There is no script, nobody tells you where to stand, what to say, when to move, nothing. When the hearse arrived I was handed the tiniest coffin I have ever seen. I gasped as I cradled my treasure and whispered "Hello." All I wanted to do was grab Mandy and run off and sit under a tree and spend one last moment together in the sunshine, just once. There were a million things I never told Taylor. There were songs to sing, there was so much I needed to say in these final moments, but our time together had passed in a fleeting glimpse, and I knew whatever I hadn't said by now was too late.

I had obviously bypassed normality, and entered some bizarre twilight zone, because I did not cry, even though it was the saddest moment of my entire life. We chose "Close to You" by the "Carpenters", as the music to say goodbye to Taylor. A beautifully simple tune that affected everybody there. It rained torrentially for the week beforehand, and it rained for a week solid afterwards, but on this particular day, the sun was shining. It finally hit me hard a week later, when we buried Taylor's ashes in her plot in the "children's" section at the cemetery. Me, Mandy, the vicar, and the rain. This time I was handed a box that was about three or four inches square that contained her ashes. Maybe it was because I had carried her coffin, which was small enough, but this was even harder for me to deal with, because there was nothing of her anymore. She was gone forever. She was a memory to those lucky enough to have met her. To the rest, she was just a name. To me and Mandy, she was our world.

Our friend Deb Thornton is a night club singer, and she asked us if she could organise a charity gig in Taylor's name, to raise money for the Special Care Baby Unit at Fairfield Hospital, where she died. It was a great idea, and offered us something to focus on, instead of holding each others hand and crying all day. Deb booked the club, arranged the acts, printed the tickets, sorted out the raffles, the prizes, everything. Mandy grew up with Deb, and I've known her for years because of the music and clubs we loved. She loved getting drunk and dancing to the loudest music, and up to this point, it was my only memory of Deb; but suddenly she was committed to a cause. She was brilliant. The night was a sell out, as people travelled from miles around, just to let us know that they cared.

My brother was working at Brian McClair's house, and somehow managed to wangle a signed Manchester United shirt off him. Not just his autograph, but the whole bloody team. Cantona, Keane, Schmeichel, Giggs, Beckham, the lot. Manchester City also let me have a signed football, and these two items, above all others, turned the raffle into a frenzy. Every ticket was sold, and the prizes were drawn. I picked the winner of the football, and I handed the prize to an ecstatic City fan. As I handed the prize over, two lads approached me. One of them said to me.

"How much is that?"

"I'm sorry mate, the football was a raffle prize."

"No, not the football, that."

The lad was pointing to the Manchester City plastic bag that the football had been in. It had the club badge on each side of the bag. I handed the bag to him and smiled.

"Here mate, you can have it."

"No fucking way. I'll give you a fiver for it."

It was a great gesture, and my eyes filled with tears. His mate jumped in.

"I'll give you six pounds."

He thrust six pounds in my hand, but his mate pushed him aside.

"Seven pounds."

His mate looked at him.

"Hold on, eight pounds."

This carried on, and I sold a plastic bag for twelve pounds. Tears rolled down my face as I hugged the strangers. In the end, I think we raised well over £1000. Deb did us both proud, and Taylor. Deb will always be very special to us, because of the selfless, honest, no bullshit type of friend she has always been.

Days turned into weeks, as we were cast beneath the darkest cloud imaginable, and the slightest task took the greatest amount of effort. Mandy cried for hours, just for a chance to hold Taylor again. I was useless; I couldn't do anything to ease the pain. I tried to be strong, but this meant that I cooked the odd meal, or went to the shops, certainly nothing heroic, because I've never been anybody's hero, not really, but it was all I could offer. I gradually got worse, and Mandy sensed it was time to help me. She managed to find the strength to put her demons to one side, and give me the love that I needed to show me the way. That might sound a bit dramatic, but at one point I honestly thought that there was no way out.

We went to a meeting of S.A.N.D.S. the Stillborn and Neo-natal Death Society. Sounds scary doesn't it? Well it does exactly what it says on the tin. It's raw, it's frightening, it's honest, it's graphic, it's ugly, it's aggressive, it's painful, it's brutal, but in the middle of the darkest recess, there is a flicker of light. Newcomers are thrown into the spotlight, as you bare your soul in front of total strangers who cry with you and then hug you like you have known them all of your life. There was an immediate bond, a tragic bond, but a bond nonetheless. We looked forward to the meetings, even though we knew there would be tears, and we made some good friends. It played a huge part in the healing process. The process isn't complete, it never will be, but you have to learn to deal with it.

Anything can trigger it, a song, a smell, anything. For me, I will always remember that United were beaten 6-3 by Southampton on the day Taylor died. Being able to deal with it might sound caustic and heartless, but it isn't. There are times when I cry. I will always remember, but if you can't deal with it, what is the alternative? It's a scary proposition. I still feel guilty when I laugh, when I get drunk, when I have a great night out, when I feel good, but I can deal with it. The feeling will never go away, I know that, but I don't want it to. It's all part of my history, and it makes me who I am, Taylor's Dad.

In March 1997, Mandy hit me with the great news that she was pregnant again. We were elated, but there was the underlying fear that the same thing would happen again. When she started losing blood early in her pregnancy, our already fragile world started to weaken at the very cracks, which were just starting to knit. The hospital wasn't prepared to take any chances, and Mandy was scanned monthly. All we could do was wait nervously, as the weeks dragged slowly into months. My boss Pete was an absolute star during this time, as he let me go whenever I needed to, no questions asked. He was there when we lost Taylor, and rather than offering me some awkward, insincere, staring at the floor condolences, he came clean, told me he didn't have a fucking clue what to say, and shared a few tears with me over a drink.

Mandy was advised to have a Caesarean section, to try and avoid the same complications, and during one visit she was given a date and booked in. We broke down crying, partly through fear, and partly through relief. As it was an "elective" section, essentially pre-booked, I could be present at the birth. I wasn't going to miss this for the world. Mandy was booked in for the 24th November 1997. This was like time travel to me. I didn't have a child, but I was given a date in the future, in fact, the precise hour, when I would witness the birth of my baby. Amazing.

November isn't really known as a cold month, not in England anyway, but my teeth were chattering as I followed Mandy to the operating theatre. I stripped off and donned my blue gown and white clogs and waited in the corridor. A nurse eventually popped her head around the door and beckoned me in. As I walked past her she shouted in my direction.

"Dad."

Me; "What is it?"

"You didn't need to strip off. The gown is supposed to go over your clothes."

She was holding back her laughter. I reached behind me and realised that my hairy arse was on show to everybody, through the gap in my gown that ran from my neck to my ankles. There was no time to change, and I jumped on to a stool next to Mandy's face. I almost broke her hand as I squeezed as tightly as possible, thinking I could will her to make our child safe. In a split second, I heard a baby crying. It was a gargled sound from deep inside Mandy's stomach. This bugger was coming out fighting alright. The crying got louder, and the Consultant shouted;

"It's a boy, and he's fine."

I looked up and saw him for the first time, my son, Jake Anthony Bell. We had been given a second chance, and all of a sudden everything changed. We argued because we both wanted to change his dirty nappies, we grappled for the pram, we both sneaked off to make his meals, so that we could feed him, and we both came home with surprise presents. Every single minute has been a wonderful experience. It's obvious that losing Taylor has made us appreciate Jake so much more, but he merits every ounce of love and affection we bestow upon him, due to him being the remarkable loving son that he is. Creeping into the room behind him while he watches Scooby Doo is scary. It's me in 1970, honestly. He loves cartoons and fast cars. He nags me all of the time, to get rid of the "Escort" and get a "Ferrari Enzo." I tell him that if we go and wash our car, it will look just like a "Ferrari"; so he jumps into his wellies, and I get a hand, cleaning the car. He can sing "Rock and Roll all Nite", and he does a mean impression of David Coverdale, "Good evening my serpents. Are you ready? I was born under a bad sign…" He tells me to chill out when things get on top, and he brushes his smile for the "ladies" when he cleans his teeth.

307

My favourite night is now a winter's evening inside, with the fire on, watching cartoons as he drifts off to sleep, safe in my arms. Sooner or later he will find out that Dick Dastardly never wins a race, and they don't catch the pigeon, not ever.

My only hope is that he remembers me as somebody that loved him as much as I possibly could, and never turned my back on him when he needed me. Whether it be the last piece of the jigsaw that has been sucked up the Hoover, or the six hundred piece Lego spacecraft that took me a day to build, before I could have a beer. There is nothing I won't do for that little guy, because the day he was born, my lottery numbers came up. The best thing is though, that they come up week after week, without fail. He knows all about Taylor, and he helps put flowers on her grave. I can't help smiling, even though I'm crying at the same time. On her last birthday, Jake had us singing "Happy Birthday" to Taylor, after we had laid the flowers and cards. When we finished singing, he shouted, "Hip Hip…" and then looked at us. Of course, we had to shout "Hooray" as loud as we could three times. He understands in his own way, and he is a great comfort to both of us, as we know that Taylor's spirit is alive inside of him.

Some of you will be shaking your head in disbelief at how I could bring the death of my daughter into the frame, to pad out a story that may never make the bookshelves, or if it does, provides a sensationalist twist to a non-descript, badly written account of absolutely nothing. I don't want your "There, there, there's", because it's far too late. Besides, I had them at the time that it mattered, from the people that mattered. I don't want any more sympathy, because I almost OD'd on it. I don't need any more sympathy. I didn't die. I told you about Taylor to put my story into some kind of perspective, because no matter how important it all seemed at the time, my life changed in a split second in 1996, when everything before that moment was washed away, just like the sandcastle you spent all day building, oblivious that the tide was on it's way in. What makes me cherish Jake so much is that I now know that I don't have all the answers, and I can't keep anybody safe, not really. All I can do is hope that I have the answers, and hope that I can keep the people under my charge as safe as possible. Beyond that, it's down to luck, fate and odds.

When people didn't know what to say, they brought God into the conversation as some kind of panacea that was supposed to make Mandy and myself feel better, and come to terms with our loss. It just wasn't that easy for me, being the sceptic that I am. The more I read the Bible, the more questions came to my mind, and it offered me no solutions or answers to my allotted "time slot" on the planet. The whole book is based on retribution, and I can't help but think that it has been painstakingly engineered for somebody's benefit, cleverly hidden behind the threat of the "Wrath of God" on the turn of each page. A cloud by day, and a pillar of fire by night? You want to get out more.

I don't care if you think I am blaspheming, because if you are the staunchest of believers, then you accept that from your viewpoint, He created me and my mind, and the questions and doubts flying around it. So, you will also be aware that I have nobody to answer to but Him. For all I know, He might be looking over my shoulder as I write this, laughing his tits off, rubbing his hands, waiting for my eyes to close for the last time. If He is, then He'd better have a good fucking excuse for taking my little girl, or there will be trouble. It's not about if He wants me, it's if I want Him. I hope He's got a comfy chair and a crate of Stella, because if He's there, we're in for a fucking long night.

# CHAPTER FORTY ONE

*"Why Do Stars Fall Down From The Sky?"*

The dream that shaped my life amounted to nothing, and doesn't come close to becoming a father, or the events that shattered our lives, but it is relevant, it is valid, and it was hugely important. I was young, happy, healthy, not ugly, and carefree. "Not Ugly" is no recommendation, just a kind of "phew" from me that I wasn't repulsive. Obviously, to some people I was, but you can't please everybody. I was confident that I wouldn't stand out in a crowd for being a great looking lad, or for that matter, being a complete ugly bastard. I could melt safely in the middle, knowing that nobody would ask anything of me, or point the finger at me, Mr. Average.

Being at either end of the spectrum forces you to rise to the challenges. A great looking lad, who learns to communicate with the gifts he has been blessed with, becomes a legend. Especially if he can sprinkle a little bit of humour over everything he does. If he can't rise to the challenge, for whatever reason, he becomes a shallow twat, who has relied on his looks, and consequently developed no personality. It doesn't matter that he is shy and a bit insecure. He has not matched the "ideal" selection criteria for a good looking lad, and he is doomed. I knew loads of lads that fell by the wayside because of this. Ugly lads that think "Fuck this, I'm only here once", turn into absolute stars. These guys have nothing to lose, so they open up, and become confident, funny, and endearing. Sadly, some retract into their shells, but I identify with the ugly guy who's going out all guns blazing, 100%.

I didn't realise it at the time, but the only factor that made any of this possible, was good health. We all breeze through life, taking for granted the gifts we possess. If you can walk, talk, see, think and hear, then anything else is a big bonus. I was lucky enough to spend my life chasing a dream with a great bunch of friends, drinking and laughing all the way. I lost sleep, wondering what I would do if I didn't "make it." What would my life become? I needn't have worried. I look back now and thank my lucky stars that I didn't "make it." If things had been different, there may not have been a Jake Bell, and that just wouldn't do, would it? I fully understand how lucky I am to have met him. Every twist and turn led me to Jake. Every girl that I turned down, or turned me down, plotted the course that led me to him. If somebody had told me that I wasn't going to "make it", but on the way, would have so much fun, and then end up with Jake, I'd have torn their arm right out of its socket for it.

For some reason, everybody seems to think that you join a band just to make money. It couldn't be farther from the truth, I know. These people live in a "safe" Phil Collins, Tina Turner, Rod Stewart, Dire Straits, world of success. I'm not slagging the artists, but some people only know mega famous, mega rich singers or bands. They have never bothered to scratch the surface to find what lies beneath the glitz and glamour of the music industry. Tina Turner wouldn't stand on the hard shoulder in the snow, smoking a fag as the A.A. man fixed her car. Dire Straits wouldn't distract a waitress at the service station, so they could all nick one extra sausage while she wasn't looking. Rod Stewart wouldn't jump into the back of a transit van, with two drunken blondes in hold up stockings, who were cadging a lift to the next town. Yeah, yeah, fucking scrub that last one off the list. Anyway, all I'm trying to say is that these people were hit by the same steamroller that hit us all. You've just got to go with it. Nobody was guaranteed any kind of success, but they ploughed on. Some went the distance, while others attempted to write a book about their failure.

People continually pointed out the cold reality of it all, that the chance of success was minimal. Sometimes it was just family and friends who genuinely cared, hoping that you hadn't bet you last dime on the spin of the wheel. Most times though, it was vindictive twats who knew you were on to something, and that you were a couple of blocks ahead of their band. Jealousy, rage and envy can simmer under the lid of a sober mind. Introduce alcohol, and it can boil over, especially as your nemesis is stood at the end of the very same bar, as you laugh out loud with your mates, while wondering whether to go for the blonde or the brunette. A simple nod or just a friendly "Hello" was all they needed to do to get a reaction, and then they were in. Thirty seconds in and their bitterness started to seep out. Conversations were cut dead, as we marshalled lads back to the "ugly" crowd. Anyway, fuck the lot of them; it's got nothing to do with money. I wish it was that straightforward. You will do anything to get on a stage and play. That's all it was ever about. If it's in your soul then you have to do it. It's the same today. The music may have changed, but dreamers are born every minute, and some of them pick up a guitar. I can't see how money could have made me any happier, I had everything. Sure, a Ferrari would get me there faster than my old Fiesta, but who wants to be the first at a party?

As I get older and wiser, music has found its natural place in my life. I still love the bands that shook me in my youth, but it is no longer the most important thing to me. Music is as valid as a crossword or a knitting pattern, to the people that love those things. It has its place. It is a way of passing time. Some people will disagree and say that music is just as important to them today, as it was twenty five years ago. That's fine, but I can't help thinking that they have clung to their music because nothing significant enough has come along to challenge it. If the last thing to affect your life was the adolescent awakening that music brought, then you will still find solace in it. There are hundreds of songs, that when I listen to them, I can pinpoint a specific time in my life, and they all bring back great memories. Rockers sang romantic songs back then, and there were always loads of songs to choose from, if you were making a tape for the girls. Similarly, the girls had their own special songs that reminded them of different guys. Lads must have to put a lot more work in now, because there are no shortcuts. "Slipknot", "Korn", and "Marilyn Manson." do not make a schmoozy tape that can get you to first base without trying. I would listen to bands, and think "Thanks lads", as I found song after song that, along with my car heater, would prove irresistible.

"Close to you" still reduces me to tears, whenever I hear it. Department stores, traffic lights, restaurants, it still gets me, but I don't mind one bit. It brings out every emotion I experienced at the time, and besides the sadness, there was also love, hope and joy. In a way, Taylor gave us Jake, and he is the light that burns brightly inside both of us. The songs that we loved brought me and Mandy together, and blessed us with our children. I only ever wanted to play music, and I didn't consider for one minute, that I might get something far greater out of it. It's better than being in the biggest band on the planet... or one of the smallest.

The legacy that music left me with has far surpassed anything I could have dreamed of, all those years ago. Music didn't fail me, it supported me all of the way, until I could walk unaided, and stand tall. I know the exact moment that it happened, and rather than feeling angry, bitter, or upset, it was a warm comforting feeling. I looked back over my shoulder.

"I guess this is my stop."